On the Rule of Law

The rule of law is the most important political ideal today, yet there is much confusion about what it means and how it works. This book explores the history, politics, and theory surrounding the rule of law ideal, beginning with classical Greek and Roman ideas, elaborating on medieval contributions to the rule of law, and articulating the role played by the rule of law in liberal theory and liberal political systems. The author outlines the concerns of Western conservatives about the decline of the rule of law and suggests reasons why the radical Left have promoted this decline. Two basic theoretical streams of the rule of law are then presented, with an examination of the strengths and weaknesses of each. The book examines the rule of law on a global level, and concludes by answering the question of whether the rule of law is a universal human good.

BRIAN Z. TAMANAHA is Chief Judge Benjamin N. Cardozo Professor of Law at St. John's University School of Law. He has written award-winning books in legal theory, and published widely in leading journals. He is Associate Editor of the Law and Society Review.

D1296022

On the Rule of Law

History, Politics, Theory

Brian Z. Tamanaha

CAMBRIDGE
UNIVERSITY PRESS

PUBLISHED BY THE PRESS SYNDICATE OF THE UNIVERSITY OF CAMBRIDGE
The Pitt Building, Trumpington Street, Cambridge, United Kingdom

CAMBRIDGE UNIVERSITY PRESS
The Edinburgh Building, Cambridge, CB2 2RU, UK
40 West 20th Street, New York, NY 10011–4211, USA
477 Williamstown Road, Port Melbourne, VIC 3207, Australia
Ruiz de Alarcón 13, 28014 Madrid, Spain
Dock House, The Waterfront, Cape Town 8001, South Africa

http://www.cambridge.org

First published 2004

Printed in the United Kingdom at the University Press, Cambridge

Typeface Plantin 10/12 pt.   *System* LaTeX 2_ε [TB]

A catalogue record for this book is available from the British Library

ISBN 0 521 84362 6 hardback
ISBN 0 521 60465 6 paperback

For Honorata

"Oni"

Contents

Acknowledgments

For helpful comments on earlier drafts of this book, I thank Jeff Sovern, Paul Kirgis, three anonymous Readers for Cambridge University Press, and two anonymous Readers procured by John Tryneski. Their critical observations helped me tighten the argument, fill in gaps, and rectify flaws. The faculties at Hofstra Law School and the University of Pennsylvania Law School invited me to present parts of this book; I thank them for their feedback. I thank Chris Borgen for his invaluable assistance with Chapter Ten. I thank Michael Freeman for inviting me to present a Public Lecture at University College London on one of the themes taken up in this book, later published as "The Rule of Law for Everyone?" in volume 55 of *Current Legal Problems* (2002). I thank William Twining for several days of intensive intellectual exchange at two separate, crucial periods in the writing of this book. William has influenced this book as well as everything else I have written or thought about in legal theory since I had the good fortune to meet him. I owe particular thanks to Brian Bix for his careful reading and insightful comments on the manuscript. His observations helped improve the book in ways large and small. Brian is one of the most astute and knowledgeable legal theorists writing today. Anyone with an interest in the subjects covered in this book would find a wealth of information in his work, starting with his book, *Jurisprudence: Theory and Context*. I also thank Finola O'Sullivan and John Tryneski for their enthusiastic support for the book. I thank Lisa Roder for her superb research assistance. I thank Jolijt and Kats for their patience, understanding, and good humor while I worked on this book.

Finally, I thank Katsugi Tamanaha, my father, for serving as my inspiration and imagined audience. My conviction is that theory is relevant to everyday life and should therefore be available to everyone. Unfortunately, most theoretical works are too dense and jargon-filled to be of interest to non-theorists. When colleagues and friends inquired why I was striving to write this book in a more generally accessible style, which (I confess) is a departure from my previous theoretical books, my response was that my goal was to write a book intelligent people like my father could read. I hope I have succeeded.

Introduction

Just over a decade ago, following the almost total collapse of communism, it seemed to many observers to be the dawn of a new age, an age in which Western ideas of freedom, democracy, individual rights, and capitalism finally would come to dominate, spreading their beneficent effects to the many blighted parts of the globe that had previously rejected them in the name of Marxism, or traditional values, or anti-Westernism, or some other self-defeating ideal. "The End of History"[1] had arrived. Peace and prosperity were about to reign worldwide.

How quickly have things turned. There has since been a bewildering array of nationalist, ethnic, religious, and political conflict, of genocide and other unthinkable atrocities, of economic crises that have threatened global financial stability, of terrorism and war, all at levels exceeding what occurred during the hottest moments of the half-century-long Cold War. New global fault lines, previously sublimated beneath the overarching confrontation between communist systems and the West, have emerged and deepened, between rich and poor countries, between North and South or East and West, between Islamic and non-Islamic countries, between liberal and non-liberal societies, between mercantilist (state-run) capitalism and free trade capitalism, between dominance by global corporations and the preservation of local autonomy, between US military, economic, political, and cultural influence and the rest of the world, at once bitterly resistant while guiltily complicit. For all but the most sanguine observers, the triumphalist confidence of the 1990s has dissolved.

Amidst this host of new uncertainties there appears to be widespread agreement, traversing all fault lines, on one point, and one point alone: that the "rule of law" is good for everyone. Among Western states this belief is orthodoxy. Listed first in the "Declaration of Democratic Values" issued by the seven heads of state of the major industrial democracies: "We believe in a rule of law which respects and protects without fear or favor the rights and liberties of every citizen and provides the setting in which the human spirit can develop in freedom and diversity."[2] In the words of US President George W. Bush, "America will always stand firm

1

for the non-negotiable demands of human dignity: the rule of law . . ."[3] It is commonplace wisdom that the defining characteristic of the Western political tradition is "freedom under the rule of law."[4]

Western promotion of the rule of law is not limited solely to the enhancement of liberty. In the early 1990s, the Western-funded World Bank and International Monetary Fund began conditioning the provision of financial assistance on the implementation of the rule of law in recipient countries. This imposition was justified on economic grounds as a means to provide a secure environment for investments, property, contracts, and market transactions.[5] At a training session of World Bank staff members and consultants, "'Rule of law' was probably the most-repeated phrase of the week."[6] Development specialists uniformly agree that absent the rule of law there can be no sustainable economic development.

Support for the rule of law is not exclusive to the West. It has been endorsed by government heads from a range of societies, cultures, and economic and political systems. Russian "President Putin continues to place judicial reform and the full implementation of the principles of the rule of law among the country's highest priorities."[7] China recently signed a UN pact for cooperation and training to develop the rule of law.[8] "Chinese leaders say they . . . support the establishment of the rule of law," a commitment underscored by the highly publicized attendance of President Jiang Zemin at a seminar on the rule of law.[9] His successor as President, Hu Jintao, observed following his selection that "We must build a system based on the rule of law and should not pin our hopes on any particular leader."[10] Robert Mugabe, embattled President of Zimbabwe, previously stated that "Only a government that subjects itself to the rule of law has any moral right to demand of its citizens obedience to the rule of law."[11] Seven months after taking office, Indonesian President Abdurrahman Wahid identified as one of his major achievements: "we are beginning the rule of law."[12] President Mohammed Khatami of Iran has made "repeated remarks about the value of a civil society and the importance of the rule of law."[13] Mexican President Vicente Fox Quesada declared that the lack of the rule of law is "the theme that worries Mexicans most."[14] Even a notorious Afghan warlord, Abdul Rashid Dostum, campaigning for a position in the post-Taliban government, was quoted as saying "Now is the time to defend ourselves not with tanks and armed corps but by the rule of law . . ."[15] These and similar testimonials have come from leaders of a variety of systems, some of which have rejected democracy and individual rights, some of which are avowedly Islamic, some of which reject capitalism, and many of which oppose liberalism and are explicitly anti-Western. The reasons they articulate for supporting the rule of law might differ, some in the interest of freedom, some in the preservation of order, many in the furtherance of economic development, but all identify it as essential.

This apparent unanimity in support of the rule of law is a feat unparalleled in history. No other single political ideal has ever achieved global endorsement. Never mind, for the moment, an understandable skepticism with respect to the sincerity of some of these avowed commitments to the rule of law. The fact remains that government officials worldwide advocate the rule of law and, equally significantly, that none make a point of defiantly rejecting the rule of law. At the very least, even in the case of cynical paeans on its behalf, the mere fact of its frequent repetition is compelling evidence that adherence to the rule of law is an accepted measure worldwide of government legitimacy.

Notwithstanding its quick and remarkable ascendance as a global ideal, however, the rule of law is an exceedingly elusive notion. Few government leaders who express support for the rule of law, few journalists who record or use the phrase, few dissidents who expose themselves to risk of reprisal in its name, and few of the multitude of citizens throughout the world who believe in it, ever articulate precisely what it means. Explicit or implicit understandings of the phrase suggest that contrasting meanings are held. Some believe that the rule of law includes protection of individual rights. Some believe that democracy is part of the rule of law. Some believe that the rule of law is purely formal in nature, requiring only that laws be set out in advance in general, clear terms, and be applied equally to all. Others assert that the rule of law encompasses the "social, economic, educational, and cultural conditions under which man's legitimate aspirations and dignity may be realized."[16] Dissidents point out that authoritarian governments that claim to abide by the rule of law routinely understand this phrase in oppressive terms. As Chinese law professor Li Shuguang put it: "'Chinese leaders want rule by law, not rule of law' . . . The difference . . . is that under the rule of law, the law is preeminent and can serve as a check against the abuse of power. Under rule by law, the law can serve as a mere tool for a government that suppresses in a legalistic fashion."[17] In view of this rampant divergence of understandings, the rule of law is analogous to the notion of the "good," in the sense that everyone is for it, but have contrasting convictions about what it is.

The theory experts have it no better. Political and legal theorists also often hold vague or sharply contrasting understandings of the rule of law. One theorist remarked that "there are almost as many conceptions of the rule of law as there are people defending it."[18] Many theorists believe that it is "an essentially contested concept,"[19] that is, a notion characterized by disagreement that extends to its core. "It would not be very difficult to show that the phrase 'the rule of law' has become meaningless thanks to ideological abuse and general over-use."[20]

The rule of law thus stands in the peculiar state of being *the* preeminent legitimating political ideal in the world today, without agreement upon precisely what it means. Bringing greater clarity to this ideal is the primary objective of this book. This ideal is too important to contemporary affairs to be left in confusion. Despite the surrounding uncertainty, it is not the case that any proposed meaning is as good as another. There is a relatively short list of plausible conceptions, each derived from a recognized historical-political context, with relatively clear elements and discernable implications.

This effort is not offered for edification alone. According to an article in *Foreign Affairs*, several decades and hundreds of millions of dollars have been expended on developing the rule of law around the world with minimal positive results.[21] If it is not already firmly in place, the rule of law appears mysteriously difficult to establish. This exploration of the history, politics, and theory surrounding the rule of law will elaborate on the circumstances of its origin and will identify its ingredients. It will not produce a formula that can be replicated in every situation, for owing to the uniqueness of each social-political context that cannot succeed. But learning about how it originated and how it functions will provide useful information for those looking for alternative paths that that might work in local circumstances.

This effort to clarify the rule of law to assist in its realization should not be interpreted as an unreserved promotion of this ideal. I share the view of many that the rule of law is a major achievement deserving of preservation and praise. But it has limitations and carries risks seldom mentioned by its advocates. A striking disjunction exists between the theoretical discourse on the rule of law and the political and public discourse on the rule of law. Theorists have observed the decline of the rule of law in the West for some time some now, beginning with A. V. Dicey over a century ago, renewed by Friedrich Hayek fifty years ago, and widely repeated by legal theorists, especially in the USA, in the past three decades. Therefore, even as politicians and development specialists are actively promoting the spread of the rule of law to the rest of the world, legal theorists concur about the marked deterioration of the rule of law in the West, with some working to accelerate its demise. This decline suggests that problems are being glossed over in its promotion.

Two particular concerns bear mention at the outset. First, some of the most vociferous champions of the rule of law, famously including Hayek, have claimed that it is incompatible with an expansive social welfare state and with the achievement of distributive justice. Theorists often tie liberalism, unrestrained capitalism, and the rule of law into an all or nothing package. However, many of the non-Western societies that wish to implement the rule of law have no desire to become liberal, and many Western societies with the rule of law are committed to the social welfare state. A host of fundamental social and political issues are thus implicated in the decision to adopt the rule of law ideal. Second, the rule of law carries the ever-present danger of becoming rule by judges and lawyers. Aside from having obvious anti-democratic implications, this raises additional concerns in societies where judges and lawyers are drawn exclusively from the elite, or from some other discrete subgroup. Countries working to develop the rule of law must be cognizant of these and other potential problems.

Equal attention will be allocated in this work to elucidating the weaknesses and strengths of the rule of law, to considering the theoretical and practical arguments for and against it. Like all ideals, there are certain social-cultural contexts for which it is ill suited, and it must be weighed against and sometimes give way to other important social values. Like all ideals, choices must be made in how the ideal is to be formulated and how it is to be implemented, choices that take into consideration immediate context and prevailing preferences.

A telling revelation of this exploration is that the rule of law ideal initially developed in non-liberal societies. This millennia-old ideal survived extraordinary changes in surrounding social, political, and economic circumstances, which led to alterations in how the ideal operated and what it was taken to represent. These changes have generated a few complicated puzzles that were not present at earlier stages. Not only will this exploration disclose how these problems arose, which is relevant to contemporary liberal societies, it will also reveal ways in which modern non-liberal societies can understand the rule of law in a fashion amenable to their situations.

This exploration will proceed chronologically, beginning briefly with Ancient Greece and Rome, then focusing more attention on the Medieval period, then on the modern rise of liberalism, ending up in the present, looking at the rule of law at the national and international levels. History, politics, and theory are interwoven throughout the book, showing up in each chapter, but they also serve as general organizing themes, delivered in sequential order. The first few chapters are thus more historical, the middle chapters more political, and the concluding chapters more theoretical.

Although a number of challenging topics in political and legal theory will be canvassed in the course of this work, an effort has been made to present the ideas and issues surrounding the rule of law in a manner accessible to readers with no theoretical background. While it is written to be of use to theorists and students, one objective of this book is to expose a general audience to the insights to be gleaned from the historical, political, and theoretical discussion. The rule of law has swept the realm of public political discourse. Given its prominence, it is essential that a thorough understanding of this ideal be available to anyone with an interest and the requisite determination to know.

1   Classical origins

Greek thought

Many accounts of the rule of law identify its origins in classical Greek thought, quoting passages from Plato and Aristotle. Though this is not incorrect, a caveat must be kept in mind. For half of a millennium, known as the Dark Ages, Greek thought was almost entirely lost to the West, until rediscovered and given new life in the high Middle Ages by religious scholars.[1] The rule of law as a continuous tradition took root more than a thousand years after the heyday of Athens. Greek ideas with respect to the rule of law are therefore best understood as exemplary models, inspiration, and authority for later periods. Many of the problems the Greeks, Plato and Aristotle in particular, grappled with so insightfully are timeless problems; hence their timeless relevance and appeal.

Fifth-century BC Athens, at the height of its glory, took great pride in being a democracy governed directly by its citizens. The overarching orientation of Athenians was toward the *polis*, the political community. Every male citizen over thirty years of age, of whatever class or wealth, was eligible to serve (for pay) on juries that decided legal cases; they also served as magistrates, on the governing Council (with a rotating head), and on legislative assemblies, with positions filled by lot. To insure accountability, magistrates presiding over cases could be charged with violations of the law by complaints from private citizens.[2] Owing to these characteristics, "democracy was synonymous for the Athenians with the 'rule of law.'"[3] Athens did not have a class of legal professionals or state officials who monopolized the production of law or the delivery of legal services. Law was – literally – the product of the activities of its citizens. Equality before the law was an important value in their system. This did not mean that the same legal standards were applied to everyone. The law recognized categories of individuals (for example, women, children, slaves, and non-citizens) with different legal implications. Rather, equality meant that the law would be applied to all in accordance with its terms without regard to whom, whether aristocrat or lowly artisan, stood before it.[4]

The danger in a popular system of this kind is that democracies can be as tyrannical as absolute monarchies.[5] Protecting against a populist tyranny, the law was accorded a status that set it apart, rendering it not easy to modify by the popular courts and legislative assemblies.[6] The role of these courts and assemblies was to respect the law and act as guardians of the law, not to declare the law as they pleased. Seen as the reflection of a transcendent order that stands behind the lived community, law enjoyed a sanctified status. "Greek philosophers and statesmen, like others before and after them, were beguiled by the dream of putting on record some system of basic law which would be so perfectly adapted to the true interests and the actual social conditions of the society for which it was framed as to be venerated as eternal and unalterable."[7] The phrase "the laws of Solon," a reference to the legendary monarch who in the sixth century BC established a body of laws and the popular courts, was used to stamp particular laws as ancient and untouchable. New laws could be passed, and old laws changed, but such enactments were subject to review. Proponents had to demonstrate the inadequacy of existing laws as a condition of passage, and all decrees of the assemblies were examined for consistency with preexisting law.[8] If legislation was found to be in contradiction with preexisting valid laws, the proponents of the legislation could be fined.[9] The result of these various mechanisms and standards was to maintain a democratic system "while subordinating the principle of popular sovereignty to the principle of sovereignty of laws."[10]

Plato was from an aristocratic family. His student Aristotle – a Macedonian, non-citizen resident of Athens – was the son of a physician and later the tutor of Alexander the Great. By the time of Plato and Aristotle, Athens had already declined from its height, having lost the war with neighboring Sparta at the close of the fifth century BC. Its citizenry were thought to have degenerated, lacking in the self-discipline and orientation to the *polis* that had made Athenian democracy so superior. Instead they were overly preoccupied with commerce and excessively indulged in enjoying the fruits obtained from Athens's maritime expansion. Underlining the risks of popular rule, Plato's teacher, Socrates, was condemned to death by Athenian democrats. Under these circumstances, Plato and Aristotle were acutely concerned about the potential for tyranny in a populist democracy; accordingly, they emphasized that the law represented an enduring and unchanging order. Plato's legal code in *The Laws* was intended to be permanent. The faith they expressed in the rule of law was in contemplation of its stability and restraining effect.

Plato insisted that the government should be bound by the law: "Where the law is subject to some other authority and has none of its own, the collapse of the state, in my view, is not far off; but if law is the master of the government and the government is its slave, then the situation is full of promise and men enjoy all the blessings that the gods shower on a state."[11] Aristotle's words on the rule of law still resonate:

Now, absolute monarchy, or the arbitrary rule of a sovereign over all citizens, in a city which consists of equals, is thought by some to be quite contrary to nature; . . . That is why it is thought to be just that among equals everyone be ruled as well as rule, and therefore that all should have their turn. And the rule of law, it is argued, is preferable to that of any individual. On the same principle, even if it be better for certain individuals to govern, they should be made only guardians and ministers of the law . . . Therefore he who bids the law rule may be deemed to bid God and Reason alone rule, but he who bids man rule adds an element of the beast; for desire is a wild beast, and passion perverts the minds of rulers, even when they are the best of men. The law is reason unaffected by desire.[12]

Aristotle raised several themes in the above passage that perennially course through discussions of the rule of law: self-rule in situations of political equality; government officials being subject to law; and the identification of law with reason, serving as protection against the potential for abuse inhering in the power to rule. His final observation, the last two sentences above, has had the most impact. Aristotle's contrast between the rule of law as reason and the rule of man as passion has endured through the ages.[13] "In Aristotle's account the single most important condition for the Rule of Law is the character one must impute to those who make legal judgments . . . It is part of such a character to reason syllogistically and to do so his passions must be silent."[14]

   Both Plato and Aristotle asserted that the law should further the good of the community and enhance the development of moral virtue of all citizens. As Plato put it, "we maintain that the laws which are not established for the good of the whole state are bogus law."[15] "Hence what is just will be both what is lawful and what is fair, and what is unjust will be both what is lawless and what is unfair."[16] Law for Plato was the reflection of a divine order, consistent with the Good. Both thinkers recognized the possibility, however, that the law might be co-opted to serve elite interests. For Aristotle, "true forms of government will of necessity have just laws, and perverted forms of government will have unjust laws."[17] He concluded that the "laws, when good, should be supreme."[18]

   Several cautions are in order to avoid the temptation of placing too modern of a spin on Plato and Aristotle. Neither advocated rebellion against the law, even against unjust laws. "There is nothing which should be more jealously maintained than the spirit of obedience to law," Aristotle counseled, for even minor transgressions, if allowed to creep in, "at last ruins the state."[19] He saw law as essential to social order and insisted on general obedience. Neither was a fan of popular democracy,[20] which they viewed as potentially the rule of the mob, uneducated and lacking in talent, susceptible to seduction by a demagogue, with a leveling effect on society.[21] Furthermore, neither was an egalitarian. They believed that people had unequal talents in political capacity, virtues, and excellence – often associated with birth status – and held that those who are superior should rule and deserve more rewards.

Their view was that the best government was the rule by the best man, not rule by law, for law does not speak to all situations, and cannot contemplate all eventualities in advance.[22] "Indeed," observed Plato, "where the good king rules, law is a hindrance standing in the way of justice like 'an obstinate and ignorant man.'"[23] The rule under law that they advocated was a second-best solution, necessitated by human weakness. Plato bid the law rule in *The Laws* as a more realistic alternative to the benevolent (philosophically educated and virtuous) Guardians he proposed to rule in *The Republic*. Aristotle advocated rule under law owing to the risk of corruption and abuse that exists when power is concentrated in single hands.[24]

Significantly, although Plato and Aristotle extolled the supremacy of law, their focus was diametrically opposite to that of the Athenian democrats mentioned at the outset, who also believed in the rule of law.[25] Plato and Aristotle were greatly concerned about restraining popular tyranny. In contrast, the Athenian democrats – the very popular government that incited trepidation in Plato and Aristotle – were predominantly worried about capture of the government by aristocratic oligarchies, which they had suffered during the brief but notorious tenure of the Thirty Tyrants, installed by Sparta following its conquest. One of these usurpers was Critias, Plato's uncle (and also a student of Socrates).[26] For Athenian democrats it was essential – a prerequisite of its supremacy – that the citizens themselves participated directly in giving rise to the law. As we shall see, the tension between these two concerns, law as a restraint on democracy and law as the product of self-government, has not lessened throughout history.

At the height of Athenian governance under the law, citizens had equality before the law; the laws were framed in general terms, not against any individual; the Council, magistrates, and legislative assemblies were bound by the law; and citizens were free to operate as they pleased outside what the law prohibited.[27] Athenians thus achieved a form of liberty under the law. This was not individual liberty in modern terms, which is a notion they did not possess,[28] but rather involved the liberty of self-rule and the liberty to do whatever was not expressly prohibited by the law.

Roman contribution

The Roman contribution to the rule of law tradition was negative as well as positive, with the negative being of much greater consequence. Cicero was the source of the positive. In *The Republic*, written in the first century BC, he condemned the king who does not abide by the law as a despot who "is the foulest and most repellant creature imaginable."[29] "How can anyone be properly called a man who renounces every legal tie, every civilized partnership with his own citizens and indeed with the entire human species."[30] A contemporary of Julius Caesar, Cicero wrote during the dying stage of the Roman Republic, as it was giving way to autocratic rule. "Everyone of standing had realized that the republic's rule of law and order had given place to the rule of the stronger."[31] Cicero's *The Laws* contains the following passage on the rule of law:

> You appreciate, then, that a magistrate's function is to take charge and to issue directives which are right, beneficial, and in accordance with the laws. As magistrates are subject to the laws, the people are subject to the magistrates. In fact it is true to say that a magistrate is a speaking law, and law a silent magistrate.[32]

It is the law that rules, he emphasized, not the individual who happens to be the magistrate. Cicero pointedly contrasted rule under a king with living under "a body of law for a free community."[33]

For Cicero the supreme status of laws hinged upon their consistency with natural law. He believed that natural law was the rule of reason. According to the rule of reason, law should be for the good of the community, should be just, and should preserve the happiness and safety of its citizens. This natural law of reason stands over positive law, indeed over all human conduct, according to Cicero. "Therefore law means drawing a distinction between just and unjust, formulated in accordance with that most ancient and most important of all things – nature."[34] Harmful or unjust rules did not qualify as "law," and hence were not supreme.[35] Cicero did not, however, support disobedience of unjust laws. He placed a premium on order. Moreover, he believed that only the wise could recognize the true law in accordance with reason.

Cicero did not advocate popular democracy, preferring instead a mixed constitution, with power divided among royalty, leading citizens, and to a much lesser extent the masses.[36] To the best citizens – the most educated and the wise – should be allocated the greater power to rule, as they are the ones with the capacity to discern the requirements of the natural law that should govern society.

Although Cicero is often cited as an important natural law theorist, and as an early advocate of the rule of law, most of his writings were lost until the early Renaissance, with the complete text of *The Republic* not located until the sixteenth century. Thus, as with Plato and Aristotle, he is less a direct ancestor in the rule of law tradition than an authority whose work was consulted and enlisted in the context of later political discussions. A key contribution Cicero made, echoing Plato and Aristotle, but put in more forceful terms, was his insistence that the law must be for the good of the community and comport with natural law. Cicero conditioned the supremacy of law on its consistency with justice.

The negative Roman contributions to the rule of law are to be found in the *Lex Regia* and the *Corpus Iuris Civilis*. A bit of historical background is necessary. The Roman Republic, governed by an aristocratic assembly, had existed since the fifth century BC, until it fell under the rule of emperors, beginning with Augustus, who reigned from 27 BC until 14 AD. In the following several centuries the Roman Empire extended its reach over the entire Mediterranean and much of Europe.

Constantine became Emperor in 306 AD, with fateful consequences for the Empire. He converted from paganism to become the first Christian Emperor, issuing an edict of toleration for Christianity, building basilicas, and, in addition to managing the affairs of state, taking a lead role in religious activities and decision-making. Emperor Constantine was a "self-styled bishop of the Christian Church,"[37] commingling secular and religious leadership in a manner that monarchs would emulate for many centuries. Constantine's other major impact was to move the capital of the Empire eastward, building a new capital in the old city of Byzantium, thereafter called Constantinople (Istanbul today). Rome had already begun its decline. In the following generations it would be overrun by successive invasions of Germanic tribes. Contrary to his desire to maintain a unified Roman Empire, Constantine's move inaugurated the Byzantine Empire, dividing the old Empire into western and eastern halves that took separate courses, never to be one again.

Now to the *Lex Regia*. The shift from Republican rule to rule by emperors was in need of legitimation. The *Lex Regia* provided this service. According to the *Lex Regia*, which purported to be an account of this transformation in rule, the Roman people expressly granted absolute authority to the emperor for the preservation of the state.[38] But the *Lex Regia* was a complete fiction, a myth made up by early Roman jurists – legal experts – to justify the power of the emperor. This fictional status (albeit not known as such) did not hinder its historical importance, however. During the Middle Ages, and later, in a feat of ambidextrous influence, the *Lex Regia* was cited by both democrats and absolutists, the former because it represented the idea of original popular sovereignty,[39] and the latter because it placed absolute authority in an emperor above the law.

Justinian became Emperor in 527. The accomplishment for which he is most remembered was the codification of Roman law. At his direction, jurists collected and systematized the existing unruly jumble of laws and legal opinions. In a span of about five years, jurists prepared and issued the *Codex*, which contained the body of rules, the *Digest*, a compilation of the writings of jurists analyzing the rules, and the *Institutes*, comprised of extracts from the first two for use in law schools.[40] These three books collectively constituted the *Corpus Iuris Civilis* (the civil code, by contrast to church canon law), more commonly known as the Justinian Code. It largely consisted of existing customs, rules, decisions and commentaries by jurists, reorganized, reconciled, and articulated in coherent, comprehensive form.

Of particular relevance to the rule of law tradition are two declarations contained in the Code: "What has pleased the prince has the force of law;" and "The prince is not bound by the laws."[41] Renowned third-century jurist Ulpian referred to the *Lex Regia* in support of these declarations, later incorporated into the Code. Under existing views there was no question that the emperor possessed law-making power; indeed Justinian issued the Code itself as an exercise of this power. And there was no question that the emperor was above the law, for he made the law. Needless to say, this understanding is the very antithesis the rule of law ideal. The Code, while effective in the Eastern Empire, was generally ignored in the West until its rediscovery and spread commencing in the twelfth century. But the notion of absolute monarchs above the law that it made explicit survived outside of the Code, and would have a continuous influence in the West, bolstered by the Code's rediscovery, throughout the Middle Ages and beyond.

The fuller picture of the emperor's power vis-a-vis the law, however, is more nuanced than these declarations might indicate. Emperors, whose legislation consisted mostly of edicts and decrees prepared by jurists, had minimal participation in actual law-making. A large bulk of the laws restated in the Code were the products of the past writings of jurists.[42] Moreover, it was generally understood that the emperor, when not exercising his law-making power, was subject to the framework of the legal tradition, though he undoubtedly had the power to modify the laws if he desired. Not every act of the emperor was considered a legal act, and irregular activities in violation of the general laws were disapproved of (keeping in mind that the emperor was not accountable to any legal institution). Even when the emperor exercised his power to alter a law, "if, wrote Ulpian in a different context, law which had been regarded as just for a long time was to be reformed, there had better be good reason for the change."[43] Reflecting this sentiment, a separate provision in the Code asserted: "It is a statement worthy of the majesty of a ruler for the Prince to profess himself bound by the laws."[44]

The reality, then, was not quite unfettered legal absolutism by emperors. The emperor was indeed above the law in theory and by general understanding, but in practice the law still mattered, and imposed constraints on regal conduct.[45] This combination – a reconciliation of law-making power with being law-bound – must be somehow achieved if the rule of law is to work. Modern legal systems have the very same tension, in that the sovereign is both the source of the law and subject to the law. In every successful arrangement there is a prevailing ethic that the good king, the good law-maker, adheres to the law.

2   Medieval roots

The rule of law tradition congealed into existence in a slow, unplanned manner that commenced in the Middle Ages, with no single source or starting point. Three contributing sources will be elaborated upon: the contest between kings and popes for supremacy, Germanic customary law, and the Magna Carta, which epitomized the effort of nobles to use law to impose restraints on sovereigns. Preliminary to considering these sources, a historical context will be laid.[1]

By convention among historians, which is imprecise and by no means unanimous, the Medieval period of the West lasted for 1,000 years, commencing with the fifth-century collapse of the Roman Empire, terminating in the course of the Renaissance of the fifteenth and sixteenth centuries.

The first several centuries of this period are known as the Dark Ages. After Constantine shifted the capital of the Roman Empire to Constantinople, the western half of the Empire entered into a long decline precipitated by waves of invasions by Germanic tribes, who were unlearned barbarians by contrast to the refined Greco-Roman civilization they overran. The fearsome Huns, hitherto unknown Asian warriors originating from the distant east, mounted an invasion that thrust far into Europe in the fourth and early fifth centuries, driving the Germanic tribes (Goths, Visigoths, Ostrogoths, Vandals) before them in to the Roman Empire. Rome, sacked more than once, became a virtual backwater, with a fraction of its former population living amidst the ruins of the once great city. In the seventh and eighth centuries the Saracen followers of Mohammed emerged from Arabia to conquer much of the Middle East, all of North Africa, and the Iberian Peninsula (modern Spain), extending into what is today southern France, thereby shutting down the previously thriving Mediterranean trade. In the nineth and tenth centuries came Norsemen (Vikings) who traveled up navigable European rivers and along the coastlines of the major seas to plunder whatever could be taken away, settling where they pleased. Hungarians (Magyars) threatened from the eastern border of Europe during the tenth century as well.

Encircled and besieged, Medieval society closed in upon itself.[2] Dispersed rural inhabitants engaged in subsistence cultivation, with scant commerce. Towns were sparsely inhabited and small, built adjacent to or within an enclosure of defensive walls erected to stave off roving gangs or sorties by neighboring lords or their errant or ambitious offspring. Towns were the location of the church, the meeting place for occasional assemblies, the abode of artisans, with small markets for exchange. For most people life was brief and lived out within a short radius of the site of their birth. Travel was unsafe owing to the ever-present threat of robbery, roads and bridges lapsed into disrepair, and tolls were exacted at town gates, bridges, docks, and roads at regular intervals, all throwing up barriers to movement, although a few hardy monks and traders did brave the perils. Itinerant merchants and their regional fairs, once common during the Roman Empire, were no more. Coinage – mostly debased silver – was minted and exchanged at a small percentage of its former volume. Feudal law and local customary law intermingled or coexisted with Roman law survivals and ecclesiastical law; local lords or powerful bishops, who presided, respectively, in their own manorial or church courts, were in effective control. There was no professional body of jurists as had existed in Roman times. Outside of the Church there was little learning.

The feudal system formed in the nineth and tenth centuries. With land and labor the only ready resources, but little active market for either, a calcified social order came into being that revolved around a complex of relationships tied to who owned or had rights over the land and who worked the land.[3] Feudal society was constituted by so-called Estates, or social classes: the nobility, clergy, and serfs.[4] Each class was thought to play a distinct and essential role within an organic society. The nobility and their vassals (or knights) possessed substantial land holdings which were divided up and allocated in various ways. Through the practice of sub-infeudation, whereby vassals further divided up the land among subordinate vassals, and so forth, multi-layered networks of relationships were created, the leading noble at the pinnacle, with everyone linked in a descending hierarchy of obligations, in which services (manual labor or military) or tributes (produce or rent) were owed by persons lower in the rung to their immediate superior in exchange for the use or control of the land. Some of the land (demesnes) the lords held themselves, with their own serfs doing the cultivation; other of their land was distributed to vassals who were required to supply, among other things, armed soldiers in times of need. Although lords and their vassals had expansive powers over serfs, they also owed them responsibilities, primarily including defending them from outside attack, presiding over the resolution of disputes, and providing for them in times of drought or calamity. The clergy, the spiritual leaders of society, were not all of the same cloth. Some were Latin-educated offspring of the aristocracy, who ran estates or monasteries with vast landholdings, including serfs, acquired by accretion through gifts and bequeaths to the Church. Bishops of standing were in effect barons, dominating the spiritual as well as temporal affairs of their cities and towns, their courts exercising a broad jurisdiction.[5] But other clergy, the local parish priests, often were from peasant stock, had halting command of classical Latin (speaking instead the vulgar languages), ran poorly endowed churches, and worked the land alongside their flock to eke out their living. The serfs toiled the land with no freedom to leave, beholden to their feudal masters, owning nothing beyond their movable possessions. In the absence of a significant market, there was no incentive, nor available technology, to produce a surplus beyond what they were obligated to supply and able to consume; there were no means to improve their condition. The feudal social order was hierarchical and fixed. The free town folk, a negligible presence during this period, were the only ones who fell outside these categories.

Kings and princes were feudal lords as well, with their own large land holdings from which they derived their wealth. They had no significant control over territory outside their immediate reaches, and possessed limited power over the nobles, who were rivals as much as subordinates. There was no governmental apparatus to speak of and no unified court system. Charlemagne, crowned Emperor in the West in 800, whose reign ended in 814, was the last great king, his Frankish kingdom disintegrating upon his death. Not until the eleventh and (more so) twelfth centuries would the incipient elements of the state system – erected upon the establishment of courts and the effective collection of taxes, facilitated by the increase of men educated in law who entered into the service of kings – come into being.[6] During the heart of the Middle Ages only the Roman Catholic Church had a semblance of an institutional presence that spanned western Europe.

The eastern Roman Empire, meanwhile, continued as a repository of learning and ancient, though also diminishing, glory, projecting its power across Greece, Serbia, Macedonia, Bulgaria, and parts of Italy and the Middle East, while becoming increasingly isolated from the West. Latin was dropped for Greek. Known to history as Byzantium,[7] the eastern Empire became Hellenized and Oriental, although its Emperors continued for centuries to look longingly westward with dreams of reuniting the Empire under unitary (eastern) rule, which Justinian partially and temporarily achieved. Of more pressing concern to the eastern Empire, however, was resisting incursions from the south from Muslims, at various times Arabs, Persians, and Turks, to which it finally succumbed after centuries of conflict, from the north and east from Bulgars, Russians, and Mongols, and from the west from their putative Christian allies, the (plundering) Crusaders passing through Constantinople on a mission to recover the Holy Land. Although the Roman popes – as well as the Germanic kings who ruled western Europe – had for centuries acknowledged Byzantine emperors as the titular head of the entire Roman Empire, over time the relationship turned antagonistic, not only because of the threat of conquest Byzantium occasionally posed to Rome, but also because its emperors appointed Patriarchs – the leaders of the eastern church – and asserted authority to decide doctrinal matters, which ran counter to the popes' claimed preeminence. The first break came in the early eighth-century iconoclast controversy, when the Pope refused to accept the Emperor's declaration that Christian icons be destroyed to avoid idolatry; the denouement of this contest over power was the eleventh-century schism, which officially and permanently separated the eastern Orthodox Church from the Roman Catholic Church.

Our concern, however, is primarily with the West, for that is where the rule of law tradition took root. As mentioned earlier, classical ideas – Greek philosophy and codified Roman law – were largely lost to the West during the first half of the Middle Ages, although vestiges of Roman law continued. The rediscovery of Aristotle's works (which had been preserved by the Muslims) and the Justinian Code, in the twelfth and thirteenth centuries, coincided with a substantial rise in the number of educated men – the founding of the University of Bologna (for law) and the University of Paris, the beginnings of Oxford and Cambridge Universities, and others.[8] Students from all over Europe converged on these centers of learning to read and discuss texts, to debate ideas in religion, science, ethics, philosophy (which were not distinct disciplines at the time), and law. Commercial activity showed signs of new-found vitality. These were the initial stages of the West's emergence from its long darkened slumber. This awakening struggled to make headway, however, in an environment steeped in Catholic orthodoxy that denigrated commerce, prohibited the charging of interest on loans (usury), and insisted upon unquestioning obedience to the Church, a conservative institution that extolled faith and viewed reason as a threat.

Aristotle (a pagan) was made acceptable to the Church by Thomas Aquinas's demonstration of the compatibility of reason and Church doctrine. Aquinas would exercise a substantial influence over subsequent Western views of law, especially of natural law. In his great thirteenth century work *Summa Theologia*, Aquinas echoed Aristotle's observations that judges should be governed by the law, rather than be left to decide matters as they will: "those who sit in judgment judge of things present, towards which they are affected by love, hatred, or some kind of cupidity; wherefore their judgment is perverted."[9] Like Aristotle, Aquinas asserted that the law is based on reason and must be oriented toward the common good. Aquinas held that an unjust positive law is "no law at all,"[10] thereby situating positive law beneath and subject to Divine Law and Natural Law. Aquinas accepted, however, that it was logically impossible for the sovereign to be limited by the positive law: "The sovereign is said to be exempt from the law; since, properly speaking, no man is coerced by himself, and law has no coercive power save from the authority of the sovereign. Thus then is the sovereign said to be exempt from the law, because none is competent to pass sentence on him, if he acts against the law."[11] Aquinas went on to assert that the sovereign can nevertheless subject himself to the law by his own will, and further that he should so do, because "whatever law a man makes for another, he should keep for himself."[12] Finally, he asserted that the sovereign, while free from the coercive power of the law, is in God's judgment limited by the positive law, and is subject to the Divine Law and Natural Law, with sanctions to be imposed by God.[13]

With this backdrop, three essential Medieval contributions to the rule of law tradition can now be conveyed.

Popes versus kings

Notions of theocratic kingship, first asserted by Constantine, made conflict between popes and kings inevitable. The Gelasian doctrine, formulated in the late fifth century, which established that secular and religious authorities had supremacy in their own respective realms, helped suppress the conflict.[14] But Justinian rejected this doctrine, as would later emperors and kings, claiming authority over the sacred owing to their own divinely ordained status; conversely, popes, from their end, asserted ultimate authority over secular leaders, a logical implication flowing from the primacy of the sacred over the profane.

Emperors performed many religious functions, including the appointment and dismissal of bishops and other church officials, and summoning and participating in ecclesiastical councils to resolve religious issues as well as determine matters of church law and policy. A number of popes were either seated by or had their selection ratified by emperors. Justinian considered himself the supreme temporal power and the supreme spiritual power.[15] "The combination of regal and sacerdotal power . . . was the hallmark of the emperor's singular position . . . The emperor's laws and decrees and commands were the laws, decrees, and commands of divinity made known through the emperor."[16] The laws were not just the product of the emperor's will, but also of Divine will, which granted them a sacred stamp. Justinian declared that "The laws originate in our divine mouth;" and the law was a "divine precept."[17] Charlemagne stated that he was "lord and father, king and priest, chief and guide of all Christians;"[18] he outlined for Pope Leo III the extent and limits of papal authority, and dictated to the Pope on certain matters of church dogma. Roman absolutism was thus overlaid with a religious cloak that rendered the emperor answerable to no one but God; certainly not to the people. Western kings and princes without the title of emperor also asserted divine authority and regularly exercised powers of appointment and taxation over local dioceses.

Roman popes similarly exerted expansive powers over both realms. Their first task was to consolidate their authority as heads of the entire Church, claiming entitlement to primacy as successors to St. Peter. Popes were also kings in their own right, filling the secular vacuum in Rome, ruling the territories of the papal states. In recognition of their monarchial status, the term *princeps* was used indistinguishably to refer to emperors, kings and popes. Roman law continued to have an influence in Rome itself during the Middle Ages, affecting the canon law of the Church as well as the Church's institutional culture, imbuing popes, many of whom were trained in law, with regal absolutism. The Church took on the "juridical and authoritarian qualities of the Roman imperial culture, with a strict hierarchy that issued binding rulings from the top."[19]

The intrepid popes went beyond mere leadership within the Church, however, to insist upon superiority over emperors, kings, and princes, reasoning that the spiritual realm took precedence over the temporal. *Dictatus Papae*, issued in 1073 by Pope Gregory VII, declared that "papal authority alone was universal and plenary, while all other powers in the world, whether emperors, Kings, or bishops, were particular and dependant."[20] Natural law and divine law, of which popes were the ultimate earthly representatives and interpreters, controlled positive law and applied to kings (by God's design). A more specific foundation for this asserted supremacy was known as the Donation of Constantine, an eighth-century forgery. According to the Donation, Constantine, mortally ill with leprosy, was cured by Pope Sylvester. In gratitude, Constantine made the Bishop of Rome the head of the Church, and he resigned his crown to the Pope before moving the capitol to Constantinople, although the Pope magnanimously returned the crown to Constantine. "The doctrine behind this charming story is a radical one: The pope is supreme over all rulers, even the Roman emperor, who owes his crown to the pope and therefore may be deposed by papal decree."[21]

This arrogation of ultimate power by popes – severely tempered in practice by their limited military strength – was not absurd in the heart of the Middle Ages, when the Holy Roman Empire of the West was united only in being Christian. The Church, it must be appreciated, encompassed everyone in Medieval society, no less emperors and kings, excluding only infidels "Medieval thought in general was saturated in every part with the conceptions of the Christian faith."[22] At the local level the bishops were the ruling authority in many towns. Society was thoroughly Christianized, with no clear boundaries to separate the secular from the religious realm.[23] "In the Middle Ages the demarcation of the sphere of religious thought and that of worldly concerns was nearly obliterated."[24]

The fraudulent Donation played an immediate role in political affairs. Pepin needed legitimation to take over from the Merovingian line that had previously ruled the Frankish kingdom. The Pope obliged Pepin's request for Church approval of his claim to the crown, culminating in Pepin's anointment with holy oil by Boniface, the Pope's representative. Pepin, in return, explicitly acknowledged the Donation "as a true statement of the valid powers of the papacy."[25] It was an arrangement of mutual benefit that reciprocally conferred legitimation.

The situation was different, however, with the coronation of Charlemagne, son of Pepin. Charlemagne was a powerful ruler who had proven his mettle as a conqueror. The reigning pope, Leo III, in contrast, was in a position of weakness, having recently been beaten by a Roman mob. Leo was determined to regain his prestige:

On Christmas day, 800, as Charlemagne rose from prayer before the tomb of St. Peter, Pope Leo suddenly placed the crown on the king's head, and the well-rehearsed Roman clergy and people shouted, "Charles Augustus, crowned great and peace-giving emperor of the Romans, life and victory!" Charlemagne was so indignant and chagrined that, according to Einhard, "he said he would never have entered the church on that day, although it was a very important religious festival, if he had known the intention of the Pope."[26]

Charlemagne "understood the constitutional implications of papal coronation and had no intention of placing himself in a position of debt or weakness to the bishop of Rome."[27]

Charlemagne's foresight was confirmed by the dramatic Investiture Conflict of the late eleventh century.[28] Henry IV, the most powerful monarch of his time, insisted on his traditional right to appoint leading church personnel within his domain, contrary to the aforementioned declaration of Pope Gregory VII that popes controlled all church matters. With the tentative support of his own church officials (who he had earlier appointed), Henry challenged Gregory. Gregory promptly deposed Henry, declaring him no longer king, threatening to excommunicate anyone who refused to comply. Although unprecedented, these actions proved effective. With his support crumbling, Henry hastened to make amends, traveling to the Pope. Forced to wait three days before receiving a papal audience, he abased himself before Gregory, promising to thereafter obey papal decrees, whereupon he was reinstated as king. Some time later Henry exacted a measure of vengeance by forcing Gregory into exile where he remained until his death, but the conflict embroiled succeeding kings and popes for decades.

Despite the justified wariness with which monarchs viewed papal claims of authority, oath-taking became an integral aspect of the coronation ceremony, thereby consolidating the understanding that the king was subject to a higher authority and operated within legal restraints. "At the time of the inauguration the ruler, on the face of it, accepted ecclesiastical notions of the nature, purpose and limitation of his kingship in so far as he agreed to undergo the whole procedure."[29] In these ceremonies kings explicitly committed themselves to upholding the ecclesiastical and mundane – customary as well as enacted – laws. "These ceremonies, controlled and performed by the Church hierarchy, incorporated the secular Germanic idea that the king's chief duty was to be guardian of the community's law; in all the rituals the king promised to perform this duty faithfully."[30] From this period onward no monarch ascended to office without taking the oath. Pepin said "Inasmuch as we shall observe law toward everybody, we wish everybody to observe it toward us;" Charles the Bold swore, "I shall keep the law and justice;" Louis the Stammerer asserted "I shall keep the customs and the laws of the nation."[31] Even Louis XIV, the exemplar of absolutist monarchy, stated in an ordinance in 1667, "Let it be not said that the sovereign is not subjected to the laws of his State; the contrary proposition is a truth of natural law . . .; what brings perfect felicity to a kingdom is the fact that the king is obeyed by his subjects and that he himself obeys the law."[32]

The significance of these repeated oaths and voluntary affirmations must not be underestimated. Monarchs thereby confirmed, time and again, that they were bound by the law, whether customary, positive, natural, or divine, not just admitting but endorsing the proposition that fidelity to the law was an appropriate standard against which to evaluate regal conduct. This routine helped render a self-imposed obligation into a settled general expectation.

The complete religious cloak on law and society in Medieval under-standings operated in another way to lay the groundwork for the rule of law, as described by Medieval scholar Walter Ullmann:

What the metaphorical use of soul and body attempted to express was that, because faith in Christ was the cementing bond of the whole Church and the exposition of the faith the business of the clergy, the law itself as the external regulator of society was to be based upon the faith. Faith and law stood to each other in the relation of cause and effect . . . Differently expressed, since every law was to embody the idea of justice, and since justice was an essential ingredient of the Christian faith, the "soul" in this allegory meant the Christian idea of justice. There can be little doubt that this thesis was the medieval idea of the "rule of law," manifested in the idea of the supremacy of law.[33]

Hence society was governed by a law identified with Christian justice; the monarch as a Christian was subject to this law, like everyone else, and made an explicit oath confirming his subjugation to the higher (natural, divine, and customary) law and the positive law. The absolutist monarch mold inherited from Roman law was thereby counteracted and trans-formed into a monarch explicitly under law.

Germanic customary law

The Germanic customary law proposition that the king is under the law has been widely identified as an independent source of the rule of law in the Medieval period, providing a counterpoise to Roman notions of absolutist monarchs. Germanic customary law influenced broad swaths of Europe beyond the native German-speaking lands, including substan-tial parts of modern England, France, and Spain, owing to the spread of the expansionary and settling German tribes, though its actual degree of penetration varied, weakest in the Latinate (Romance language) regions. The bulk of law in the Medieval period was customary law, not statutory or positive law. Mostly unwritten, customary law obtained special sanc-tity by virtue of its claimed ancient pedigree, which during the Medieval period was one of the most powerful forms of legitimation. Moreover, customary law carried strong connotations of consent of the people, in virtue of the fact that it (per definition) enjoyed widespread recognition and compliance. Even legislation, to the limited extent that it existed, was generally understood not as the creation of new law, but rather as the declaration and clarification of existing unwritten customary law. The pri-macy of customary law did not prohibit legal change; it required only that such change be consented to by those affected. According to Medieval-ist Frits Kern, Germanic views of the supremacy of law were reconciled with Romanist views that law is the will of the sovereign through the understanding "that the monarch has absorbed the law into his will."[34]

Kern offered this summary:

In the Germanic State, Law was customary law, "the law of one's fathers," the preexisting, objective, legal situation, which was a complex of innumerable subjective rights. All well-founded private rights were protected from arbitrary change, as parts of the same objective legal structure as that to which the monarch owed his own authority. The purpose of the State according to Germanic political ideas, was to fix and maintain, to preserve the existing order, the good old law. The Germanic community was, in essence, an organization for the maintenance of law and order.[35]

The monarch and state existed within the law, for the law, and as creatures of the law, oriented toward the interest of the community. A king was a guardian of the law who did not have the power to declare new law by his leave, a view that would have been considered "blasphemous, for the law, like kingship, possessed its own sacrosanct aura."[36] The later permeation of Germanic customary law with Christian understandings solidified the identification of law with justice, as described in the previous section. There was a "fusion of law and morals,"[37] a sense that "that law was in its nature more than a mere command, that it implied justice and a right recognized but not created by it . . ."[38]

The legendary Germanic "right of resistance," according to which any king who breached the law was subject to abandonment by the people, was a stark manifestation of the belief of the supremacy of the law over kings. "The king and his people both stood under a mutual obligation to preserve the law from infringement or corruption and in some cases when the king clearly failed to do his duty we find his subjects taking matters into their own hands and deposing him."[39] The key underlying notion was fealty, in which both ruler and ruled were bound to the law; law imposed reciprocal, albeit unequal, obligations that ran in both directions, including loyalty and allegiance. This notion ran through the gamut of social relations of the feudal system. A ruler who breached this law forfeited the right to obedience of his subjects.[40] Among other obligations, the king was bound to honor feudal obligations, and contracts, and could not lightly seize the property of others.[41] "A man may resist his king and judge when he acts contrary to law and may even help to make war on him . . . Thereby, he does not violate the duty of fealty."[42]

Some Medieval scholars assert that the impact of these customary law views has been exaggerated, and it is impossible to separate the influence of these views from those mentioned in the preceding section, which commingled and reinforced one another. But even skeptics acknowledge that they mattered. During most of the Medieval period there was a real tradition of the sovereign being limited by law, albeit not always honored in practice. "Most jurists did not conclude that the prince's absolute power transcended natural or divine law, or the normal, established, 'constitutional' order."[43] Deviations from the law required "cause." Keeping in mind that the king could not be brought before a legal institution to answer for violations, the consequence of these views is that the king was not entirely free to disregard the law. Beyond binding kings, princes, and their officers, as indicated, customary law applied to everyone, including local barons and their aristocratic brethren who presided in manorial courts, confirming and solidifying the everyday sense that no one was above the law.

The Magna Carta

No discussion of the Medieval origins of the rule of law would be complete without a mention of the Magna Carta, signed in 1215, ten years before the birth of Aquinas. Although it stands on its own as a historical event with reverberating consequences in the rule of law tradition, the Magna Carta also epitomized a third Medieval root of the rule of the law, the effort of nobles to use law to restrain kings.

There is no disputing the historical significance of this oft-mentioned document, but historians are split over when it acquired this significance and whether it was deserved.[44] Far from embodying the notion of liberty for all for which it has become renowned, the document was the product of concessions forced upon King John by rebellious barons interested in protecting themselves from onerous exaction by the King to finance his losing war effort in France. The document is occupied with details about the privileges of substantial land-holders. Detractors assert, further, that the significance of the document was relatively minor until given a glorified mischaracterization in the seventeenth century by Coke "and made into the symbol of the struggle against arbitrary power."[45] Supporters contend, in response, that the Magna Carta had contemporary and ongoing significance, considering that – notwithstanding almost immediate repudiation by King John – it was confirmed by later monarchs and parliaments numerous times, and was referred to in public discourse over the course of centuries on multiple occasions. Moreover, supporters assert, while acknowledging that the immediate participants were the King and barons, the latter represented the interests of all free men, as stated in the document itself.

For present purposes this debate need not be resolved. Then and now the Magna Carta symbolized the fact that law protected citizens against the king. Clause 39 is the historic provision:

No free man shall be taken or imprisoned or disseised or outlawed or exiled or in any way ruined, nor will we go or send against him, except by the lawful judgement of his peers or by the law of the land.[46]

This language confirmed that the barons were not subject to the king's justices, who were notorious for doing his bidding, and confirmed that decisions must be based upon ordinary law, not upon the desires of the king. Regular courts were thus identified as the proper preserve of lawful conduct.[47]

A few decades later, influenced by the Magna Carta, Henry of Bracton began writing his treatise *On The Laws and Customs of England*.[48] Therein penned Bracton this famous formulation of the rule of law:[49]

For his is called *rex* not from reigning but from ruling well, since he is a king as long as he rules well but a tyrant when he oppresses by violent domination the people entrusted to his care. Let him, therefore, temper his power by law, which is the bridle of power, that he may live according to the laws, for the law of mankind has decreed that his own laws bind the lawgiver, and elsewhere in the same source, it is a saying worthy of the majesty of a ruler that the prince acknowledge himself bound by the laws. Nothing is more fitting for a sovereign than to live by the laws, nor is there any greater sovereignty than to govern according to law, and he ought properly to yield to the law what the law has bestowed upon him, for the law makes him king.[50]

In addition to subordinating the king to law, the Magna Carta has been credited with promoting the notion of the due process of law, which is significant in US constitutional analysis.[51] Although these words are not actually used in clause 39, the phrase "due process of law" was used in a statute in 1354, and came to be identified with the phrase "the law of the land."[52] Over time it acquired the connotation that at least a minimal degree of legal procedures – those that insure a fair hearing, especially the opportunity to be heard before a neutral decision-maker – must be accorded in the context of the judicial process.

Finally, the Magna Carta has also been identified as the source of constitutionalism – the structuring of the fundamental relationship between a government and its people in legal terms. The English long held a myth about an ancient unwritten constitution based upon customary law and understandings. The Magna Carta added a foundational written piece (which some thought detracted from the ancient one). In the UK, where the notion of parliamentary sovereignty prevails, the Magna Carta does not officially possess a higher legal status, and its terms have been superceded several times by ordinary statute. Still, in a popular sense it is thought of as a higher form of law, certainly at least clause 39, which is nigh untouchable, and it has been referred to in such terms on many occasions over the centuries.[53]

Much of the Magna Carta's actual influence on the rule of law tradition, it should be emphasized, came after the Medieval period. But it did stand for the rule of law during this period. "Repeated confirmations of Magna Carta, when demanded by the community and granted by the monarchs, reiterated the idea that the king, like his subjects, was under the law."[54] Equally important, it added a concrete institutionalized component within the positive law system – an ordinary court and jury of peers – to the earlier mentioned abstract declarations about natural law and customary law.

The dilemma bequeathed by this medieval legacy

It has been asserted: "The principle foundation on which medieval political theory was built was the principle of the supremacy of law."[55] The foregoing exploration suggests that this came about in several ways – by monarchs taking oaths to abide by the divine, natural, customary, and positive laws; by a pervasively shared understanding that everyone, kings included, operated within a framework of such laws; by Romanic, Germanic, and Christian ideals that the good king abides by the law; by kings entering agreements (voluntarily or under duress) to accord others the protections of ordinary legal processes; by others having an interest in tethering kings (as well as barons) within legal restraints; and by monarchs recognizing that they obtained legitimacy by claiming to be bound by, and by acting consistent with, the law. Although the preceding discussion was organized in terms of separate contributions, in reality they comprised intermingled influences that were anything but separate. Within these roots, however, was also laid a hidden dilemma that would sprout and grow large only when the surrounding Medieval trappings fell away.

With the sixteenth-century Reformation, shattering the hegemonic grip of the Church, and eighteenth-century Enlightenment, hearkening the rise of reason and science, a general social-cultural partitioning of the sacred and temporal came about, in steps at first imperceptible but in hindsight large, unwinding the Medieval intertwining of the two. Divine law and natural law were separated from positive law, the former two losing their authority over affairs of state. With the vast expansion of the state – that accelerated only after the Medieval period – also came an increase in the volume and scope of legislation and a consequent decrease in the proportion and prestige of customary law. Anglo-American views of the common law as an autonomous body of law comprised of custom, reason and legal principle survived into the late nineteenth century, but also suffered decline. Long-standing conceptions that legislation did not create new law but merely declared preexisting natural law or customary law were superceded entirely, supplanted by the view that law is the product of legislative will to be shaped as desired, known as an "instrumental" view of law.

Troublesome implications for the rule of law resulted from these changes. In the Medieval period monarchs were considered bound by positive law in large part because natural law, divine law and customary law demanded it. These sources of law also set limits upon and controlled positive law. A key characteristic they shared is that all were beyond the reach of monarchs. As these others lost their significance, positive law was left standing on its own legs. "The more law comes to be thought of as merely positive, the command of the law-giver, the more difficult is it to put any restraints upon the action of the legislator, and in cases of monarchial government to avoid tyranny."[56] This changes everything, for if positive law is a matter of will, changeable as desired, it would seem that there can be no true legal restraint on the law-maker. Aquinas said as much.

"How can the rule of law be compatible with sovereign legislative authority?"[57] This is the age-old question of how – or indeed whether – the government can be limited by law when it is the ultimate source of law. The enduring significance of, and possible answers to, this question will become apparent in the course of this work.

Rise of the bourgeois

The transition in Europe from the Middle Ages, through the Renaissance and the Enlightenment, to the modern era, was not the uninterrupted flowering of the rule of law and democratic institutions, culminating in the birth of liberalism. For a time, centered around the seventeenth century, absolutist monarchies prevailed in much of Europe.[58] Their authority was bolstered by the doctrine of the Divine Right of Kings. By asserting appointment directly from God, this doctrine was aimed at freeing the king from the Church. Its implications went further, removing all restraints from the king, including law: "Hence the Prince or the State which he represents is accountable to none but God, and political sovereignty 'is at all times so free as to be in no earthly subjection in all things touching the regality of said power.'"[59] "[K]ings were 'above the law,' because they made the laws and were responsible for their actions only to God."[60] Among other manifestations of their right to unfettered rule, monarchs exercised the royal prerogative to preside over cases of consequence, and the dispensing power, which entitled them in specific instances to hold the law in abeyance.

The rule of law ideas elaborated earlier in this chapter were not completely squelched, however. Although monarchs acted above the law under compelling circumstances, in many routine respects, despite absolutist declarations, they continued to operate within legal restraints.[61] What helped preserve these restraints, aside from the recognition by monarchs that it was in their interest to be seen to conform to the law, was the increase in numbers and professionalization of lawyers and judges, a process that had begun in the Middle Ages. At least in England, which by the time of royal absolutism had a centuries-old legal tradition, with its own system of education and body of knowledge,[62] courts could withstand or parry attempts at regal interference. This capacity was in evidence in a decision issued by Coke in 1607, which denied King James I the power to decide a case already under the purview of the Court, regardless of his acknowledged ultimate authority over law: "the Judges are sworn to execute justice according the law and custom of England . . . the King cannot take any cause out of any of his Courts, and give judgement upon it himself."[63] Law had become, or was well on the path to becoming, an established, regularized institutional presence substantially shaped by the increasingly autonomous legal profession. Courts were at the center of this institutional complex and judges served as the guardians of and spokesman for the law.

No attempt will be made to elaborate on the sources of the transformation from feudalism, through absolutist monarchies, to liberalism, which occurred under various circumstances and timing across Europe, and would take the discussion far beyond the scope of this work.[64] However, one factor – the rise of the merchants, of the bourgeois – will be briefly addressed, because it plays an important part in the emergence of liberalism.[65] As with much of the historical discussion herein, a broad brush will be used to recount these developments, foregoing nuance and bypassing differences.

Commencing in the twelfth century, the rise of towns as the centers of economic activity, an increase in population and commerce, and the consequent accumulation of wealth by merchants, prompted developments that finally broke the stranglehold of the feudal system,[66] which lost its total social dominance by the end of the thirteenth century and finally expired in the West by the seventeenth century. Merchants had no place in the land-based, agrarian, hierarchically fixed feudal order. Left out of feudal categories, they were free. But this exclusion also provided them with limited protections and little political power. The cities, which their activities built, enriched, and enlivened, had no right of self-government.

Merchants increasingly chafed under a feudal system that gave priority, status, and control over the courts to the landed nobility, who applied restrictive, obsolete laws and procedures in a self-interested manner that inhibited the activities of the merchants. Nobles – land rich but money poor – envied, and strove to inhibit or siphon off, the wealth of the merchants. Remember that the medieval Church – its bishops major land owners with economic clout and legal and political power to supplement their religious authority – was also aligned against commerce, disparaging it as an unworthy activity and stultifying the availability of commercial credit through its prohibition of usury.

Monarchs had persistent conflicts of their own with the landed nobility.[67] In addition to being potential rivals, the nobility resisted when called upon for military or financial contributions due to the monarch as feudal overlord (pace the Magna Carta). This resistance rendered tenuous the fiscal condition and military might of monarchs, who derived most of their resources from their feudal holdings. The nobility also was not compliant when asked by monarchs to authorize a tax in support of a war effort. This recalcitrance forced some monarchs to sell off their land holdings to raise necessary revenues, which further undermined their strength.

A common interest – their common opponent – resulted in an unspoken alliance between monarchs and merchants. Monarchs increasingly obtained a greater proportion of their income through the more reliable means of substituting fee-generating state courts for baronial courts, procuring loans from wealthy merchants, and taxing commercial activities (especially customs taxes). Thus it was in the monarch's interest to facilitate the efforts of merchants, who were often also commercial lenders. Monarchs supported the attempts of the cities, led by the merchants, against the opposition of the nobles, to become self-governing corporations or franchises.[68] Owing to the demands of merchants for cheap labor, it became imperative for serfs – multiplying in number – to be available for work. Freedom was conferred upon anyone who resided in a city for more than a year. "City law not only did away with personal servitude and restrictions on land, but also caused the disappearance of the seignorial rights and fiscal claims which interfered with the activity of commerce and industry."[69] "The factor of a changing economic structure operated . . . everywhere including England, where rational procedures of proof were introduced by the royal authority especially in the interests of the merchants."[70] Practices and rules merchants followed in their transactions with one another in the markets or regional fairs, enforced in their own tribunals, were subsequently recognized by courts.

As commerce increased and wealth grew, the accompanying inflation sapped the economic power of the nobility, who were dependent for their income on fixed feudal rents that could not be easily increased. When the basis of wealth shifted from the possession of land to buying and selling goods, the nobility were caught in an economic vise: suffering from a relative decrease in the value of their income, yet required to support the lifestyle and large retinue expected of persons of high social standing. Land came on the market for sale to satisfy the demands of the merchants, for whom land ownership still represented wealth and standing, as well as to meet the financial needs of the nobles. Nobles who would not deign to engage in commercial activities, or to enter marriages with successful merchant families (an arrangement of reciprocal advantage, trading money for prestige), faced decline. As dramatic evidence of their precarious condition, in some locations all of the nobles became indebted to town merchants.[71] Lords actually came to have an interest in freeing their serfs, for this freedom had to be bought; and the change in status allowed lords to effectuate a favorable transition from traditional payment by serfs in services or produce to payment in money of rent (or face eviction); lords in effect were transformed into bare landlords, freed from their preexisting host of responsibilities toward their former serfs.

Once these various factors gathered momentum, the demise of the feudal system in the West was fated. Facilitating the economic activities of the merchants led, over time, to an entirely new society and set of legal institutions, away from a fixed-at-birth status of the feudal social order, toward individual striving and the accumulation of wealth, revolving around the market, commercial credit, financial instruments, property rights, and the enforcement of contracts. The above scenario did not occur everywhere; nor is it the whole story.[72] When merchants viewed the monarch as the greater threat, they allied themselves with the nobility against the monarch; at times monarchs and nobles took on the merchants and lenders; in later periods, protectionist town guilds comprised of groups of artisans engaged in sustained conflicts with external merchants (who were favored by monarchs owing to their economic benefits); workers who rebelled against merchants to improve their conditions and pay were put down by monarchs or nobles who feared disorder; plagues, crop failures, and wars intermittently decimated the population, making labor scarce, dampening demand, disrupting commercial progress. Thus there was no single or straight path. Whatever other factors were involved, the culmination of these developments was the rise of the bourgeois, with a concomitant recognition of their interests in politics and law. This lies at the heart of liberalism.

3   Liberalism

Liberalism was born in the pre-modern period of the late-seventeenth and eighteenth centuries. Like any political theory, there are competing versions of liberalism, ranging from the social welfare liberalism of John Rawls, to the libertarian liberalism of Robert Nozick, to the conservative liberalism of Friedrich Hayek, to the pluralistic liberalism of Isaiah Berlin, to the egalitarian liberalism of Amy Gutman. The picture is further complicated because liberalism consists not just of a political theory and system of government, but also a culture, an economic theory, a psychology, a theory of ethics, and a theory of knowledge.[1] Notwithstanding this variety and complexity, every version of liberalism reserves an essential place for the rule of law. And the rule of law today is thoroughly understood in terms of liberalism.

Above all else liberalism emphasizes individual liberty.[2] Put in classic terms by John Stuart Mill: "The only freedom which deserves the name, is that of pursuing our own good in our own way, so long as we do not attempt to deprive others of theirs, or impede their efforts to obtain it."[3]

The liberal social contract tradition, formulated most influentially by John Locke, explains the origins of law and the state in idealized terms. Life without law (in the state of nature) is insecure and prone to disputes; keeping the peace requires laws, and unbiased law enforcers and judges. Autonomous individuals choose to enter a mutually binding covenant to form a government authorized to promulgate and enforce a body of laws in the interest of preserving order, thereby exchanging their natural freedom for living under a legal system, while retaining their basic rights and liberties. What renders the arrangement legitimate is their consent. Consent respects the autonomy of individuals even as they become subject to the dictates of the law.

Equality is a companion of liberty within liberalism by virtue of the moral equivalence accorded to all individuals as autonomous rights-bearing beings. Everyone must be treated with equal respect and dignity, due as human beings with the inherent capacity for reason and moral conduct. Equality within liberalism entails that citizens possess equal political rights and be entitled to equality before the law. Liberty and equality require that the government remains neutral on the question of the good: "Since the citizens of a society differ in their conceptions, the government does not treat them as equals if it prefers one conception to another, either because the officials believe that one is intrinsically superior, or because one is held by the more numerous or more powerful group."[4]

This chapter will provide an introduction to the main themes in liberalism to supply a background for the ensuing discussion of historical and contemporary theories on the rule of law in liberal systems. An important reminder is necessary to offset this lengthy focus on liberalism: while liberal systems cannot exist without the rule of law (as will be explained), the rule of law can exist outside of liberal systems. None of the accounts of the rule of law discussed in the previous two chapters – Greek, Roman, and Medieval – related to liberal systems. The liberal orientation of the rule of law differs markedly from these pre-liberal sources. In liberalism the rule of law emphasizes the preservation of individual liberty. Not so in the Greek or Medieval understandings of the rule of law, which contain nary a mention of individual liberty. In Greek conceptions liberty meant collective self-rule, and supremacy was accorded to law because it was effectuated by the citizens themselves and reflected and enforced the community morality and tradition. In Medieval understandings the rule of law was oriented to containing rapacious kings, and emphasized that law must be for the good of the community. For both historical sources primacy was accorded to the community, not the individual. In societies oriented toward the community, or in fixed hierarchic societies, restraining the tyranny of the government does not enhance the liberty of individuals to be or do what they wish. Surrounding social and cultural constraints render such liberty irrelevant if not inconceivable. "The sense of privacy itself, of the area of personal relationships as something sacred in its own right, derives from a conception of freedom which, for all its religious roots, is scarcely older, in its developed state, than the Renaissance or the Reformation."[5] Owing to its individualist emphasis, a consistent thrust underlying liberal thought is fear, fear of impositions by others, and especially fear of the state.

Four themes of liberty

The familiar liberal story told above begins by placing individuals in an unenviable predicament: it appears to require that liberty be sacrificed in the interest of personal security and social order. After all, in the absence of law an individual would be absolutely free. Giving up liberty to further self-preservation is a dubious exchange if the result is to be subject to legal oppression; it is like willingly entering a jail cell for the safety offered behind bars. Liberals counter that if everyone is absolutely free, then no one is truly free, owing to the threat that we pose to one another. Even if this were correct – by no means obvious – to be told that one is free after submitting to law should evoke suspicion. Is it not more candid to admit that under law we are not free, but the benefits that law brings are worth the trade off? Modern liberal democracies offer a fourfold answer to this question.

First, the individual is free to the extent that the laws are created democratically. Citizens have thereby consented to, indeed authored, the rules they are obliged to follow. The individual is at once ruler and ruled. Individuals thus rule themselves. "[O]bedience to a law one prescribes to oneself is freedom,"[6] Rousseau declared. "A people, since it is subject to laws, ought to be the author of them."[7] Moreover, presumably under a democracy citizens would not enact laws to oppress themselves; their power to make law is, accordingly, their own best protection. Self-rule is "*political liberty.*" Representative democracy is the modern manifestation of self-rule in the West. This is akin to the classical Greek understanding of liberty, although importantly different in that theirs was a direct, not representative, democracy. In the contemporary world it lies behind the manifold examples of yearning and agitation for independence from alien rule or from rule by a majority group with a different cultural identity or religion. The realization of political liberty requires the opportunity for real participation in collective decisions with respect to the governing political and legal structure, and it implies the right to vote and eligibility for political office, and the protection of freedom of speech, assembly, and association.

Second, the individual is free to the extent that government officials are required to act in accordance with preexisting law. This requirement promotes liberty by enabling individuals to predict when they will be subject to coercion by the state legal apparatus, allowing them to avoid legal interference in their affairs by not running afoul of the law. Citizens are subject only to the law, not to the arbitrary will or judgment of another who wields coercive government power. This entails that the laws be declared publicly in clear terms in advance, be applied equally, and be interpreted and applied with certainty and reliability. The seminal example of this is the prohibition against criminal punishment in the absence of a preexisting law. This is "*legal liberty.*" Montesquieu framed it best: "Liberty is a right of doing whatever the laws permit[.]"[8] It is the freedom to do whatever the laws do not explicitly proscribe. Legal liberty is the dominant theoretical understanding of the rule of law in modern liberal democracies, as will be later elaborated.

Third, the individual is free in so far as the government is restricted from infringing upon an inviolable realm of personal autonomy. Often the protections are known as civil rights or liberties, and are contained in bills of rights or human rights declarations. These restrictions may be substantive (strictly prohibiting government incursion within the protected sphere), or only procedural (the government must satisfy a high burden, like demonstrating compelling necessity, before interference is allowed). This is *"personal liberty."* Personal liberty constitutes the minimum degree of autonomy individuals retain even after they consent to live under law. It consists of the protections necessary to allow the achievement of Mill's "freedom to pursue our own good in our own way." This is what prohibits the liberal state from imposing on everyone in society a particular version of the good. Personal liberty, when recognized, is uncertain in scope and variable in content. Routinely there is disagreement with respect to the contours of the protected sphere, as well as with regard to how those contours should be determined. It usually includes the freedom of religion and conscience, freedom of speech and political belief, freedom from torture or cruel punishment, and freedom to determine one's life pursuits and values. Robust versions are phrased in terms of an expansive zone of privacy or dignity. The US Supreme Court phrased it thus: "Liberty presumes an autonomy of self that includes freedom of thought, belief, expression, and certain intimate conduct."[9] The essential underlying idea is that individuals are entitled to integrity of body and mind free from government interference. This notion is "the standard view of freedom in the liberal tradition."[10]

Finally, freedom is enhanced when the powers of the government are divided into separate compartments – typically legislative, executive, and judicial (horizontal division), and sometimes municipal, state or regional, and national (vertical division) – with the application of law entrusted to an independent judiciary. This division promotes liberty by preventing the accumulation of total power in any single institution, setting up a form of competitive interdependence within the government. The separation of the judicial apparatus from other government institutions has particular significance. Allocating the application of law to an independent judiciary insures that a consummately legal institution is available to check the legality of governmental action. This is the *"institutionalized preservation of liberty."* It entails institutional structures and processes that have been devised to enhance prospects for the realization of the liberty of citizens through the effective division of government power. This is qualitatively different from the previous three, in that it is a structural arrangement for enhancing liberty rather than a type of liberty itself.

Each of the first three forms of liberty, in their own way, vindicates a different shade of self-determination. Political liberty allows individuals to determine (collectively) the rules under which they live. Legal liberty allows individuals to do whatever they wish with knowledge of, and consistent with, these rules. Personal liberty insures individuals the minimum degree of autonomy they require to be who they want to be. None of these liberties, however, is absolute. The first entails the participation and cooperation of others; the limits of the second are set by the proscriptions of standing laws; the scope of autonomy provided by the third is bounded by the equivalent autonomy of other individuals as well as by the necessities of the state. A separate set of limits is imposed on persons thought incapable of self-determination, as with children, mental incompetents, and criminals, and, in previous times, women, slaves, and colonized subjects. To exercise the liberty of self-determination people must have the capacity for self-determination. Measures like mandatory education, for this reason, can be imposed on youth without offending their liberty.

Modern liberal democracies answer the skeptical question posed earlier – how is an individual under law still free? – by offering a tight combination of these four themes. In a democracy citizens create the laws under which they live (political liberty); government officials take actions against citizens in accordance with these laws (legal liberty). In the first respect they rule themselves; in the second they are ruled by the laws which they set for themselves. Citizens, therefore, are at no point subject to the rule of another individual. Moreover, citizens possess a specially protected realm of individual autonomy that restricts the reach of law (personal liberty). Liberal democracies typically carry out this combination by utilizing some form of separation of powers, in particular with an independent judiciary (institutionalized preservation of liberty). Almost without exception (the UK being a prominent partial exception), this arrangement is set out in a written constitution, binding on government officials and citizens and enforced by independent courts. As is evident, this liberal construction is thoroughly legalistic. Law is the skeleton that holds the liberal system upright and gives it form and stability.

Tensions among the liberties

Although these four answers are often found together, that is neither required nor an easy matter. Legal liberty, personal liberty, and institutionalized preservation of liberty, may all coexist without political liberty, for example, in a system in which laws are established by a non-democratic (philosophical or scientific) elite, as utopian political philosophers have dreamed. Indeed sound arguments can be made that an elite-designed system is more likely to maximize legal liberty and personal liberty than a democratic system. The unease this suggestion generates – even if the potential for corruption of the elite guardians could somehow be eliminated – demonstrates the significance attached to political liberty. Self-rule is widely preferred even if that means being ruled poorly.

Legal theorists have often made the point that legal liberty (as the rule of law) may exist without political liberty (democracy). "The mere commitments to generality and autonomy in law and to the distinction among legislation, administration and adjudication have no inherent democratic significance."[11] "A nondemocratic legal system . . . may, in principle, conform to the requirements of the rule of law better than any of the legal systems of the more enlightened Western democracies."[12] Some theorists have further argued that, owing to a growing assertiveness on the part of judges, "the Rule of Law has functioned as a clear check on the actual impact and expansion of a rigorous democracy."[13] The relationship between the rule of law and democracy is asymmetrical: the rule of law can exist without democracy, but democracy needs the rule of law, for otherwise democratically established laws may be eviscerated at the stage of application by not being followed.

Legal liberty may easily exist without personal liberty. Non-liberal regimes with the rule of law demonstrate this. To say that a citizen is free within the open spaces allowed by the law says nothing about how wide (or narrow) those open spaces must be. Legal liberty is not offended by severe restrictions on individuals, for it requires only that government actions be consistent with laws declared in advance, imposing no strictures on the content of the laws. Benjamin Constant remarked two centuries ago, pointing out the inadequacy of Montesquieu's account of liberty: "No doubt there is no liberty when people cannot do all that the laws allow them to do, but laws could forbid so many things as to abolish liberty altogether."[14] A regime with oppressive laws can satisfy legal liberty by meticulously complying with those laws. In such systems, the more legal liberty is honored the worse for personal liberty. The relationship is again asymmetrical: personal liberty cannot exist without the rule of law, at least when the former is framed in terms of legally enforceable rights.

Perhaps the most formidable problem in the combination of liberties is the potential conflict between personal liberty and political liberty. As Isaiah Berlin observed, "there is no necessary connexion between individual liberty and democratic rule. The answer to the question 'Who governs me?' is logically distinct from the question 'How far does government interfere with me?'"[15] The goal of personal liberty is to curb the application of governmental authority against individuals, whereas the goal of political liberty is to seize control of power to exercise that authority.[16] The concern of the former is tyranny against the individual, which is no less tyrannical when the product of democracy. The concern of the latter is to determine who gets to shape the social and political community through legislation, an objective that is inhibited by the limits set by personal liberty. Drawn in the sharpest terms, this conflict represents the battle between two contesting ideologies: collective self-rule in the interest of the community versus the desire of individuals to be left alone. "These are not two different interpretations of a single concept, but two profoundly divergent and irreconcilable attitudes to the ends of life . . . These claims cannot both be fully satisfied."[17]

Liberals have traditionally held liberty of the individual as preeminent whenever it has come into conflict with democracy. Most early liberals were against popular democracy – not widely instituted until the twentieth century – which they viewed with trepidation as leading to rule by the ignorant masses, a threat to the property of the elite, an invitation to disorder. Even apparently strong pro-democratic sentiments expressed by liberals, like Kant's assertion that a citizen has a "lawful freedom to obey no law other than the one to which he has given his consent," are usually less generous than they might appear; for Kant disqualified from voting all "passive" citizens, which included apprentices, servants, all women, sharecroppers, and more generally all "persons under the orders or protections of other individuals."[18] Some prominent modern liberal theorists have argued that the gravest threat to personal liberty is posed by representative democracy.[19] "Inasmuch as poor voters always and everywhere outnumber rich ones, in theory there are no limits to the democratic state's ability to ride roughshod over the rights of private property."[20] Not surprisingly, considering these fears, when liberal theorists (like Kant) insisted on consent to law, what they often meant was not actual consent but rather a form of hypothetical consent – what people would consent to if they were exercising proper reason.[21]

These tensions among the four liberties are unavoidable but not intractable. Every liberal democracy mediates them in various ways. Another fundamental tension within liberalism is the tension between liberty and equality. Whenever an unequal distribution of assets (including wealth and talent) exists, liberty may have to yield to some degree to insure greater equality. Reconciling the tension between these two liberal values, which is the great burden of liberal social welfare states, will be addressed in later chapters, for it is featured in the claimed Western decline of the rule of law.

Socio-cultural context of liberalism

Liberalism cannot be fully grasped without taking into consideration the cluster of ideas that revolved around the eighteenth-century Enlightenment.[22] The primary creed of the Enlightenment was the application of reason and science to banish ignorance and superstition.[23] Isaac Newton's physics, which produced a few laws that could predict the location and motion of all matter on earth and in the heavens, demonstrated the extraordinary power of science to expose the previously opaque mysteries of nature. After this grand achievement everything was thought accessible to human understanding. The Enlightenment *Philosophes'* distinctive contribution was to extend the application of reason and science to the social, political, legal, economic, and moral realms. They believed that a science of man could be developed which would allow government and society to be designed to give rise to a more just, rational existence. For the most ambitious and optimistic, the ultimate goal was nothing less than the creation of a perfect society. Custom, tradition, and the teachings of the Church, which hitherto had been the leading sources of authority, henceforth were subjected to critical scrutiny. Government and law, and every other social institution, had to be rationally justified, or discarded. The concrete satisfaction of individual and social interests in the here and now took center stage, displacing God and promises about rewards in the hereafter.

The internecine battles among Christians wrought by the sixteenth-century Reformation helped pave the way for the coming Enlightenment and liberalism. It openly challenged Church orthodoxy, which had enjoyed 1,000 years of dominance. Protestantism promoted a kind of individualism in its assertion of a personal relationship with God, unmediated by the Church. The clashes between Protestants and Catholics culminated in slaughters and mutual exhaustion, ultimately forcing a truce based upon tolerance.[24] The very fact of the dispute evidenced the insecure foundation for knowledge provided by religion. Since Medieval Christianity constituted a total world-view, encompassing politics, law, morality, economics, as well as natural phenomena, doubt thrown upon Church teachings could not be sequestered from seeping into a more general questioning of all aspects of existence.

The most consequential casualty of this total questioning, a bedeviling legacy that continues to the present, was the destruction of moral certainty. In the Medieval view, moral right and natural law could be discerned from Biblical revelation (as interpreted by the Church), or through the application of reason implanted in man by God. Enlightenment philosophers were confident that a new secular grounding for moral right and natural law could be found through the application of reason to the study of human nature, which they believed to be universal. This effort ran aground for a combination of reasons.

The exploration of the non-Western world that occurred contemporaneously with the Enlightenment revealed an unexpected variety of customs and moral systems. If commonality was lacking, then some values and traditions must be right and others wrong, but there was no evident standard by which to adjudge one moral system superior to another. Many philosophers assumed the superiority of Western civilization, while others idealized "primitive" systems as a lost, purer state of human existence. Some insisted that a common core of moral beliefs existed beneath the apparent variation among cultures. But David Hume's monumental philosophical argument separating the *is* from the *ought* – to the effect that normative propositions are statements of a qualitatively different kind that cannot be deduced from descriptive propositions – ruined the attempt to derive moral norms based upon shared customs or morality. The fact that a moral norm is widely followed does not, of itself, mean that it should be followed. The practical wisdom of this philosophical point can be seen in the fact that slavery was commonly practiced by cultures, and the subordination of women is still widespread. Hume's argument, furthermore, appeared to disqualify any moral system grounded exclusively in human nature, for that builds upon the *is*, upon descriptive propositions of who we are as humans, to say how we *ought* to act. Another formidable problem was that humans do much that is evil (apparently by nature), so an examination of human nature alone could not establish what was proper moral conduct. A minimalist natural law, built around the conditions necessary for survival in a human community, is a more viable strategy, but it would lack any higher aspirations, hardly deserving of the name morality. A more ambitious natural law focused on human flourishing must first determine what human flourishing means, and must identify a way to select from among or rank the possible alternative versions, for which no uncontroversial answers could be given.

A severe blow to the Enlightenment utopian project was delivered by the Romantics, who challenged the very coherence and desirability of universality, and (with Hume's help) the scope of reason, advocating in their place particularity, will, creativity, and passion. They glorified cultures as wholes unto themselves, each with its own unique and incommensurable life world and values. "But if we are to have as many types of perfection as there are types of culture, each with its ideal constellation of virtues, then the very notion of the possibility of a single perfect society is logically incoherent."[25]

With the failure of the Enlightenment attempt to establish absolute or universal moral principles, many philosophers turned away from the classical search for the ultimate good, rejecting the view that any such single good exists, or at least that it could be identified with certainty. One outcome of this logic was the recognition of moral pluralism, which when taken to the extreme slides to moral skepticism (an extreme that many Enlightenment thinkers abhorred).[26] Another response to this logic was the nineteenth-century rise of utilitarian moral theory, grounded on the notion that the good is whatever people desire or take pleasure in; accordingly, society and its institutions should be designed to maximize the total aggregate quantity of pleasure (minus pain) of individuals within society. Yet another response was the shift to an emphasis on procedures: given that the content of moral principles elude certainty, perhaps there can instead be agreement on fair procedures to be followed when making decisions affecting society. Liberalism, as will become clear in following chapters, is substantially procedural in bent.

The liberty central to liberalism can now be better understood. As indicated, it is the liberty to pursue one's own vision of the good. Whether this is understood as the best way in which to maximize aggregate pleasure, or as a default position forced upon us by the failure to identify universal moral principles, or as the right position to take given the conclusion that there are many alternative forms of the good attached to different cultures or forms of life,[27] the result is the same: liberalism is constructed in a manner that accommodates moral pluralism.[28]

Moral pluralism can function within liberalism in two alternative forms, which can also exist together. The primary Western form involves a pluralism of moral views among the individuals within a liberal (individualist) culture; a secondary form exists when more than one distinct community or culture (liberal or non-liberal) coexists within the ambit of a single system. In either case the liberal state purports to be neutral with respect to the alternative circulating visions of the good. That is, it cannot adopt and promote as the state sanctioned good or religion one vision over others, with the important caveat that it may prohibit or sanction those that perpetuate violence on others or threaten the survival of the liberal state. Competing visions of the good are left to exist – thrive, develop, change, or wither – in the marketplace of cultural ideas. Liberal tenets are not offended, at least not in most versions of liberalism, when the state utilizes subsidies or education to encourage certain social goods, like art and music, or actively promotes or inculcates in youth liberal values like tolerance and individual autonomy, but the state may not apply coercion on behalf of any particular set of values.

This explicitly neutral stance does not mean that liberal systems are completely neutral – in two important respects they are not. Western liberal regimes take the position that neutrality is the *right* principle upon which to construct a government and system of laws.[29] Repeal of this neutrality by those who wield government power cannot be allowed. Were this not the case, liberalism might fail to reproduce itself, which would occur if an anti-liberal, anti-tolerant group prevailed in a democratic election and proceeded to institute a non-liberal regime. Liberal systems are not neutral in the further respect that the primacy accorded to individual rights sets limits upon the extent to which a community-first-and-foremost orientation can be implemented. Owing to these reasons, illiberal sub-communities that exist within overarching liberal structures may see themselves in conflict with the overarching liberal system, and fear it to be corrosive of their community values.

Liberal neutrality, it must be emphasized, represents a radical shift from prior views of the state and the law. Under classical Greek views the state and law were seen as properly oriented to the promotion of the (aristocratic, warrior) virtues and community life; under the Medieval view their role was thought to be the creation and perpetuation of a Christian life and community on earth. In both cases the law was seen as reflecting a substantive vision of the good and a common way of life with a common end. Under the liberal view, it is not necessary that there be a common way of life beyond agreement that individuals are better off if they leave each other alone to pursue whatever ends they desire. Rather than a community integrated by shared values, it amounts to an aggregation of individuals held together by a mutual non-interference pact.

Communitarianism compared with liberalism

Another way to understand liberalism is by way of contrast to communitarianism – presented here in simplified terms – which is commonly identified in political theory as its antithesis.[30] The starting point of communitarianism is the community, not the individual. Communities preexist and survive the births and deaths of individual members. Communities have a presence or being of their own which constitutes more than just the agglomeration of individuals. Communities have an interest of their own – survival of the community way of life – which is more than and different from the aggregated interests of each individual. The culture, language, and history of the community are the cradle within which individuals are reared. The identities of individuals are shaped and determined by their place within the community. Notions of the good are generated by the community and its shared way of life. Life meaning for individuals is provided by their role in perpetuating or contributing to the common life of the community, not from self-realization as an autonomous self-creating individual. Indeed individuals are neither autonomous nor self-determining, but rather are creatures of the communities that bear, nurture, and envelop them throughout life. The choices they make are from among socially generated alternatives and are based upon socially derived values. Primacy in the communitarian understanding is thus accorded in various ways to the community rather than the individual.

In a communitarian system law is a reflection of shared community values and interests. Legislation is a matter of discovering or declaring those values and interests immanent in the life and culture of the community.[31] The law is emphatically not neutral but conforms to and enforces the community way of life and interests. In the presence of pervasively shared values and customary law, legislation need not be as prominent or voluminous. Adjudication of conflict is not so much rule-oriented as it is oriented to achieving an outcome that furthers the community interest. Significantly, in contrast to the driving liberal obsession of fear of government tyranny, it is not essential in a communitarian system that there be restraints on government power. The state is not set against individuals but instead is an extension of community that should not be hobbled in the collective achievement of the common good.

Liberalism and capitalism

Liberalism has been called a "bourgeois" political theory for reasons of its origins and its content. Its articulation by Locke followed upon and coincided with the newly found prominence of the merchant class in the towns and cities of England.[32] As described in the previous chapter, the bourgeois engaged in a long struggle against the privileges of the nobility, fighting laws that inhibited their activities and accorded them no status. An individualist political theory that champions liberty and the protection of rights, especially the rights of contract and property, including the right to sell one's own labor, as Locke's theory did, mirrored the interests of the bourgeois.[33] The right of property promoted and protected their accumulation of capital; the right to work for wages undercut feudal restrictions that held back the supply of labor; freedom of contract restrained government interference in merchants' contractual arrangements with workers and with one another; enforcement of contracts provided security for their transactions.[34] Above all else, merchants required predictability and reliability in the enforcement of contractual and property rights as a means to calculate the anticipated benefits of commercial transactions and to secure the fruits of their enterprise.[35]

Scientific support for economic liberalism was provided by Adam Smith, who argued that individuals pursuing their own interests in a market allowing free exchanges and price and wage competition would (as if by an invisible hand) lead to a situation beneficial for all. Individuals benefit because they engage in the type and level of productive and consumptive activities consistent with their desires and abilities. Society benefits because wealth is maximized: only goods that promise a profit are produced, in the desired amounts, at the ideal combination of cost, price and quality, and are distributed to those who value them the most (as measured by their willingness to pay). Whatever does not satisfy these strictures will suffer the natural corrective sanction of failure. This system of "natural liberty" would be vastly superior to planning by the government, which would be inefficient if not impossible, and would impinge upon the natural rights of property and contract of individuals.[36] The key flaw of planning is that the government lacks the capacity to know the multitude of different desires of individuals; whereas the market, through innumerable voluntary individual exchanges, operates as a mechanism for registering such desires. Accordingly, the government should supply a framework of laws that protect property and contract, it should establish a sound monetary system and assure competition and a free market, and for the rest stay out of the way. "The appeal this doctrine made to its generation hardly requires any emphasis. It told the business man that he was a public benefactor; and it urged that the less he was restrained in the pursuit of his wealth, the greater the benefit he could confer on his fellows."[37] These economic arguments offer another way of encouraging everyone to pursue their own good, now in the interest of all, and to structure a government and laws that facilitate this pursuit.

The connection between liberalism and capitalism, so described, is direct and intimate. Liberalism is about freedom; capitalism is an economic system built upon freely made economic exchanges. The liberty advocated by political liberalism implies an unspecified but considerable degree of economic liberalism. Individuals in society are routinely occupied with social, political and economic activities that cannot be sharply separated from one another. Inventing, producing, buying, selling, accumulating, consuming, are among the primary goods pursued by people in capitalist societies while exercising their liberty. Hence the liberty championed by liberalism is substantially played out in the economic arena.

Liberalism, it is fair to conclude, expresses "a view of politics that is required by and legitimates capitalist market practices."[38]

To forestall a common misconception, it should be emphasized that political liberalism is not necessarily committed to a laissez faire (non-interference) view of government.[39] Hayek, one the twentieth century's foremost champions of classical liberalism, stated this unequivocally: "Probably nothing has done so much harm to the liberal cause as the wooden insistence of some liberals on certain rough rules of thumb, above all the principle of laissez faire."[40] Hayek argued that, in addition to establishing a background legal framework for the market, government participation and regulation is necessary when competition and pricing mechanisms do not suffice in the provision of public goods and infrastructure, as in the building of roads, and dealing with deforestation or pollution.[41] He asserted, further, that "there can be no doubt that some minimum of food, shelter, and clothing, sufficient to preserve health and the capacity to work, can be assured to everybody."[42] And he advocated a state-sponsored system of social insurance to protect individuals against calamities.[43] Contemporary conservatives who advocate little or no regulation forget what Hayek well understood, that the liberal state preserves a substantial role for law.

A concluding caution

A libertarian, a person who accords freedom the utmost value, might be dismayed by the liberal portrayal that law serves as the great preserver of liberty. Libertarians see law largely as an imposition on liberty. Jeremy Bentham – not himself a libertarian, but an unfailing advocate of taking a clear-eyed view of the law – insisted that liberty "is not anything produced by positive Law. It exists without Law, and not be means of Law."[44] Libertarians believe law should establish the minimum conditions necessary for social order, an allowance that distinguishes them from anarchists. Nothing more. Liberty exists when the law is *silent*.[45] Less law means greater freedom. From this standpoint, legislation, regardless of democratic origins, is always a threat; the rule of law serves legislation; and individual rights are too minimalist to offer much protection.

Modern social theorists have reported an increasing "juridification" of liberal societies – an unprecedented penetration of social life by state law, extending ever deeper into the affairs of individuals.[46] If this phenomenon is indeed taking place, it might be argued that there is less liberty in liberal societies, regardless of their vaunted legal protections, than in many absolutist regimes of the past, in which legislation was scarce and the legal apparatus mostly inactive or weak. This charge can be rebuffed, at least initially, by recognizing that it is inapt to compare modern capitalist, mass society with the vastly simpler conditions of bygone days. But the point merits serious contemplation. It carries, moreover, an implicit warning: do not be beguiled by legitimating theoretical accounts that might distract one from perceiving the situation in a less idealized, more realistic way.

4   Locke, Montesquieu, the Federalist Papers

Three majestic early works, standing above all others in stature and influence, cemented the integral place of the rule of law in liberal systems: Locke's *Second Treatise of Government* (1690), Montesquieu's *Spirit of the Laws* (1748) and *The Federalist Papers* (1787–88) by Madison, Hamilton, and Jay. This chapter will present a summary exegesis of each contribution. They have decisively shaped the modern rule of law in Western liberal democracies. Following this exegesis will be a brief examination of the rule of law in nineteenth-century England. England deserves special mention, for it has achieved the longest-running continuous tradition of the rule of law, it was the home of Locke, it provided the prime exemplar for Montesquieu, its culture influenced the authors of the *The Federalist Papers*, and it was the tradition within which Dicey made his arguments about the modern decline of the rule of law (taken up in the next chapter). It is also an instructive test case, inconsistent in important respects with the framework set out in *The Federalist Papers*, that operates contrary to a number of popular contemporary assumptions about what the rule of law requires. To conclude this chapter a presumption contained within these accounts – the presence of a well-established legal profession – will be drawn out.

But first a mention of the seventeenth-century giant of political theory, Thomas Hobbes, who casts a shadow on liberalism as well as on the rule of law. Although he initiated the social contract tradition later developed by Locke, liberals understandably prefer to categorize Hobbes as a pre-liberal thinker. Under his account, the sovereign created by the original contract wields absolute untrammeled power (though bound in conscience by natural law). The *only* right individuals retain post-contract is to resist the sovereign if they are threatened with death.

The sovereign (whether a monarch or a parliament) is not subject to legal limitation, according to Hobbes, for sensible as well as logical reasons.[1] Anything less than an absolute sovereign would perpetuate the uncertainty of the state of nature by encouraging challenges to authority, defeating the purpose of the arrangement. Order will result only if everyone bows before a single acknowledged power holder who answers to no other higher earthly force. Never mind the temptation for such a sovereign to ignore legal restraints. It was also illogical, according to Hobbes, to suggest that a sovereign can be bound by law. He defined law as the command of the sovereign.[2] The creator of law cannot be limited by the law for the plain reason that the law may be altered at the law-maker's will. Echoing Aquinas – considered by many to be the antipode of Hobbes – he observed that "he that is bound to himself only, is not bound."[3] Hobbes raised a further acute argument against the possibility of the rule of law,[4] conveyed here by Jean Hampton:

A rule is inherently powerless; it only takes on life if it is interpreted, applied, and enforced by individuals. That set of human beings that has final say over what the rules are, how they should be applied, and how they should be enforced has ultimate control over what these rules actually *are*. *So human beings control the rules*, and not vice versa.[5]

Hobbes denied the very possibility of a complete antinomy between the rule of law and the rule of will at the moment of interpretation and application. "There must always be somebody – not some text but some *body* – who has the final word."[6] Hobbes also rejected the separation of powers, which would generate conflict within the divided sovereign, handicapping its ability to preserve social order.[7]

A formidable collection of objections to various aspects of the rule of law were thus articulated by Hobbes just as it was to become the center-piece of the liberal system.

Locke's preeminent role for law

Locke's *Second Treatise of Government* is widely credited with being the single most influential formulation of liberal theory. His imagined state of nature was more benign than Hobbes's. Guided by reason, individuals enjoyed perfect freedom and equality, and were governed by natural laws. According to these natural laws, one must preserve oneself, and not harm others in their enjoyment of life, health, liberty, and possessions.[8] Under this natural liberty individuals are free to pursue their own vision of the good.[9] Everyone also possesses the right to punish and seek restitution for violations of their natural rights by others. Although people generally abide by the laws of nature, transgressions inevitably occur. The right personally to enforce the law against violators is what creates a problem. In the absence of an impartial judge, conflicts cannot be resolved to the satisfaction of the parties, since everyone would be biased in his or her own favor. Disputes would fester, threatening peace and security. To avoid this individuals would join together to form a government and accord it the power to make, execute, and apply laws for the public good, "and all this for the preservation of property of all the members of that society, as far as is possible."[10]

Locke summarized:

And thus all private judgment of every particular member being excluded, the community comes to be umpire, by settled standing rules, indifferent, and the same to all parties; and by men having authority from the community, for the execution of those rules, decides all the differences that may happen between any members of that society concerning any matter of right; and punishes those offences which any member hath committed against the society, with such penalties as the law has established . . .[11]

His design involved a limited delegation of power, for limited purposes, from individuals to the government, revocable by them if the government failed to meets its obligations. He specified a separation of powers between legislature and executive – though not a separate judiciary – to assure that the government acts according to duly enacted standing laws. And he argued that absolute monarchy is inconsistent with civil society because such a monarch would judge his own cases, continuing in a state of nature in relation to the people.[12] Finally, consistent with the consensual nature of the civil society, Locke held that legislation should be established by majority vote.[13]

Liberalism under Locke was consummately legalistic, as captured in his observation that "Where-ever law ends, tyranny begins."[14] He contrasted the rule of law with subjection to the will of another: "freedom of men under government is, to have a standing rule to live by, common to every one of that society, and made by the legislative power erected in it; a liberty to follow my own will in all things, where the rule prescribes not; and not to be subject to the inconstant, uncertain, unknown, arbitrary will of another man . . ."[15] Standing laws were crucial to his scheme:

Absolute arbitrary power, or governing without settled standing laws, can neither of them consist with the ends of society and government, which men would not quit the freedom of the state of nature for, and tie themselves up under, were it not to preserve their lives, liberties and fortunes, and by stated rules of right and property to secure their peace and quiet . . . [F]or all the power the government has, being only for the good of the society, as it ought not to be arbitrary and at pleasure, so it ought to be exercised by established and promulgated laws; that both the people may know their duty, and be safe and secure within the limits of the law; and the rulers too kept within their bounds . . .[16]

This is a succinct formulation of legal liberty and constitutional government.

Locke did not, however, specify any actual limits on the legislative power. He did not advocate explicit protection for individual rights. Nor did he articulate the independence of the judiciary as a separate branch, and he failed to identify any mechanism (like judicial review), short of revolt, which could invalidate illegitimate government action.[17]

Locke attached particular significance to the right of property. The *Second Treatise* leaves no doubt about its primacy: "The great and chief end, therefore, of men's uniting into common-wealths, and putting themselves under government, is the preservation of their property."[18] Although he used the term property broadly to include life and liberty – in the sense that individuals owned themselves – there is no question that he means primarily property in the sense of possessions. Locke's "state is a society of property owners."[19]

This leads to a related point. Although he wrote expansively on behalf of the "people" and "freemen," and he believed humans had the inherent capacity for reason, Locke was not an unreserved egalitarian. In his other writings, typical of the elite views of his time, Locke expressed a lower opinion of the non-propertied laboring class as lacking in reason.[20] Leo Strauss elaborated Locke's view of equality and its connection to property:

> Equality, he thought, is incompatible with civil society. The equality of all men in regard to the right of self-preservation does not obliterate completely the special right of the more reasonable men. On the contrary, the exercise of that special right is conducive to the self-preservation and happiness of all. Above all, since self-preservation and happiness require property, so much so that the end of civil society can be said to be the preservation of property, the protection of the propertied members of society against the demands of the indigent – or the protection of the industrious and rational against the lazy and quarrelsome – is essential to public happiness or the common good.[21]

The people that counted for the purposes of ruling were those with estates. The democracy Locke advocated, his majority consent for legislation, was the consent of property holders, to whom the franchise was limited at the time, a small fraction of English society (estimated at only 3 percent of the population[22]); "Locke was assuming that only those with property were full members of civil society and so of the majority."[23] This likely explains why Locke did not promote any direct protections of individual rights. Since the consent required was that of a majority of property owners, this "was a sufficient safeguard of the rights of each, because he assumed that all who had the right to be consulted were agreed on one concept of the public good, ultimately the maximization of the nation's wealth . . ."[24]

More flesh has now been put on the earlier assertion that liberalism is a bourgeois political theory. "Locke's doctrine of property is directly intelligible today if it is taken as the classic doctrine of 'the spirit of capitalism[.]'"[25] Stripped to its basics and construed uncharitably, the system he espoused might be characterized as the supremacy of law created by property holders to, above all else, insure the preservation of their property. Adam Smith, another towering eighteenth-century liberal thinker, wrote in candor that:

Laws and government may be considered in this and indeed in every case as a combination of the rich to oppress the poor, and to preserve to themselves the inequality of the goods which would otherwise be soon destroyed by the attacks of the poor, who if not hindered by the government would soon reduce others to an equality with themselves by open violence.[26]

Karl Marx, father of modern Communism, who occupies the opposite pole from Smith on the political economy spectrum, could not have made the point more trenchantly. Marx accused the liberal state and law of operating in favor of bourgeois property interests: "your jurisprudence is but the will of your class made into a law for all . . ."[27] Marx's collaborator, Friedrich Engels, elaborated: "As the state arose from the need to keep class antagonisms in check, but also arose in the thick of the fight between the classes, it is normally the state of the most powerful, economically ruling class, which by its means becomes also the politically ruling class, and so acquires new means of holding down and exploiting the oppressed class."[28]

Viewed in this light the liberal rule of law is less self-evidently attractive (at least to the non-elite). It would be a mistake, however, to take this apparent partiality toward property owners, at least at its inception, as a sufficient reason to reject liberalism or the rule of law, or to condemn Locke. Liberals have argued, in defense, that law is in fact neutral, standing above the class conflict, and that individuals as well as society are much better off, among other reasons, because the property-preserving orientation of liberalism maximizes wealth as well as liberty, as will be articulated later. Nor do these observations detract at all from Locke's extraordinary legacy. The arguments and ideals he espoused were seized upon by others to further liberalism and the rule of law in the interest of individual liberty to a greater extent than any other early political theorist, rivaled only by Montesquieu. The liberal system he helped build is not captive to his understanding or the circumstances of his time. These observations do suggest, however, that it must be considered whether the fullest benefits offered by the rule of law and liberalism extend only as far as the distribution of property within society.

Montesquieu's contribution

Montesquieu began his discussion of liberty by observing that it has been given many meanings. He asserted that equating democracy with liberty is an error in which "the power of the people has been confounded with their liberty."[29] Liberty, moreover, is not the right to do whatever one pleases, for then everyone would be under constant threat owing to others doing the same. Each of us has liberty only if all are restrained from doing harm to one another. The law then creates a scope of secure action within which individuals may do as they please. "Liberty is a right of doing whatever the laws permit[.]"[30] This, again, is the classic statement of legal liberty. "Montesquieu identifies liberty with a life lived under the rule of law."[31]

But more is necessary to preserve freedom than legal liberty, for the laws can be onerous, allowing little room for permissible conduct. Liberty exists, according to Montesquieu, only if people are secure from tyranny. No less than monarchies or aristocratic oligarchies, he observed, democracies "are not in their own nature free."[32] A moderate government provides the greatest liberty. To prevent abuse, the government should be constituted in a manner such that "power should be a check to power."[33] His prescription was a separation of powers:

When the legislative and executive powers are united in the same person, or in the same body of magistrates, there can be no liberty; because apprehensions may arise lest the same monarch or senate should enact tyrannical laws, to execute them in a tyrannical manner.

Again, there is no liberty, if the judiciary power be not separated from the legislative and executive. Were it joined with the legislative, the life and liberty of the subject would be subject to arbitrary control; for the judge would then be legislator. Were it joined to the executive power, the judge might behave with violence and oppression.

There would be an end of everything, were the same man or the same body, whether of the nobles or of the people, to exercise those three powers, that of enacting laws, that of executing the public resolutions, and of trying the causes of individuals.[34]

An independent judiciary was central to Montesquieu's scheme. "The idea is not so much to ensure judicial rectitude and public confidence, as to prevent the executive and its many agents from imposing their powers, interests, and persecutive inclinations upon the judiciary. The magistrate can then be perceived as the citizen's most necessary, and also most likely, protector."[35] The judiciary is the point of most direct confrontation between the government, law, and the individual, and it can therefore serve as the best barrier against lawless governmental actions.[36] Montesquieu suggested, as a means to restrict their power, that judges (and juries) should be drawn from the people to sit for a temporary duration. And he insisted that judgments be rendered strictly according to the law: "Were they to be the private opinion of the judge, people would then live in society, without exactly knowing the nature of their obligations."[37]

Montesquieu elaborated on how English culture and society was a counterpart to the liberal legal system. "The central feature of the English way of life, and a chief purpose of its constitution, is the free pursuit of commerce."[38] He characterized the English as "all passions being unrestrained, hatred, envy, jealousy, and an ambitious desire of riches and honours."[39] The English readily assert their independence; they easily give up friends for more advantageous alliances; almost everything can be sold for a price; people are esteemed for riches; everyone speaks their mind; they are engaged in selfish competition. Despite the lack of an orientation toward the good of the community, it does not come apart because everyone works within a common political framework that allows all to pursue their ends, understanding that they have an individual and shared interest in making it work.[40] In Montesquieu's portrayal, the English are too busily engaged in enterprise to seize the governmental apparatus to oppress others, though they do take opportunities to promote legislation that furthers their own economic interest.[41]

This is bourgeois culture. In almost every relevant respect this society was contrary to the classical ideal of a society oriented toward virtue and the community. But Montesquieu was not contemptuous of it: "[T]he spirit of commerce is naturally attended with that of frugality, economy, moderation, labour, prudence, tranquility, order, and rule."[42] This provided the cultural backdrop for the law, that enhanced the liberty of English citizens by facilitating their transactions, enforcing their agreements, protecting their property, and otherwise leaving them be. Montesquieu thought a commercial culture to be a freer culture. Although an entire way of life is not transferable, commerce can be transferred, and in this possibility Montesquieu saw the prospect for the spread and increase of liberty in other societies.[43]

Historians agree that Montesquieu misread the actual extent of separation of powers in England, which he exaggerated, and his portrayal of English culture has been challenged as failing to appreciate the significance of virtue, honor, and (at least a modicum of) a prevailing orientation to the whole. None of that matters. His formulation of the separation of powers, the emphasis he placed on the judiciary as the preserve of the rule of law, his statement of legal liberty, and his insight that there is a complementary connection between the surrounding culture and the law, are of enduring moment. More immediately, his ideas, together with Locke's, had a major influence on the designers of the US Constitution.

The Federalist Papers

The Federalist Papers is a "classic of liberalism."[44] Written by Alexander Hamilton, James Madison, and John Jay, it was a piece of advocacy to urge adoption of the proposed US Constitution. But it was also a work in political theory with the task of translating the ideas of liberal theorists into an operating government structure and set of institutions.

Madison formulated the central quandary with which they wrestled:

To secure the public good and private rights against the danger of such a [majority] faction, and at the same time to preserve the spirit and form of popular government, is then the great object to which our inquiries are directed.[45]

Both Madison and Hamilton, in various writings, openly worried about the threat democracy posed to contract and property rights, concerns that had been reinforced by recent events in state legislatures.[46] Citing historical instances of abuses by democracies, Madison wrote: "Hence it is that such [direct] democracies have ever been spectacles of turbulence and contention; have ever been found incompatible with personal security or the rights of property; and have generally been as short in their lives as they have been violent in their deaths."[47] They understood that the so-called "self-rule" of democracy was something of a fiction that contained a risk of institutionalizing domination by some over others. "For those who govern are not necessarily the same 'people' as those who are governed, and democratic self-government is not the government 'of each by himself' but, at best, 'of each by the rest.'"[48] When factions exist in society, democracy in practice can be the rule of the more populous, or more organized, or more powerful, over the lesser group.

Despite these worries, *The Federalist Papers* did not question that the government should and must be democratic. It channeled the aforementioned concerns into constructing ways to control democracy for the protection of individual liberties. Three mechanisms were identified. First, representative democracy, rather than direct, would allow the representatives to exercise deliberation and wisdom when enacting laws, resistant to the passions that sway direct democracies. Second, two kinds of divisions would be installed as a means to check power with power: a vertical separation of powers, separating state from federal governments, would help restrain the states, which are closer to the masses and thus more susceptible to popular abuse; a horizontal separation, separating legislative, executive, and judicial functions, and further dividing (internally) the legislative branch, into a popular body and a more elite body, with different methods of selection and different tenures.[49] The animating principle behind these various divisions was to make it difficult for the governmental apparatus to be captured by any particular group and wielded against others. "[T]he society itself will be broken into so many parts, interests and classes of citizens, that the rights of individuals, or of the minority, will be in little danger from interested combinations of the majority."[50]

The third mechanism was judicial review of legislation, articulated by Hamilton:

> By a limited Constitution, I understand one which contains certain specified exceptions to the legislative authority; . . . Limitations of this kind can be preserved in practice no other way than through the medium of courts of justice, whose duty it must be to declare all acts contrary to the manifest tenor of the Constitution void. Without this, all the reservations of particular rights or privileges would amount to nothing.[51]

Hamilton applied logic to establish judicial review. A constitution is "a fundamental law."[52] The supremacy of the Constitution would be vitiated if contrary legislation could not be invalidated; otherwise ordinary legislation could trample constitutional restrictions with impunity. This reasoning, while persuasive, does not of itself determine who or which body should have the power to declare invalidity. Nominating the court for this role, Hamilton offered the prudential argument that the judiciary is the weakest branch, with no army or wealth at its disposal, that poses no threat to the others; and, furthermore, that "the interpretation of the laws is the proper and peculiar province of the courts."[53]

Notably, *The Federalist Papers* did not advocate a Bill of Rights. A few miscellaneous protections were explicitly set forth in the Constitution – the prohibitions against *ex post facto* laws, bills of attainder, and the impairment of contract, and the writ of *habeas corpus* – but it contained no explicit list of protected rights. Hamilton argued that a Bill of Rights was unnecessary, and perhaps dangerous.[54] The government had only limited powers, with the entire constitutional design operating to protect individual rights. Including explicit protections might suggest that the government otherwise did have such power, and would have the effect of narrowing the protection to only that which was stated in the rights.[55] Notwithstanding Hamilton's opposition, a Bill of Rights, which had already been included in several state constitutions, was soon added to the US Constitution by amendment.[56]

A written constitution, democratic elections, explicitly articulated individual rights, the separation of powers, and judicial review of legislation, are today thought to be essential to liberalism and the rule of law. Chief

Justice John Marshall, when finding that judicial review was constitutionally required, despite no mention of it in the Constitution itself, observed that constitutions secure "a government of laws, and not of men."[57] A written constitution establishes legal controls on the law-maker. Although constitutions can be altered through amendment, the higher hurdles that must be overcome to do so means that ordinary law-making does operate under legal limitation. Judicial review provides the mechanism through which this legal limitation is effectuated. Construing the judiciary as the oracle of the law, this presents the law itself as speaking. In modern liberal democracies, the binding constitution replaces the role formerly fulfilled during the classical Greek and Roman, and Medieval periods, by divine or natural law, or the ancient code, or customary law, in providing legal constraints on the sovereign.

The case of England

For most of its history – at least prior to its entry into the European Union and its incorporation of the European Convention on Human Rights[58] – England has not possessed many of the just described features: it had no written constitution, no explicit bill of individual rights (in the modern sense), and no judicial review. Yet it is the acknowledged birthplace of liberalism and the bastion of the rule of law. A brief exploration of the English case will provide insights into the social connection to the rule of law.

For many centuries, the ordinary common law was thought to set legal limits on sovereign law-makers.[59] Law was found, not made, according to this understanding. The common law, it was said by English jurists, was the product of custom from time immemorial, and represented the working out of legal principles through the application of reason by judges. It is beside the point that this claim was something of a myth,[60] for it was often repeated and widely believed. This legal framework applied to all government conduct. Even the rhetoric on both sides of the English Civil War (which influenced Hobbes) and the Glorious Revolution (which influenced Locke), in the mid- and late seventeenth-century, was saturated with arguments that drew from the common law.[61] At the time there was no sharp separation between public and private law; the common law rules of, for example, contract, trust, and liability for harm, were applied equally in actions between citizens and between citizens and government officials.[62] Accountability of government officials to ordinary law in ordinary courts was the cornerstone of this understanding.

A constitution establishes the basic powers and limits of a government and the relationship between a government and its citizens. In this sense

England has had an *unwritten* constitution for centuries, comprised of seminal documents like the Magna Carta, key legislation like the Act of Settlement (the relationship between the monarch and parliament), the Septennial Act (the duration of parliament), the Habeas Corpus Act, and especially the general corpus of common law rules, all bolstered by a shared complex of understandings and conventions about law and government. This constitution served as the functional equivalent of the written US Constitution in the sense of a law that sets limits on the law-makers.[63] Coke's decision in *Doctor Bonham's* case testified to this understanding, when he declared that "the common law will control acts of parliament, and sometimes adjudge them to be utterly void."[64] The basic idea was that the common law, a body of private law reflecting legal principles, established the fundamental legal framework. Legislation, from this standpoint, posed a threat to the integrity and coherence of the common law – enactments in derogation of the common law were therefore strictly construed by judges.

In the nineteenth century, under the influence of Jeremy Bentham and other law reformers, attitudes toward law in England changed, following upon the general shift in views wrought by the Enlightenment. Law came to be seen as the product of sovereign legislative will – a theory of law identified with Hobbes and John Austin called "legal positivism" – there to serve current social purposes. Law was made, not found; its utility mattered more than its heritage in custom or tradition. This is an instrumental view of law,[65] in contrast to the view that law reflects a timeless unalterable body of legal principles or emanation from the culture or nation. Locke's argument for parliamentary sovereignty, its authority derived by delegation from the people, prevailed. Judicial review of legislation was repudiated. There was no justification for judges possessing the authority to override the will of the people expressed in legislation. Any part of the common law could be altered by ordinary legislation, as could any fundamental legal document, including the Magna Carta, or indeed any constitutional provision. "Parliamentary sovereignty is therefore an undoubted legal fact."[66]

England, then, had a constitution in the sense of setting out a fundamental structure of government and the legal rights and liberties of the citizens, but not one contained in a single written document, not supreme over ordinary law-making, and not protected by judicial review.[67] The rule of law, in the general sense expressed by Justice Marshall of a government under law, prevailed despite the complete absence of features thought to be essential.

One explanation, following Montesquieu's lead, points to something deep set in the English culture and society, centuries in the making: the widely shared belief and commitment, among the public and government officials, that the government operates within a limiting framework of law. Hence the law ruled. The rule of law existed owing to a widespread and unquestioned belief in the rule of law, in the inviolability of certain fundamental legal restraints on government, not to any specific legal mechanism. This answer to the ancient puzzle of how the law can limit itself is that it does not – attitudes *about* law provide the limits.

Hayek observed that the rule of law is not itself a legal rule, but a political ideal. "It will be effective only in so far as the legislator feels bound by it. In a democracy this means that it will not prevail unless it forms part of the moral tradition of the community, a common ideal shared and unquestioningly accepted by the majority."[68] Dicey, another leading theorist of rule of law, characterized these limits on law-makers as "political" or "moral," not "legal."[69] However it is characterized, the crucial point remains that even the unlimited law-maker is hemmed in by a legal framework that cannot be violated or easily altered. As Isaiah Berlin observed, "What makes [Great Britain] comparatively free, therefore, is the fact that this theoretically omnipotent entity is restrained by custom or opinion from behaving as such. It is clear that what matters is not the form of restraints on power – whether they are legal, or moral, or constitutional – but their effectiveness."[70]

The legal profession

Though seldom given detailed attention by liberal theorists, all liberal accounts of the rule of law presuppose the presence of a robust legal tradition. Alex de Tocqueville's classic study, *Democracy in America*, published a half-century after the independence of the USA, emphasized the danger of populist tyranny posed by democracy. Helping to mitigate this risk, according to de Tocqueville, was the legal profession. With a specialized body of knowledge that emphasized rationality and an orientation to the values of legality, lawyers were a reckonable social force. He wrote: "Men who have made a special study of the laws derive from this occupation certain habits of order, a taste for formalities, and a kind of instinctive regard for the regular connection of ideas, which naturally render them very hostile to the revolutionary spirit and the unrelenting passions of the multitudes."[71] De Tocqueville expressed faith in the tempering influence the legal profession exercised over law-making, as judges and elected legislators, and was reassured that many private and political disputes in US society ultimately made their way into the legal arena for resolution.

Other theorists have recognized the relevance of the professional legal culture. Judith Shklar wrote:

> Legalism is, above all, the operative outlook of the legal profession . . . The tendency to think of law as "there" as a discrete entity, discernibly different from morals and politics, has its deepest roots in the legal profession's views of its own functions, and forms the very basis of most of our judicial institutions and procedures.[72]

These characterizations suggest that if the rule of law is to function effectively – especially the crucial feature that judges be committed to following the law – a necessary contribution is to be found within the attitudes and orientation of those trained in law. Judges, if not lawyers more generally, must be imbued with the sense that their special task and obligation is fidelity to the law.

Theorists have cautioned, however, that the legal profession has its own interests (personal and group) that influence its production of the law. Bentham castigated lawyers for collectively engaging in a fraudulent enterprise designed to extract "out of the pockets of the people, in the largest quantity possible, the produce of the industry of the people."[73] Sociologist Max Weber observed that the financial interests of legal professionals led English courts – in the name of protecting the common law – to undermine legislation aimed at law reform.[74] Law was kept obscure, unclear, and inaccessible – factors which militate against the requirements of the rule of law – to keep lawyers indispensable as intermediaries and facilitators. These concerns are in addition to familiar worries, taken up in a later chapter, that the legal profession serves the interests of the elite class, which provides them the most lucre, turning the law to the benefit of these masters.

The legal profession, then, is located at the crux of the rule of law. In contemporary societies persons trained in law comprise a notable social force that monopolizes legal activities. Given that liberal theorists uniformly allocate a special place for an independent, neutral judiciary as the final preserve of the rule of law, the rule of law could not conceivably function without this group committed to the values of legality. This position, however, also renders the legal profession, judges in particular, uniquely situated to undermine the rule of law.

5   Conservatives warn

Beginning at the end of the nineteenth century and continuing through the late twentieth century came loud and repeated warnings from theorists about the decline of the rule of law. It is an odd paradox that the unparalleled current popularity of the rule of law coincides with widespread agreement among theorists that it has degenerated in the West. Theorists on both ends of the political spectrum, right and left, have concurred on this diagnosis, though the former have lamented this decline while the latter have celebrated it. Given that the rule of law is widely prescribed as the elixir for many political and economic ails, it is essential to understand the nature of and reasons for this decline. The arguments of the political right will be taken up in this chapter.

Liberalism versus socialism

The observed decline of the rule of law is directly linked to the grand ideological contest between liberalism and socialism of the past 150 years. Mid-nineteenth-century England was the highpoint of classical liberalism. A free market in the production, distribution, and exchange of goods and services substantially prevailed, with relatively limited government interference. According to historian Eric Hobsbawm,[1] the engine of economic progress during this period was the development of the railroad. It generated increases in steel production (to build rails and cars) and coal mining (to fuel the engines); it encouraged innovations in machine-building and engineering; it prompted the creation of new financial devices for capital accumulation (to finance projects). The resulting rail network revolutionized travel for both persons and goods, especially cotton and textiles, increasing the bulk of goods transported and lowering the costs of transportation, opening up new markets for trade. Manufacturing towns grew, generating opportunities for employment that lead to a population transfer from rural to urban areas (coinciding with an increase in population), throwing together strangers in large numbers, altering the community and family structure. Each of these developments in turn led to multiple others.

This expansion of commercial activity spread its rewards unequally; creating great wealth for a few industrial magnates; comfortable wealth for a measurable upper middle class of successful merchants and their professional facilitators (lawyers and bankers); less comfortable but still adequate wealth for the growing number of servants, teachers, store clerks, and others in the service industry; and no wealth but at least minimally sufficient food and shelter for the masses of working poor who manned the steel mills, textile factories, and coal mines. During this period an unprecedented amount of new wealth was generated in England, and to a lesser but still substantial degree elsewhere in Europe and the USA. All boats were raised, though everyone in the boats of the working poor, children included, had to paddle vigorously, and were threatened at every moment with capsize, whether by illness, industrial accident, or being thrown out of work.

During this period the bourgeois enjoyed an unprecedented influence in cultural, economic and political affairs:

They believed in capitalism, in competitive private enterprise, technology, science and reason. They believed in progress, in a certain amount of representative government, a certain amount of civil rights and liberties, so long as these were compatible with the rule of law and with the kind of order which kept the poor in their place.[2]

England, with a vast colonial empire, dominated the world economically and politically. Moreover, its citizens enjoyed more wealth, as well as freedom, than citizens any where else, although the USA matched the latter and was catching up in the former. Such success was considered self-evident proof, except to the willfully blind, of the correctness of liberal theory in both economic and political aspects.

Liberalism had hardly a moment to enjoy its apotheosis before its retreat began, slowly at first then with increasing momentum in the final quarter of the century. Two factors will be mentioned that contributed to this shift, both identified at the time by liberal theorist John Stuart Mill as compelling reasons to take socialism seriously.[3] The first factor was the large numbers of perpetually insecure working poor toiling long hours in abominable conditions doing body-and-mind-numbing work. They suffered from ill heath and exhaustion and lived in overcrowded, unsanitary housing, many making their lives more palatable through excessive alcohol consumption, a combination that routinely resulted in premature aging and death. And the rewards for their labor were meager, often little more than necessary to maintain adequate shelter and to buy enough bread to supply sufficient calories to get up and go to work the next day. It is not coincidental that Marx and Engels lived in England when they developed their theories about the alienation of labor and the harsh edge of capitalism, which were plain for all to see. In the long run, it seemed to social observers at the time, power must reside with the many, and the masses would not put up with their intolerable state indefinitely. What especially galled the workers was the striking disparity between their lives and that of those in the better neighborhoods across town who lived off the bounty produced by their sweat. To its detractors, capitalism was not just harsh, it was unfair, in that those who benefited most, the capitalists, appeared to labor the least and be the least deserving.[4] Furthermore, the liberal economic system was morally bankrupt, charged opponents, based on a spiritually impoverishing, heartless, selfish, anti-social view that would eventually shred the bonds of society. "It is the principle of individualism, competition, each one for himself and against all the rest. It is grounded on opposition of interests, not harmony of interests, and under it everyone is required to find his place by a struggle, by pushing others back or being pushed back by them."[5] In the 1870s and 1880s, finally flexing its long dormant political muscles, labor began to organize, and strikes broke out across Europe.[6]

The second factor was the expansion of the eligible electorate. Despite its generously egalitarian rhetoric, the actual practice of democracy in Europe reserved the power of the vote for the elite, a privilege they jealously guarded. The ideology of liberal democratic theory, however, particularly the notion of individual equality it builds upon, led to the gradual extension of the franchise to others,[7] involving first a lowering of the property qualification, then including non-propertied wage earners, and finally (in the early twentieth century) allowing women to participate. Mill predicted the likely consequences of a broader extension of suffrage, providing a taste of the prevailing fears:

The great increase of electoral power which the [Reform Act of 1867] places within the reach of the working class is permanent . . . It is known even to the most inobservant, that the working classes have, and are likely to have, political objects which concern them as working classes, and on which they believe, rightly or wrongly, that the interests and opinions of the other powerful classes are opposed to theirs. However much their pursuit of these objectives may be for the present retarded by want of electoral organization, by dissensions among themselves, or by their not having reduced as yet their wishes into a sufficiently definite political shape, it is as certain as anything in politics can be, that they will before long find the means of making their collective electoral power effectively instrumental to the promotion of their collective objects.[8]

Consequent upon the economic and social dislocation generated by the great depression that occurred in the final quarter of the nineteenth century were a series of reforms designed to ameliorate the sorry condition of the working poor. "[T]he demand from below for protection against 'capitalists' by the 'little men,' for social security, public measures against unemployment and a wage minimum for the workers, became vocal and politically effective."[9] In England and gradually elsewhere across Europe, government-imposed or sponsored initiatives included limits on working hours, old age pensions, health insurance, workman's compensation for accidents, universal education with school meals, and more. Government bureaucracies created to administer these programs began their inexorable growth. Classical liberalism gave way to the social welfare state.

Resistance to social welfare initiatives took many forms, but the one pertinent here was the argument pressed by conservatives that these developments spelled the doom of the rule of law. The two most influential theorists who pressed this argument were English constitutional law giant A. V. Dicey, and Austrian-English (long-term US resident) political theorist Friedrich Hayek, winner of the Nobel Memorial Prize in Economics.

Backlash from Dicey

As a political ideal, the rule of law was largely neglected, taken for granted more than a subject of discussion. Dicey's *Introduction to the Study of the Law of the Constitution*, initially published in 1888, contained the first prominent modern formulation and analysis of the rule of law in a liberal democratic system.[10]

Dicey articulated the rule of law in terms of three overlapping aspects. His first and main articulation was: "no man is punishable or can be lawfully made to suffer in body or goods except for a distinct breach of law established in the ordinary legal manner before the ordinary Courts of the land. In this sense the rule of law is contrasted with every system of government based on the exercise by persons in authority of wide, arbitrary, or discretionary powers of constraint."[11] Three distinguishable ideas are blended by these observations. His comments centered upon the notion that there can be no punishment without a preexisting law. But he also made the separate point that the ordinary courts were the proper institution in which cases must be heard. The infamous Star Chamber served as a historical warning in England about the potential for abuse inhering in special judicial tribunals. "In England the rule of law is coterminous with the cognizance of ordinary courts: it is the rule of the judicature."[12] Dicey made the further point that the exercise of discretionary powers by government officials to impose constraint on individuals is inconsistent with the rule of law. Discretion and law, for Dicey, are antithetical. The judge is a mere conduit for announcing what the law requires. "Judicial power, as contradistinguished from the power of laws, has no existence," wrote Chief Justice Marshall of the US Supreme Court, expressing this same idea. "Courts are mere instruments of law, and can will nothing."[13]

The second aspect of the rule of law, according to Dicey, is that everyone is equal before the ordinary law. His primary concern was that public officials (the monarch excepted) should not have special immunities or privileges, that is, they should be held accountable by ordinary private causes of action before ordinary courts for their official conduct no different from everyone else.

Dicey's third aspect is less a separate element than a description of the underlying source of the rule of law, building upon his emphasis on the jurisdiction of ordinary courts. He considered the rule of law to be a product of the multitude and totality of "judicial decisions determining the rights of private persons in particular cases brought before the Courts."[14] Dicey asserted that the English constitution is characterized by the rule of law owing to this feature. For example, he argued that England had a freer press than in any other country because the primary sources of constraint on the press were ordinary libel causes of action, which were heard by judges and juries, and therefore not subject to direct governmental control.[15] Owing to its entrenched, disbursed nature, renewed every day in decisions made in ordinary courts, Dicey considered this common law tradition, taken in its entirety, to be a more secure basis for liberty than the enactment of written constitutions, for it could be overturned only in the unlikely event of a complete revolution. Through this argument, Dicey promoted private law over public law as the key to protecting citizens.

In the "Introduction" to the ninth edition of his book, reviewing the changes that had ensued in the three decades since initial publication, Dicey complained: "The ancient veneration for the rule of law has in England suffered during the last thirty years a marked decline. The truth of this assertion is proved by actual legislation, by the existence among some classes of a certain distrust both of the law and of the judges, and by a marked tendency towards the use of lawless methods for the attainment of social or political ends."[16] The specific target of Dicey's ire – posing a dire threat to the rule of law – was the expansion of administrative action resulting from the developing social welfare state. What concerned Dicey was not just that ordinary courts were precluded from reviewing the bulk of administrative actions, but also that courts were ill-suited to such review because it would involve issues of policy, management, expertise, and efficacy, which were not legal in nature.

Administrative agencies were (and are) created by legislation that typically granted resources and broad powers to agency officials to effectuate a policy mandate or implement a social program, powers which often include the issuance of regulations, binding orders, enforcement actions, and determinations in individual cases. Hence they made discretionary decisions and combined legislative, executive, and judicial powers in a single body. Local Government Boards, the Board of Trade, the Board of Education, Land Commissioners, Commissioners of Revenue, Commissioners of Insurance, and other agencies with expansive portfolios reaching ever further into daily social life, all visited consequences on individuals that were largely unreviewable by ordinary courts. The result was a huge increase in the range of government action without effective legal restraint.

Dicey was not isolated in having this concern. Another alarmed commentator wrote in 1914 that the "passing away of the 'rule of law' may seem to many honest observers to be the mark of the hour":[17]

In a word, our administrative departments not only administer; they also legislate, and they are tending more and more to exercise judicial functions. It is this exercise of judicial functions by the executive departments, removing as it does a large field of legal issues from the cognizance of the Courts, which seems to many to involve an escape from the rule of law, and therefore in its essence wrong.[18]

Setting aside questions of whether Dicey's analysis of the situation was correct, about which doubts have been raised,[19] within the terms of his understanding the threat posed to individual liberty and the rule of law by the social welfare state and its administrative apparatus was manifest. Many others agreed.

Hayek elaborates

Hayek's Version of the Rule of Law

A half-century after Dicey, Hayek pressed a more sophisticated case for the same point. In his period classic, *The Road to Serfdom*, published in 1944, Hayek identified the rule of law as the cornerstone of liberty.[20] Identical to Dicey, Hayek saw a connection between "the growth of a measure of arbitrary administrative coercion and the progressive destruction of the cherished foundation of British liberty, the Rule of Law."[21]

Hayek offered a concise and highly influential definition of the rule of law: "Stripped of all technicalities, this means that government in all its actions is bound by rules fixed and announced before-hand – rules which make it possible to foresee with fair certainty how the authority will use its coercive powers in given circumstances and to plan one's individual affairs on the basis of this knowledge."[22] This is the notion of "legal liberty." The rule of law in this sense promotes liberty by allowing individuals to know the range of activities – those not prohibited by the law – in which they are completely free to do as they please without being exposed to government coercion. Foreknowledge of the limits of permissible conduct is the key element of this freedom.

According to Hayek, all rule of law systems possess three attributes: "the laws must be general, equal and certain."[23] *Generality* requires that the law be set out in advance in abstract terms not aimed at any particular individual. The law then applies, without exception, to everyone whose conduct falls within the prescribed conditions of application. When elaborating this attribute, Hayek quoted Rousseau's description of generality: "When I say that the province of the law is always general, I mean that the law considers all subjects collectively and all actions in the abstract; it does not consider any individual man or any specific action."[24] Hayek added that the separation of powers between legislature and judiciary is virtually mandated by the attribute of generality, for only in this manner can the law be set out in abstract terms in advance of its application to any particular individual; legislative and judicial separation thus is by implication also an "integral part" of the rule of law.[25] *Equality* requires that the laws apply to everyone without making arbitrary distinctions among people. When distinctions do exist (as in male but not female conscription for armed services), Hayek insisted that to be legitimate they must be approved by a majority of people inside as well as outside the group targeted for differential treatment.[26] *Certainty* requires that those who are subject to the law be able to predict reliably what legal rules will be found to govern their conduct and how those rules will be interpreted and applied. Predictability is a necessary aspect of the foreknowledge that enables freedom of action.

Hayek acknowledged that it was impossible for any legal system perfectly to attain these three attributes, but he believed that they could nonetheless be approximated. These aspects of the rule of law preserve liberty as follows: "when we obey laws, in the sense of general abstract rules laid down irrespective of their application to us, we are not subject to another man's will and are therefore free. It is because the lawgiver does not know the particular cases to which his rules will apply, and it is because the judge who applies them has no choice in drawing the conclusions that follow from the existing body of rules and the particular facts of the case, that it can be said that laws and not men rule."[27] Hayek (like Dicey) postulated a fundamental antithesis between law and discretion, and he equated discretion with arbitrary will. In this understanding, as historian Frederic Maitland put it, even bad general laws are better than untrammeled will: "Caprice is the worst vice of which the administration of justice can be guilty; known general laws, however bad, interfere less with freedom than decisions based on no previously known rule."[28]

Hayek accepted that modern governments must exercise discretion if they are to function efficiently. His concern was with the narrower category of coercive actions by administrative officials that have an impact on private citizens and their property. And even these actions do not necessarily fall afoul of the rule of law, according to Hayek, as long as the discretion exercised by officials is pursuant to legal rules that possess the qualities of generality, equality, and certainty, and as long as their decisions are subject to judicial oversight.[29] The problem was that too often these legal restraints were absent. Moreover, any administrative authority that tries to achieve particular policy results in concrete situations involving the application of coercion inherently violates the rule of law, Hayek insisted, because the generality requirement cannot be satisfied.[30] "This pursuit of 'social justice' made it necessary for governments to treat the citizen and his property as an object of administration with the aim of securing particular results for particular groups."[31] According to Hayek, the growth of administrative actions in this respect had "already led very far away from the ideal of the Rule of Law."[32] Hayek was especially alarmed by, and poured scorn upon, what he considered to be the constant campaign against this ideal by Progressives in the name of social justice.[33]

Hayek Against Substantive Equality and Distributive Justice

While pressing his attack on administrative actions, Hayek argued that the related goals of substantive equality and substantive (or "distributive") justice are inherently inconsistent with the rule of law.[34] Substantive equality is the notion that equality requires treating differently situated people differently in order to account for the inequality of their situations (by contrast to formal equality, which treats everyone the same, making no accommodation for differences in circumstances). Distributive justice is the notion that there must be a fair distribution or allocation of goods in society, with fairness determined in accordance with some standard of merit or desert. These ideas are connected in that unfair distributions often lead to unequal situations, and vice versa. To put it in more concrete terms, people born rich or born poor cannot be said in moral terms to have deserved, respectively, their relative material advantages and disadvantages (distributive injustice); to be treated equally the dis-advantage suffered by the poor person must somehow be offset or taken into consideration (substantive equality). Other forms of inequalities also exist that cannot be blamed upon unjust social distributions of wealth, like disparities in physical and intellectual talents and in upbringing.

Hayek's first objection to distributive justice was that there is no accepted system of values according to which a society can determine what is a fair distribution, so the views of some will have to prevail over others.[35] Even in a society with a consensus on a system of values, conflicts will arise between incommensurable values, and there will inevitably be dissenters from the majority. Hayek's second objection was that any such system would by necessity be particularistic because the infinite variety of situations that arise cannot be governed by general rules established in advance. Distributive justice is thus inherently inconsistent with the rule of law. Substantive equality violates the rule of law for the same reason, and additionally because the differential treatment it entails violates the equality requirement (understood in formal terms). Even if society were massively to equalize the starting point of all individuals – say by dis-tributing all resources equally and creating a uniform education system (never mind the complexities involved, and never mind the imposition on the rich it entails) – inequalities would immediately come about owing to innate differences, so never-ending particularistic adjustments could not be avoided.

Hayek recognized and unapologetically embraced the inequitable implications of his position:

A necessary and only apparently paradoxical, result of this is that formal equality before the law is in conflict, and in fact incompatible, with any activity of the government deliberately aiming at material or substantive equality of different people, and that any policy aiming directly at a substantive ideal of distributive justice must lead to the destruction of the Rule of Law. To produce the same result for different people, it is necessary to treat them differently . . . It cannot be denied that the Rule of Law produces economic inequality – all that can be claimed for it is that this inequality is not designed to effect particular people in a particular way.[36]

Lamentable as the resulting disparity might be, Hayek asserted, the poor in liberal societies still had more absolute wealth than the supposedly equal masses in socialist societies, and they enjoyed greater freedom, including the freedom to take initiatives which would improve their eco-nomic position. And he allowed that the government could provide a minimum level of support for the unfortunate in society, since this can be established in non-coercive ways (he did not consider taxation to supply public services the market does not provide to be coercive[37]).

Hayek's View of the Common Law and Legislation

At first blush Hayek's view of the rule of law appears to be inconsistent with common law systems, which consist substantially of judge-made law. Early on Hayek expressed this concern: "there is some inherent conflict between a system of case law and the ideal of the Rule of Law. Since under case law the judge constantly creates law, the principle that he merely applies pre-existing rules can under that system be approached even less perfectly than where the law is codified."[38]

Almost two decades later Hayek altered his position to assert that the common law was in fact the bastion of liberty and rule of law, characterizing the common law in a manner resonant with Dicey's description. Hayek applied the "invisible hand" idea of the market to the common law, elaborating the view that the law is a self-correcting spontaneously grown order that inures to the benefit of all while not being the intentional product of anyone.[39] Individuals interact within society informed by and pursuant to norms, rules, customs, and practices that no one creates but in accordance with which all live. These rules and practices develop in an evolutionary process in response to the needs of social intercourse.[40] Law is a crystallization of these customs and norms of order. It is therefore an emanation from, and integral aspect of, the society to which it is attached.[41]

According to Hayek, the common law is constructed by accretion of the decisions of judges dealing with individual cases:

> The efforts of the judge are thus part of that process of adaptation of society to circumstances by which the spontaneous order grows. He assists in the process of selection by upholding those rules which, like those which have worked well in the past, make it more likely that expectations will match and not conflict. He thus becomes an organ of that order. But even when in the performance of this function he creates new rules, he is not the creator of a new order but a servant of an existing order. And the outcome of his efforts will be a characteristic instance of those "products of human action but not of human design" in which the experience gained by the experimentation of generations embodies more knowledge than was possessed by anyone.[42]

The primary orientation of common law judges, according to Hayek, is to come to a decision that matches general expectations in society about the application of legal rules and notions of justice. Judges accomplish this by identifying legal rules and principles that explain the pattern of previously decided cases. Judges in such situations are not legislating, since they are merely making explicit what was already immanent within the existing law, so the separation of powers is not violated, and the decisions are not unpredictable. When there is no answer to be found, either in the rules or principles or shared notions of justice, the judge grounds the decision upon the articulation of a rule or principle which would garner the most general assent.[43] Hayek's characterization of the common law resounds of the old Medieval view that the law is discovered, not made.

Building upon this understanding of the common law, Hayek expressed a skeptical view of legislation, no doubt owing in part to the fact that the social welfare state he bemoaned was built entirely by legislative initiatives. His main criticism came down to an irremediable lack of knowledge by legislators: no one knows or could know enough about happenings in society to anticipate the full consequences of legislative initiatives, not just because of the infinite interactions that comprise social life, all a function of individualistic context-based knowledge, incentives, and calculations, but also because every action in turn generates innumerable reactions, and so forth. The common law is superior because it builds piecemeal in response to immediate situations, with regular feedback – the supply of new cases reacting to previous decisions – and having the capacity to make adjustments, thus operating in a manner that processes a totality of knowledge that no individual or group could possibly possess.[44]

Hayek allowed that there was a proper, though limited, role for legislative modifications of the common law. The most frequent situation that called for legitimate legislative reform, according to Hayek, was to remedy instances of capture of the common law by particular interests. "There can be no doubt that in such fields as the law on the relations between master and servant, landlord and tenant, creditor and debtor, and in modern times between organized business and its customers, the rules have been shaped largely by the views of one of the parties and their particular interests – especially where, as used to be true in the first two of the instances given, it was one of the groups concerned which almost exclusively supplied the judges."[45]

Hayek on Justice, Democracy and Bills of Rights

Justice for Hayek was parasitic upon private law rules of property, contract, and torts, and criminal law prohibitions. Justice *is* the enforcement of preexisting law.[46] Rules of just conduct are primarily concerned with enforcing settled expectations with respect to property ownership and how transactions are governed. His standard for justice is substantively empty in that it entails no moral evaluation, and must satisfy no standard other than universalization. "Justice is thus emphatically not a balancing of particular interests at stake in a concrete case, or even of the interests of determinable classes of persons, nor does it aim at bringing about a particular state of affairs which is regarded as just."[47] Hayek's justice is another permutation of the rule of law.

Hayek expressed support for democracy, although occasionally in tepid in terms. He lauded democracy as "one of the most important safeguards of freedom," the only peaceful way to change government thus far discovered by human societies.[48] He emphasized, however, that democracy can easily turn tyrannical. He observed that what prevails in the legislative process is often not in fact the product of majority will but of special interests. Modern democracies, encouraged by the instrumental view of law, have increasingly come to view legislation as a tool to be used to apportion the spoils of government among winners in the political process; the result is often particularistic rather than general, taking from some in favor of others, frequently treating people unequally. Hayek's solution was that all legislation should be limited by the rule of law; specifically, the test for valid legislation should be that it must satisfy the requirements of generality, equality, and certainty.[49] This check, he believed, would eliminate all legislation favoring specific groups, and would result in an overall reduction in legislation because these requirements are not easily met.

Hayek granted that Bills of Rights have been beneficial to the cause of liberty.[50] But he asserted that the rule of law provides the "most effective protection" against the violation of individual rights, superior even to explicit Bills of Rights, because those who govern would be reluctant to adopt oppressive rules that, as required by generality and equality, would also apply to themselves.[51] "Such a clause [requiring adherence to the rule of law] would by itself achieve all and more that the traditional Bills of Rights were meant to secure; and it would therefore make any separate enumeration of a list of special protected fundamental rights unnecessary."[52]

Few theorists have expressed so much unshakable faith in the rule of law. The rule of law, according to Hayek, is the mainstay of liberty, preserving the freedom to do what one pleases outside of what the law prohibits. It is the essence of justice. It is an effective shackle that can keep democracy from becoming tyranny. It provides greater protection for the individual than Bills of Rights. Hayek's conception of the rule of law is formal, not substantive, in the sense that he did not include any specific requirements with respect to the content of the law. However, he derived important substantive implications from it: his version of the rule of law ruled out attempts to achieve substantive equality and distributive justice, and "would of course make all socialist measures for redistribution impossible."[53]

The social welfare state endures

Hayek's and Dicey's call to man the ramparts in defense of the rule of law against the encroaching social welfare state was an abject failure, though perhaps it is premature for a final reckoning. Not taking evident heed of their warnings, the growth of the administrative state continued apace, and indeed accelerated in the course of the twentieth century in the USA and England, the countries in which they wrote, and elsewhere in the liberal West. Resulting economic and social regulation addressed an array of complex subjects – like pollution control, consumer protection, and workplace health and safety – leading to greater resort to open-ended discretionary standards, and increased decision-making by experts.[54]

Coinciding with this expansion, however, administrative actions have also undergone a degree of legalization. The Administrative Procedures Act, enacted mid-century in the United States, and the development of Administrative Law in England,[55] instituted legal checks on administrative activities. Such checks were mostly procedural, and judges reviewing administrative actions in the USA evinced a strong deference to administrative decisions owing to their presumed expertise. Administrative agencies also established sharper internal separations of functions, especially in creating independent administrative courts that resemble ordinary courts of law.

Despite persistent hand-wringing by conservatives, intermittently erupting in episodes of deregulation and welfare reform – as in the Reagan-Thatcher era – the fundamental planks of the social welfare state remain unscathed, although the rate of expansion has slowed if not halted. A political theorist provided the following summary of the state of affairs relative to the rule of law as the twentieth century came to a close:

Evidence continues to mount that crucial components of the rule of law are disintegrating under the conditions of the contemporary regulatory state. In every capitalist welfare state law takes an increasingly amorphous and indeterminate form as legal standards like "in the public interest" or "in good faith" incompatible with classical liberal conceptions of the legal norm proliferate. Everywhere a troublesome conflation of traditional parliamentary rulemaking with situation-specific administrative decrees results; everywhere bureaucratic and judicial discretion grows. If a minimal demand of the rule-of-law ideal was always that state action should take a predictable form, contemporary democracies do poorly living up to this standard.[56]

6   Radical left encourages decline

While the political right laments the degeneration of the rule of law in the West, radical left theorists encourage this decline. Their opposition builds upon the communitarian reaction to liberalism and upon on the negative implications of the rule of law in liberal systems, especially those related to distributive justice and formal equality. It is liberalism and capitalism that the radical left most resents, and the rule of law is attacked for the service it provides in bolstering this political and economic system. This chapter will concentrate on arguments raised amongst legal theorists in the USA, where the theoretical challenge to the rule of law has been most vociferous. Such severe criticism could only be produced in a country in which lengthy acquaintance with the rule of law confers intimate familiarity of its limitations, and also leads to a sense of security that encourages forgetfulness about its benefits.

The 1960s and 1970s witnessed a massive social upheaval in the USA, related to the fight for civil rights, protests against the Vietnam War, refusal to comply with the draft, and resistance against school busing, mixed in with broader concerns about the dire economic future (stagflation and the oil crisis), the corruption of politics (Watergate), and the sexual revolution and mind-altering drugs. President John F. Kennedy and Robert Kennedy, his brother and political heir apparent, had been assassinated. Civil rights leader Martin Luther King was murdered. Body bags of US soldiers and napalmed Vietnamese villages flashed across the television screen, ending US innocence. Bombings and bank heists, the Weathermen and the Chicago 7, brought the unfamiliar specter of political terrorism. Malcom X and the Black Panthers frightened white America. All of this was played out on television, unifying the country in the conviction that it was deeply rent, seized in the grip of a multifaceted crisis, perhaps the first stage in the decline of a great nation.

Law was caught up in the thick of this national schism, castigated from both directions. For the left, too often the law was on the wrong side, showing its authoritarian face, protecting power and privilege, answering peaceful marches and sit ins with angry police and national guardsmen brandishing batons, bayonet-mounted rifles, and snapping dogs. For the right, rampant civil disobedience encouraged disrespect for the law and threatened social disorder, to which the law responded meekly and indecisively, reaping further lawlessness. The left cheered the Warren Supreme Court as the sole legal institution taking a progressive (albeit modest) stand for social justice, and feared that the successor Burger Court would erase the little good that was accomplished; whereas many in the legal establishment, conservative as well as mainstream, condemned Warren Court justices as activists rewriting the Constitution to advance their personal political views.[1] All sides thought it evident that a "crisis of legal liberalism" and deterioration of the rule of law were at hand.[2] The agonizing time they lived in felt like an epochal transitional moment between "the breakdown of the old order and the creation of a new one."[3]

The Critical Legal Studies Movement – its mantra "law is politics," its target "legal liberalism" – was born out of this social conflagration. The founding members of the movement were law students at elite institutions during the 1960s and new law professors during the 1970s. They watched in disgust as their erstwhile allies, mainstream liberal-leaning law professors, too often lined up on the law and order side of the upheaval. They were determined to expose legal liberalism for the fraud that it was. The philosophical prophet of the movement, Roberto Unger, published *Knowledge and Politics* (1975), a theoretical critique of liberalism, and *Law in Modern Society* (1976), an elaborate account of the decline of the rule of law in modern liberal societies, launching the initial fusillade against liberalism and the rule of law.

Liberty and equality viewed from the radical left

As the radical left saw it, liberalism promised liberty and equality, but instead surreptitiously led to new forms of domination and inequality and cloaked them in legitimacy. The liberal obsession on protecting individual freedom from government oppression creates a sharp public-private distinction. Liberal vigilance is directed against the tyrannical application of public power. Within the private realm, short of physical violence toward others or forcibly taking their property, individuals are free to do as they please (and within the "private" confines of the family, even violence was condoned, in the form of spousal abuse). That is what liberty is about.

Liberty can be exercised in ways harmful to others, however, a potential enhanced when people are encouraged to pursue their self-interest and indulge their own vision of the good. When corporations become as powerful as the government, when work conditions more pervasively effect one's existence, the abstract threat that the government might arbitrarily apply coercion recedes in immediacy; but not only does liberalism have little to say to protect individuals from oppression in the work environment (the government's regulatory authority is limited to health and safety concerns), it actually throws up barriers against such protections as impermissible interference in the private arena. Similarly, although liberalism and capitalism made substantial inroads against inequality based upon ascriptive social hierarchies tied to birth status, new inequalities based on unequal distributions of wealth and talent were established.[4] An aristocracy of blood or hereditary caste was exchanged for one based upon talent and economic class. The new inequalities, the disparity between rich and poor, could reach levels unimagined under the old inequalities, but again liberalism throws up barriers against government attempts at redress as interference in the private arena. Private domination and unequal distribution of wealth and talent complement one another: the greater the wealth and talent the greater capacity to dominate others, which in turn generates more wealth. Especially the poor, less able, less educated, or social outcasts get short shrift under liberalism. Under the old aristocracies the elite were at least bound to an ethic of social responsibility; for the new moneyed aristocracy the only ethic was "pursue your objectives," which they were told was (incidentally) good for society as well. Besides, since everyone had an equal opportunity to get rich, those who failed were deserving of their fate.

Rather than liberty for all, from the standpoint of those at the bottom, liberalism liberates some – those with economic power – to dominate others – those without. The public power of law is inordinately at the call of those at the top of the new hierarchies. They can afford highly-priced lawyers to utilize the legal system on their behalf; they can distribute campaign contributions to sway legislators to enact their interests in the law. Public resources thereby reinforce the advantage already enjoyed by those with superior private resources. Liberalism amounts to rule by and in the interests of the economic elite, all the while claiming to be neutral.

To the extent that these new forms of domination and inequality are acknowledged by liberalism, as indicated earlier, they are excused as unavoidable side effects that come with the benefits of liberty and formal equality. The trade-off is perhaps unfortunate but still preferable, liberals assert. Government domination can be absolute, including the infliction of physical pain or death or severely circumscribing freedom of movement and choice, which is not allowed to private domination. Private domination is better left to be contested among private forces than dealt with through the application of public power; for liberty would be the first casualty of allowing public officials to make determinations about the types and limits of permissible private domination. Redressing economic inequalities, furthermore, given differences in natural abilities, would involve an intolerable degree of continuous interference by the government, would kill work incentive owing to diminishing its rewards, and consequently the economic pie would shrivel, impoverishing everyone. Under liberalism individuals at least have the *opportunity* to move from one economic class to another, which status hierarchies or the enforced equality of communist systems foreclosed. People are free to be rich (or poor), even if it is admittedly far easier for the rich and their progeny to stay rich than for the poor to become rich. Finally, liberals add, thanks to economic efficiency brought by the free market, in absolute material terms the poor in capitalist societies are still better off than they would be under other economic-political systems. Witness the mass of people from around the world clamoring to immigrate, legally or otherwise, to the USA, providing forceful testimony against critics.

This response is cold comfort to the losers in the system. Private oppression can pervasively affect one's life. Inequality hurts no matter how it is constructed. Knowledge of the strong odds that children who attend poorly funded failing schools will likely end up in prison, prematurely dead, or in low-wage, mindless jobs, and live in crowded tenements or trailer parks, slowly crushes the hope of parents that their children may achieve a better life. Poverty amidst plenty is especially tough to swallow, and hardly consoled by the abstract possibility of the freedom to become rich. And it is no consolation to be told that other people or other places are even worse off.

These are familiar complaints about liberalism, as reflected in the eloquent century-old passage below from Mill:

No longer enslaved or made dependent by force of law, the great majority are so by force of poverty; they are still chained to a place, to an occupation, and to conformity with the will of an employer, and debarred by the accident of birth both from the enjoyments, and from the mental and moral advantages, which others inherit without exertion and independently of desert. That this is an evil equal to almost any of those against which mankind have hitherto struggled, the poor are not wrong in believing.[5]

The liberal ideals of equality and liberty can be vehicles to press for the reform of liberalism. Equality contains an irrepressible ambiguity: "formal equality" means treating everyone alike; "substantive equality" means treating differently situated people differently to equalize their positions in recognition of those differences. Conservatives talk exclusively about formal equality, but both are defensible understandings of equality. If a person or group is in an unequal competitive position owing to social forces, treating them as formally equal will simply confirm the preexisting inequality and is therefore patently unfair. The left has used this argument to promote affirmative action in employment and higher education for disadvantaged groups as a means to rectify disparities in early educational opportunities or disadvantages visited by racial or ethnic discrimination. Liberty contains an analogous ambiguity, though one less often utilized by reformers. Self-determination can be understood, in negative terms, to mean that individuals should be left alone by government to live as they desire; self-determination can also be understood, in positive terms, to mean that the government is obligated to empower individuals – to assist them in acquiring the tools necessary to become self-determining – in order that their liberty may be fully enjoyed. Also building upon the liberty ideal, civil rights have been utilized to impose limited restraints in the private arena – to protect individuals from infringement upon their rights by other individuals, prohibiting racial, ethnic, sexual, and religious discrimination in situations of employment and public accommodations, among others. This effort, however, comes up against the right of association that allows private clubs to exclude others, and the right of free speech that allows the expression of hatred against other groups. A revealing peculiarity of US protections of civil rights against private violations is that they have been enacted by Congress based upon powers granted by the Commerce Clause of the Constitution, justified not on their own merits but because discrimination interferes with interstate commerce. Critical opponents of liberalism, pointing at liberal protections of private domination and the half-hearted effort to rectify abuses, dismiss attempts to use liberal ideals (like rights) as merely serving to perpetuate the survival of a system that is corrupt and must be abandoned.

Legal realists and the instrumental approach to law

Legal Realism, the label for a collection of like-minded legal theorists who burst on the scene in the first third of the twentieth century, was the intellectual forerunner of the Critical Legal Studies Movement. The immediate objective of the Realist attack was to break resistance by courts to social welfare legislation grounded in arguments that tampering with common law doctrines or legal principles would violate liberty, infringe upon property rights, and hamper the market. Legal Realists systematically critiqued two central props of nineteenth-century legal thought, which the rule of law also rested upon: conceptual formalism and rule formalism.[6]

Conceptual formalism was the notion that legal concepts and principles like freedom of contract, property ownership, fault and duty in torts, had a necessary content, and consisted in relationships within the total complex of rules and concepts to form a coherent and integrated whole body of law. It was the task of the judge to discover, by identifying and formulating the principles that emerge from the cases, and applying legal reasoning thereto, what these concepts and rules consisted of and required. Much of the analysis was abstract, presented with an air of objectively determined conceptual necessity.[7] Legal Realists argued, to the contrary, that legal concepts were malleable, filled in by implicit theories or assumptions held by judges, or determined by unacknowledged choices made by judges.[8] This point was highlighted in the dissent of Justice Oliver Wendell Holmes in *Lochner* v. *New York*.[9] The Supreme Court invalidated state legislation that set limits on the working hours of bakers – permitting no more than ten hours a day or sixty hours a week – on the grounds that it violated the freedom of employers and employees to contract for whatever hours they mutually desired. The reality, which the New York State legislature recognized but the Supreme Court did not, is that the workers had no real freedom to bargain over the terms of their employment. Holmes famously declaimed that the judges were reading laissez faire economic theory into the Constitution, where it did not belong. The Realists taught that the content of a legal concept was not something to be found as a matter of internal logic, but instead must be constructed to further the realization of social purposes, with an awareness of its potential impact on social reality.

Rule formalism was the idea that rules were applied by judges in a mechanical fashion to determine the right answer in every case, without discretion on their part and without the interjection of their values. The Realists argued that there were gaps and contradictions in the law, that rules often had exceptions which allowed for contrary outcomes, that there was flexibility when judges formulated the rule purportedly laid down in a previously decided case, that many rules were ambiguous, that when going from a general rule to application in a particular case there could be more than one reasonable alternative, in sum, that the interpretation of rules was often indeterminate, anything but mechanical, and open to choices and subject to influence from the values of the judge. This interjection of choice was concealed by rule formalism. Realists suggested that often judges came to a decision first, then worked backward to locate legal rules and construct legal arguments in support of the decision. Urging greater candor, the Realists wanted this process to occur openly, the better to evaluate judges' decisions.

Realist arguments, which denied that the law alone determines cases, raised significant doubts about claims made on behalf of the rule of law. Formalists had directly tied the conceptual necessity of legal concepts and mechanical rule application to liberty under the law. Prominent nineteenth-century legal thinker David Dudley Fields stated:

If the decision of litigated questions were to depend upon the will of the Judge or upon his notion of what was just, our property and our lives would be at the mercy of a fluctuating judgment, or a caprice. The existence of a system of rules and conformity to them are the essential conditions of all free governments, and of republican government above all others. The law is our only sovereign. We have enthroned it.[10]

Following the Realist attack it appeared that the contrast between "rule of law" and "rule of man" was not as sharp as previous rhetoric suggested.

To replace formalist understandings, Realists advocated an instrumental view that characterizes law as a tool to achieve desired social objectives.[11] Law can be shaped in any way necessary towards this end. This was a marked change from preexisting views of law. As indicated in earlier chapters, for much of Western history law was seen as something to be discovered rather than made, a reflection of preexisting customs or community morality, of natural law principles, of the internal nature of legal concepts and principles, or of the necessities of the market and natural liberty. The instrumental view of law was first promoted by Jeremy Bentham in the late eighteenth century under the banner of legal reform.[12]

An instrumental view of law within liberalism poses unique difficulties, however. In the absence of agreement over the good, it is problematic to identify shared social objectives the law should promote. Bentham was not troubled by this because for a convinced utilitarian achieving the social good was a matter of maximizing the aggregate of individual pleasures. But utilitarianism is a controversial moral theory not necessarily endorsed by (though often associated with) liberalism. Realists sometimes (overly) optimistically suggested that social science might be able to identify the social good, or at least how its achievement could be facilitated through law, but nothing came of this. The instrumental view of law, in the absence of agreement upon a common good, implies that law is a matter of compromise or contest between group interests within the democratic process, with no integrity unto itself. Spoils go to the winners.

With the advent of World War II, presented at home as an epic battle between good and evil, the Realists retreated from – or at least quieted – the most radical implications of their arguments.[13] The pragmatic and instrumental approach to law promoted by the Realists was tarred with the charge of "relativism." It became imperative for the US legal establishment to reaffirm that law was not just politics, that it possessed integrity and embodied moral principle. Legal Realism in its most virulent form departed the scene, though various theorists carried on their work, and the force of their argument could not be completely suppressed.

The mainstream dilemma

The 1954 Supreme Court decision of *Brown* v. *Board of Education*,[14] in which the Court invalidated legally enforced racial segregation as unconstitutional, plagues mainstream legal theory to this day. The framers of the Equal Protection Clause apparently did not understand it to invalidate racial segregation,[15] which was a common practice at the time. Soon after enactment of the Clause segregation was upheld as valid by the Supreme Court in *Plessy* v. *Ferguson*,[16] with no subsequent change in the Constitution. Freedom of association could be invoked with equal weight by those who desired segregation or those who wanted integration. The *Brown* decision arguably was not supported by legal principles or reasoned elaboration or neutral principle.[17] Hence the decision could not be reconciled comfortably with pre-existing Constitutional law and understandings. Yet it was undoubtedly correct from a moral standpoint, at least in the view of many in the mainstream of legal academia. Other progressive Warren Court decisions raised the same dilemma: morally correct in content, as far as many mainstream legal academics were concerned, but nigh impossible to justify in purely legal terms. These decisions, evidently a product of the political views of the justices, were the antithesis of the rule of law, according to infuriated critics, one more indication of its breakdown.

Providing a justification for the reforms brought by the Warren Court was the challenge that confronted mainstream liberal legal theorists. Two different strategies applied to this task will be conveyed. The first claimed that the Court's decisions were indeed consistent with the rule of law, while the second asserted that the court was modifying the rule of law to evolve to a higher legal order.

Ronald Dworkin, beginning in the 1970s,[18] argued that the rule of law was not at all threatened by the actions of the Warren Court. The problem was not with the Court's activist stance in declaring new constitutional interpretations. Rather the prevailing "rule book" conception of law was incorrect. Law consists of more than just rules. It also consists of immanent moral/political principles embodied within or standing behind the rules and cases. These moral principles are present even when not previously stated or recognized. The US legal system, when viewed from a broader perspective, constitutes a coherent and integrated scheme of rules and principles that reflect the moral life and vision of the community. By Dworkin's account, judges render decisions regarding principles but do not thereby decide matters of policy, and the principles they identify are within the law (broadly conceived), so the law still rules. Thus the morally principled Warren Court decisions were correct and consistent with the rule of law.

Two key assumptions are contained in Dworkin's account: that the community in fact possesses a shared, coherent set of overarching moral and political principles; and that "the rule book represents the community's efforts to capture moral rights."[19] Dworkin's description, similar to Hayek's mentioned earlier, is the latest in a long tradition of presenting law in idealized terms, as representing the customs and morals of the community, and/or reflecting moral principle and reason.[20] In a deeply pluralistic society, however, Dworkin's account has questionable purchase, for there are competing sets of moral principles. Moreover, when an instrumental approach to law prevails, where legislation reflects the winners in political contests, the assertion that law represents the community's moral rights or that it will form a coherent whole merits skepticism. Unless the same group (the majority? or the elite?) or groups with coalescing views and interests routinely prevail in legislative contests, an overarching coherence of the mass of legislation could not easily come about. Even if Dworkin is correct that the US legal tradition shares a core set of political principles, or even if an overlapping consensus exists that spans the pluralism, sharp disagreement on fundamental issues still exists, as will be discussed later, so Court decisions on these subjects seem difficult to include within his broader view of the law.

A second strategy to legitimate the Warren Court took a different tack. *Law and Society in Transition* (1978), written by legal sociologists Philippe Nonet and Philip Selznick, confirmed the contemporary decline of the rule of law, but construed this change as positive, situating it in a three-stage shift from Repressive Law (authoritarian, arbitrary rule of some over others), to Autonomous Law (the rule of law), to Responsive Law (greater consideration of substantive justice). The rule of law had the virtue of placing limits on government actions, and rendering them more predictable. However, the generality of rules that enhances predictability also results in over-inclusiveness and under-inclusiveness – a rule stated in general terms will apply to some situations that do not fit the purpose behind the rule, and will fail to cover some that do. Consider a simple illustration. Setting the minimum driving age at sixteen is intended to limit drivers to the class of people who are physically and emotionally mature enough to handle the demands of driving, but there will be some younger than sixteen who have these characteristics and some older who lack them. Applied in these cases, the rule is unfair, or at least operates counter to its intended purpose. If the objective behind the legal rule, or if considerations of fairness and justice, are taken into account, situations will arise in which the rule should not be followed. The generality, equality, and certainty of the law would be diminished to a degree in a system that allows such case-by-case determinations.

Modern US law (prominently including the Warren Court), according to Nonet and Selznick, was engaged in a shift to the responsive law stage, characterized by placing a greater emphasis on achieving the purposes and principles that underlie a legal and social order. "Thus a distinctive feature of responsive law is the search for implicit values in rules and policies."[21] Under a regime of responsive law the system becomes more outcome oriented, rather than strictly rule oriented. Legality remains the prime value in the system, but not rigid formalism, such that it will sometimes give way to considerations of purpose, principles, justice, and fairness.

It is wrong to think that Dworkin, or Nonet and Selznick, represented the mainstream view of legal academics or theorists. There was, and continues to be, no consensus mainstream view, a lengthy state of theoretical contestation about law which is unprecedented. What Dworkin, and Nonet and Selznick, did capture of the mainstream was, first, dropping the hollow denial that political decisions played no part in legal decisions, and, second, sending the reassuring message that it was nonetheless "law," still worthy of support. There is evidence that judges have indeed become more open to consideration of purposes and justice, while holding to a core legal orientation, which is the intuition that underlies both theories.[22] The main difference in their accounts, which otherwise have much in common, is that Dworkin construes the situation in a way which acknowledges in no reduction in the "legal" character of the system, while Nonet and Selznick embrace the reduction as an evolutionary advance.

Radical left on the breakdown of the rule of law

Instead of searching for ways to paint these developments in positive terms, the radical left went on the offensive. Borrowing from his ideological opponents, Roberto Unger adopted Dicey's first two elements as his definition of the rule of law: that the law must be set out in advance in general terms, and that cases should be heard in ordinary, autonomous courts of law.[23] Unger asserted, with Hayek, that "the rule of law has been truly said to be the soul of the modern [liberal] state."[24] Moreover, he cited to,[25] and echoed, Hayek's and Dicey's argument that the social welfare state was bringing about "the dissolution of the rule of law."[26]

Unger elaborated on how the problems they identified went beyond the administrative context pervasively to infect the law. Two crucial changes in law were generated by the social welfare state, according to Unger. First, judges were asked increasingly to apply open-ended standards like fairness, good faith, reasonableness, and unconscionability. Second, courts – not just administrative officials – were increasingly asked to engage in purposive reasoning, that is, to render decisions about how best to achieve legislatively established policy goals, a process which immersed judges in making choices from among a range of alternative means with different value implications. According to Unger, these two changes were inconsistent with the traditional judicial role of formal rule application, and departed from the ideal of a regime of rules with the qualities of generality, equality, and certainty:

> Open-ended clauses and general standards force courts and administrative agencies to engage in ad hoc balancing of interests that resist reduction to general rules . . .[27]
>
> Purposive legal reasoning and nonformal justice also cause trouble for the ideal of generality. The policy-oriented lawyer insists that part of interpreting a rule is to choose the most efficient means to the attainment of the ends one assigns to it. But as the circumstances to which decisions are addressed change and as the decisionmaker's understanding of the means available to him varies, so must the way he interprets the rules. This instability of result will also increase with the fluctuations of accepted policy and with the variability of the particular problems to be resolved. Hence, the very notion of stable areas of individual entitlement and obligation, a notion inseparable from the rule of law ideal, will be eroded.
>
> The quest for substantive justice corrupts legal generality to an even greater degree. When the range of impermissible inequalities among social situations expands, the need for individualized treatment grows correspondingly. No matter how substantive justice is defined, it can be achieved only by treating different situations differently.[28]

These new demands placed on judges had the additional effect of eroding the autonomy of law, since judges increasingly went outside the domain of legal rules and legal reasoning to consult external sources of knowledge like social science, to discern the lay sense of justice, and to engage in efficiency analysis, when rending decisions. "As purposive legal reasoning and concerns with substantive justice began to prevail, the style of legal discourse approaches that of commonplace political or economic argument."[29] Serious questions emerge about the legitimacy of such judicial decision-making. It offends political liberty to have unelected judges make decisions no different in kind from those made by legislatures.

Further complicating matters was the fact that the shift in thinking was only partially achieved. The instrumental rationality typical of purposive reasoning was melded with rule application. "In these situations, the courts and agencies are caught between two roles with conflicting demands: the role of the traditional formalist judge, who asks what the correct interpretation of the rules of law is, and the role of the calculator of efficiencies, who seeks to determine what course of action will most effectively serve a given goal . . ."[30] The result is a legal system that contains "an unstable oscillation between generalizing rules and ad hoc decisions."[31]

Longing for community

Informed by a simultaneous revolt against liberalism taking place within political theory,[32] radical left legal theorists argued that liberalism is irredeemably flawed owing to its starting presupposition of autonomous individuals joining together to form a legal order to facilitate the pursuit of their own vision of the good. Critical legal scholars argued that in a myriad of ways the liberal approach to society and law failed to appreciate the role of community. People are born to, nurtured by, and always exist within communities; they take their language, morals, roles, and very patterns of thoughts from communities; their identity is a function of how others in the community view them; solidarity with others, expressed in friendship and altruism, gives meaning to life; they love others and need love from others; individuals are social beings through and through. All of this was forgotten by liberalism's hyper-individualism.

Critical scholars contended that the liberal rule of law system, explicitly constructed in individualist terms, harbors within it communitarian impulses struggling for recognition. Critical theorist Duncan Kennedy claimed that this created a "fundamental contradiction" within liberal law, a contradiction manifested in the combination of rule orientation and substantive justice:

I argue that there are two opposed rhetorical modes for dealing with substantive issues, which I will call individualism and altruism . . . One formal mode favors the use of clearly defined, highly administrable, general rules; the other supports the use of equitable standards producing ad hoc decisions with relatively little precedential value. [These] opposed rhetorical modes lawyers use reflect a deeper level of contradiction. At this deeper level, we are divided, among ourselves and also within ourselves, between irreconcilable visions of humanity and society, and between radically different aspirations for our common future.[33]

On this view, the rule of law was not just fraudulent – since in many cases the complex of rules and standards allow contrasting outcomes – it was incorrigible, for it systematically privileged individual autonomy at the expense of community solidarity.

Many radical left theorists took the view that the solution lies in enhanced community, which would solve the contradictions within liberalism by aligning the interests of the individual with the interests of society. Unger explained why:

Community is held together by an allegiance to common purposes. The more these shared ends express the nature of humanity rather than simply the preferences of particular individuals and groups, the more would one's acceptance of them become an affirmation of one's own nature; the less would it have to represent the abandonment of individuality in favor of assent and recognition. Thus, it would be possible to view others as complementary rather than opposing wills; furtherance of their ends would mean the advancement of one's own. The conflict between the demands of individuality and of sociability would disappear.[34]

Not only is there no conflict between individual good and the social good under these circumstances; the rule of law is no longer preeminent in a community of shared values. The dominant orientation in situations of conflict, instead of strict rule application, will be to come to an outcome that furthers the shared community purpose. The will of one conforms to the will of all, so discretion by judges and government officials is no longer a problem but a positive feature that enhanced their ability to promote the common good.

This idealized vision fails to account for the main feature of modern society that liberalism accommodates: the fact of pluralism. It requires a significant commonality amongst the interests and goods of constituent individuals (far more so than Dworkin's account), as well as an alignment of the interests of individuals with that of the community, all of which is dubious in modern society. Unger was aware that society must radically change if his vision was to work. Despite the notable negatives they bring, however, individualism and pluralism are also in many ways attractive to members of contemporary society. If liberalism makes the error of too much individualism, Unger perhaps makes the opposite error of too little, with potentially chilling implications. To his credit, Unger recognized the totalitarian and suffocating potential inherent in the promotion of greater community, and he acknowledged that all too often the supposedly shared community values are really values that promote the interests of some over others. He warned that the communitarian goal may be chimerical and dangerous.[35]

The radical left agreed upon the flaws of liberalism and the rule of law, but offered few concrete alternatives. "Critical feminists" urged that the content of legal rules should explicitly incorporate currently excluded values like altruism, caring, love, responsibility for others;[36] "legal pragmatists" urged that the generality of the rule of law should be modified to allow for greater consideration of context-specific factors and more substantive justice.[37] For the most part critical legal theorists attacked liberalism and the rule of law without proposing what should supplant them.

Critical theorists weathered a sharp backlash from mainstream legal academics, the most intemperate of whom charged the critics with nihilism and suggested that they did not belong in law schools.[38] A more penetrating response was the argument by race theorists that critical scholars failed to appreciate the indispensable service liberal rights provided in the social and legal battles waged by minorities to improve their social position.[39] Critical scholars also failed to contemplate whether the purported contradictions and instabilities they identified could be moderated in a manner such that the system could remain predominantly rulebound while more open to justice and fairness, as Nonet and Selznick suggested was in fact occurring, to accommodate individualism as well as a sense of community. Their goal was to de-legitimate the entire system rather than to find ways in which it might work better by ameliorating the flaws they identified.

Indeterminacy and the rule of law

The radical left did more than just point out the decline of the rule of law. It attempted to further this decline by pressing the indeterminacy thesis, picking up a theme first raised by the Legal Realists. The debate over the indeterminacy of law was especially lively in the 1980s and early 1990s, spawning a sizable body of literature that covered a range of subjects, from the indeterminacy of language,[40] to the indeterminacy of standards, to the indeterminacy of particular areas of the law. Fortunately much of the discussion can be bypassed. When the initial heat subsided, general agreement emerged among disputants over the presence, though not the precise extent, of indeterminacy, with remaining disagreement focused mostly on how indeterminacy was to be characterized and whether it threatened the ideal of the rule of law.

The indeterminacy thesis – which centers upon courts – asserts that, in a significant subset of cases, the law does not produce a single right answer, or (less stringently phrased) that the available body of legal rules allows more than one outcome, and sometimes contradictory outcomes. Indeterminacy exists in the failure of law to *determine* the outcome in these cases. Owing to said indeterminacy, the decision made by the judge must be the product of influences other than the legal rules. Signs of this indeterminacy are the presence of rules that can lead to different outcomes, gaps in the rules, the ready availability of exceptions to rules, the openness of legal standards, all reflected in the seeming ease with which skilled lawyers are able to formulate arguments on both sides of a case. The fact of regular disagreement over the law among judges, seen in dissenting opinions and splits among courts, is irrefutable evidence of the presence of indeterminacy.[41] The currently reigning Rehnquist Supreme Court, to cite the most visible example, has issued many contentious decisions by 5–4 votes, falling along predictable political lines.

Law is supposed to decide cases, not the person who happens to be the judge. Aristotle identified man with passion and law with reason; Locke contrasted rule by law with rule by the arbitrary will of another; Chief Justice Marshall denied that the will of judges influence the law. That is the point of the slogan: "the rule of law, not man." All of these accounts, and countless more, characterized rule application by judges in the same terms: the judge speaks the law – the judge is the law personified. This image trades on the fear of being subject to the authority of another. But the indeterminacy thesis punctures the image that the dignified black judicial robe is what matters, not the individual underneath. This argument is the latest reiteration of Hobbes' observation that human beings have final say over the rules they are interpreting and applying.

The main response put forth by opponents of the indeterminacy thesis was to point out the substantial degree of predictability in law.[42] There are many "easy cases," cases in which lawyers can reliably anticipate the likely outcome, in which there will be little or no disagreement among judges. Such cases are routinely resolved prior to court proceedings owing to this predictability. Cases not so resolved are often the result of gaps or faults in empirical proof, not uncertainties about law. Claims about rampant indeterminacy were exaggerated because critical theorists overemphasized appellate cases, the routine grist of law professors, which indeed showed a greater proportion of disagreement, but represented a small, misleading sampling of the totality of cases.

Critical legal scholars agreed that the bulk of cases were predictable. But they made three further points. First, the plentiful supply of easy cases might still be determined by influences other than exclusively the legal rules, factors like the shared socio-economic background of elite, white, male judges. Second, a fair number of cases, even if not a majority, were not easy cases, for which prediction was difficult, wherein judges must select from among alternative possible outcomes, none compelled by the legal rules. Third, situations initially thought to involve an easy case could be transformed into a problematic one, with sufficient motivation and skill exercised by lawyers or judges who wished to obtain a different outcome. Furthermore, critical legal theorists pointed out, hard cases tended to involve hotly contested social issues, which made their salience greater even if they occurred on a less frequent basis than predictable cases.

Opponents of the indeterminacy thesis had ready answers for the second and third arguments by critical theorists. They point out that *all* legal systems have an unavoidable degree of indeterminacy, owing to the openness of language, the generality of rules, and the fact that not every situation can be anticipated or provided for in advance. Consider the legal rule: "No vehicles permitted in the park."[43] Automobiles and mopeds are obviously disallowed under this rule, but bicycles or skateboards are less certain. Consider a more carefully drafted law that prohibits "motorized vehicles" from the park. Bicycles and skateboards are permitted, but what about a motorized wheelchair (or one kept in the manual mode)? Or what about a battery-operated toy car? Or an old tank permanently lodged in the park as a war memorial? Or an ambulance called to pick up an injured visitor? Although its application will be evident in routine cases, the legal rule does not provide an unequivocal answer to every possible situation. Despite the unavoidable open texture of language and rules, however, experience demonstrates that people reliably communicate through language and routinely understand and follow rules. Rules work. They are regularly adhered to and they guide conduct. When ambiguities and doubts exist in a given situation of rule application, they are resolved through reasoned analysis. Hence indeterminacies, given that they exist, do not inevitably defeat the determinacy of a legal system. The charge of indeterminacy cannot be successfully made if the argument remains at an abstract level (the level at which it is most plausible). To have bite it must be shown that existing legal rules form a pervasive mess of contradictions, which critical theorists have not demonstrated.

A related response by defenders of legal determinacy was that critical scholars set a higher bar than the rule of law requires.[44] Although legal rules sometimes do allow more than one outcome, these outcomes usually can be ranked in strength of legal support. Even if not compelled or exclusively correct, a decision based upon the strongest option will still be determined (or guided) by the law.

Finally, in response to the third point, defenders conceded that it is impossible to prevent a determined bad faith judge from manipulating the rules to achieve a desired outcome. All legal systems rely upon judges possessing the integrity not to exploit the latent indeterminacy in language and legal rules. Judges must be committed to fidelity to the law, and must have as their primary interpretive orientation to seek out the correct understanding of the legal rules. Unless corruption or ineptitude pervades the judiciary, the rogue judge will be checked (though not in every instance) by the presence of other judges, either sitting on the same panel or at higher levels of appellate review.

Most critical scholars did not strongly contest these responses. So the debate over the indeterminacy thesis narrowed to the issue of the sources of the acknowledged substantial degree of predictability in law. Critical scholars attributed the source of this predictability to factors other than the law, especially the shared socio-economic background of judges in the USA (upper middle class or elite white males). Critical scholars also identified indoctrination into the legal culture as a source of predictability:

The legal culture shared by judges and theorists encompasses shared understandings of proper institutional roles and the extent to which the status quo should be maintained or altered. This culture includes "common sense" understandings of what rules mean as well as conventions (the identification of rules and exceptions) and politics (the differentiation between liberal and conservative judges.[45]

This is a conventionalist explanation for the predictability in law.

Many opponents of the indeterminacy thesis agreed with the conventionalist explanation for the predictability in law. All meaning is conventional in this sense. Not only is it proper, therefore, but inevitable that indoctrination into a shared legal tradition would be essential.[46] Legal professionals constitute an interpretive community with a shared legal language, culture, and sets of beliefs, which stabilize the interpretation and application of rules. What appears to be indeterminate rules when viewed in the abstract, will, in the context of application, be determinate, because shared conventions within the legal tradition (backed up by institutional constraints, like appellate review) rule out certain interpretations as unacceptable. The legal rules cannot be seen, at least not within the bounds of general plausibility, in ways disallowed by surrounding legal conventions. Offending opinions "will not write." This explanation expands what it means to be a part of the "law" beyond the rules to include the entirety of the legal culture and tradition.

This explanation for the prevalence of easy cases must compete with the alternative explanation that judges' decisions are predictable owing to the fact that they share an elite background, which leads them to interpret and apply law in like ways in the interests of elite domination. This would not be an acceptable source of legal determinacy, for what matters then would not be the legal tradition itself but the particular social backgrounds of the judges. An additional unresolved question exists as to whether the legal tradition more broadly is itself socially influenced by elite interests.

In the past generation or so US law schools opened seats to previously excluded groups, and the same is beginning to occur with the judiciary. When combined with the acknowledgment that a majority of cases are predictable, and that the legal tradition is a major reason for this uniformity, the indeterminacy thesis has lost much of its punch. Though far from conclusive, empirical studies appear to indicate that, in courts below the Supreme Court, there is less indeterminacy (when measured by interpretive disagreement) than critical scholars contended.[47] There is little discussion of the indeterminacy thesis in legal theory circles today.

The indeterminacy thesis does not necessarily threaten one core aspect of the rule of law. Recall that predictability was, for Hayek, *the* key way in which the rule of law preserves liberty: it allows people to plan and take action with notice of what will subject them to legal coercion. This is legal liberty. An indeterminate *and* unpredictable legal system would fail in this respect. An indeterminate legal system that is nevertheless predictable – whatever the source of the predictability – will continue to preserve legal liberty.

That the debate among legal theorists over indeterminacy has fizzled out should not be taken to mean that it was much ado about nothing. To the contrary, it confirmed that indeterminacy is an ever-present potentiality within law. It also confirmed that the possibility of indeterminacy need not undermine the predictability of a legal system. Its most important lesson was that if judges are seated on the bench who have few qualms about exploiting the latent indeterminacy of law to favor personal or political objectives, the law is defenseless.

7   Formal theories

Now that the history and political context have been conveyed, it is possible to lay out the alternative theoretical formulations of the rule of law in circulation today. There is no shortage of competing formulations, but they can be pared down to two basic categories, known by theorists as "formal" versions and "substantive versions," each coming in three distinct forms. Here is the full complement:

ALTERNATIVE RULE OF LAW FORMULATIONS

Thinner - - - - - - - - - - - - - -> to - - - - - - - - - - - -> Thicker

FORMAL VERSIONS:	1. **Rule-by-Law**	2. **Formal Legality**	3. **Democracy+ Legality**
	– law as instrument of government action	– general, prospective, clear, certain	– consent determines content of law
SUBSTANTIVE VERSIONS:	4. **Individual Rights** – property, contract, privacy, autonomy	5. **Right of Dignity and /or Justice**	6. **Social Welfare** – substantive equality, welfare, preservation of community

These alternative theoretical formulations will be elaborated in a progression that runs from thinner to thicker accounts, by which I mean moving from formulations with fewer requirements to more requirements. Generally speaking, each subsequent formulation incorporates the main aspects of preceding formulations, making them progressively cumulative.

It is standard within legal theory to separate rule of law conceptions into formal and substantive branches. This description of the contrast will help serve as a preliminary guide to the excursion:

Formal conceptions of the rule of law address the manner in which the law was promulgated (was it by a properly authorized person . . .); the clarity of the ensuing norm (was it sufficiently clear to guide an individual's conduct so as to enable a person to plan his or her life, etc.); and the temporal dimension of the enacted norm (was it prospective . . .). Formal conceptions of the rule of law do not however seek to pass judgment upon the actual content of the law itself. They are not concerned with whether the law was in that sense a good law or a bad law, provided that the formal precepts of the rule of law were themselves met. Those who espouse substantive conceptions of the rule of law seek to go beyond this. They accept that the rule of law has the formal attributes mentioned above, but they wish to take the doctrine further. Certain substantive rights are said to be based on, or derived from, the rule of law. The concept is used as the foundation for these rights, which are then used to distinguish between "good" laws, which comply with such rights, and "bad" laws which do not.[1]

The basic distinction can be summarized thus: formal theories focus on the proper sources and form of legality, while substantive theories also include requirements about the content of the law (usually that it must comport with justice or moral principle). While the distinction is informative, it should not be taken as strict – the formal versions have substantive implications and the substantive versions incorporate formal requirements. For reasons that will be articulated, a majority of Anglo-American legal theorists have adopted the second formal version, what I have labeled "formal legality." This chapter will cover formal conceptions, with substantive conceptions following in the next.

Rule *by* law

The thinnest formal version of the rule of law is the notion that law is the means by which the state conducts its affairs, "that whatever a government does, it should do through laws."[2] A more apt label for this version is "rule *by* law." One extreme version holds that "all utterances of the sovereign, because they are utterances of the sovereign, are law."[3] Understood in this way, the rule of law has no real meaning, for it collapses into the notion of rule by the government. "It has been said that the rule of law means that all government action must be authorized by law . . . If government is, by definition, government authorized by law the rule of law seems to amount to an empty tautology, not a political ideal."[4] Every modern state has the rule of law in this narrow sense.

It is indeed an aspect of the rule of law ideal that the government acts through law, and this is a partial meaning of the German *Rechtsstaat* (law state),[5] but no Western legal theorist identifies the rule of law entirely in terms of rule *by* law. Rule by law carries scant connotation of legal *limitations* on government, which is the *sine qua non* of the rule of law tradition. Nonetheless, a few contemporary regimes apparently adopt this understanding. Chinese legal scholars have claimed that this is the Chinese government's preferred understanding of the rule of law,[6] although this take on the rule of law is not held by the Chinese alone.

"Some Asian politicians focus on the regular, efficient application of law but do not stress the necessity of government subordination to it. In their view, the law exists not to limit the state but to serve its power."[7]

The emptiness of formal legality

One might be tempted to castigate rule *by* law as an authoritarian distortion of the rule of law tradition, but the conception favored by most legal theorists – formal legality – the version espoused by Hayek, is also quite compatible with ruthless authoritarian regimes. Joseph Raz, a leading contemporary legal theorist, emphasized this point:

A non-democratic legal system, based on the denial of human rights, on extensive poverty, on racial segregation, sexual inequalities, and racial persecution may, in principle, conform to the requirements of the rule of law better than any of the legal systems of the more enlightened Western democracies . . . It will be an immeasurably worse legal system, but it will excel in one respect: in its conformity to the rule of law.[8]

The law may . . . institute slavery without violating the rule of law.[9]

These assertions will shock many users of the phrase. It should be recalled, however, that the USA adhered to the rule of law even when slavery was legally enforced, and racial segregation legally imposed. What makes this account of the rule of law compatible with evil is the absence of any separate criteria of the good or just with respect to the content of the law.

Raz followed Hayek when he identified "the basic intuition" underlying the rule of law: "the law must be capable of guiding the behavior of its subjects."[10] He derived the elements of the rule of law from this idea. According to Raz, these elements include that the law must be prospective, general, clear, public, and relatively stable. To this list Raz added several mechanisms he considered necessary to effectuate rules of this kind: an independent judiciary, open and fair hearings without bias, and review of legislative and administrative officials and limitations on the discretion of police to insure conformity to the requirements of the rule of law. The first set of requirements, also found in Hayek and Unger, is a standard statement of the dominant formal version of the rule of law.[11] Lon Fuller, a prominent legal theorist of a generation ago, presented a highly influential formulation of the rule of law, which he called "legality," in similar terms, requiring: generality, clarity, public promulgation, stability over time, consistency between the rules and the actual conduct of legal actors, and prohibitions against retroactivity, against contradictions, and against requiring the impossible.[12]

Raz, Fuller, Hayek, Unger, and all others who adopt this version, agree that the rule of law furthers individual autonomy and dignity by allowing people to plan their activities with advance knowledge of its potential legal implications.[13] This was Montesquieu's conception of liberty under law – freedom to do what the law permits – legal liberty. "But it has no bearing on the existence of spheres of activity free from governmental interference and is compatible with gross violations of human rights."[14] "It says nothing about how the law is to be made: by tyrants, democratic majorities, or any other way. It says nothing about fundamental rights, about equality, or justice."[15] It imposes only procedural requirements, only restrictions about the form that law must take.

The fact that this version of the rule of law has no content requirements renders it open to a range of ends. Fuller asserted that the notion of formal legality is "indifferent toward the substantive aims of the law and is ready to serve a variety of such aims with equal efficiency."[16] Theorists have identified this neutrality as a reason to recommend the formal over the substantive version: "a relatively formal theory is itself more or less politically neutral, and because it is so confined, is more likely to command support on its own terms from right, left, and center in politics than is a substantive theory which not only incorporates the rule of law formally conceived but also incorporates much more controversial substantive content."[17] This substantively empty quality has been identified by theorists, and by the World Bank and other development agencies, as what renders it amenable to universal application.[18]

Adherents of this version of the rule of law are in substantial agreement about its requirements and its implications, except for two points: on how to understand the equality requirement, and on whether the rule of law itself represents a moral good.

Two understandings of the equality requirement can be found in the literature. Hayek held that equality prohibited the enactment of laws that made arbitrary distinctions among people. The problem with this restriction is that it requires a substantive standard to determine what counts as "arbitrary." Another serious problem is the reality that law makes a multitude of distinctions all the time that could have been drawn differently. Progressive taxation, for example, imposes different tax percentages pegged at various income levels, all of which could have been otherwise. Owing to these difficulties, most formal accounts apprehend the equality requirement in another sense (also used by Hayek): a law applies equally to everyone according to its terms (whatever those might be), without taking account of wealth, status (government official or public), race or religion, or any other characteristic of a given individual. Everyone is equal before the law no matter who they might be.

The morality of formal legality

The second area of disagreement – is the rule of law a moral good? – is more hotly disputed; it bears on whether a government that institutes the rule of law deserves the obedience of its citizens. Fuller argued that the rule of law itself is a moral good, in that it enhances individual autonomy.[19] Furthermore, he asserted that the rule of law has an "affinity with the good,"[20] meaning that legal systems with these formal characteristics will more likely also have laws with fair and just content. "There will be at least some values and principles in the official culture to which the citizen can appeal in his complaints about injustice, and some tensions which he can exploit to embarrass the regime."[21] At a minimum, the procedural requirements of the rule of law prohibit the government from acting in an entirely ad hoc arbitrary fashion. "A tyranny devoted to pernicious ends has no self-sufficient *reason* ['(other than tactical and superficial)'[22]] to submit itself to the discipline of operating consistently through the demanding processes of law . . ."[23]

However, a strong counter-argument can be made that the formal rule of law is morally neutral. Raz presented it:

A good knife is, among other things, a sharp knife. Similarly, conformity to the rule of law is an inherent value of laws, indeed it is their most important inherent value. It is of the essence of law to guide behavior through rules and courts in charge of their application . . . Like other instruments, the law has a specific virtue which is morally neutral in being neutral as to the end to which the instrument is put.[24]

Like a knife, which is neither good nor bad in itself, but can be used to kill a man or to slice vegetables, the morality of law is a function of the uses to which it is put. The rule of law in the service of an immoral legal regime would be immoral. Clarity and consistency of application with respect to pernicious laws – like legalized slavery – makes the system more evil, enhancing its draconian efficiency and malicious effect. Whether a legal regime merits support, from this perspective, is not a question of whether it respects the rule of law (though that may be a part of the evaluation), but of the moral import of the content of laws, their application, and their consequences.

This debate is not an abstract matter of interest only to theorists. Authoritarian regimes that adhere to formal legality have existed.[25] Given the unparalleled legitimacy currently enjoyed by the rule of law, it would behoove a tyrannical regime with oppressive laws to institute the rule of law – accepting the inconveniences it imposes – in order to claim the allegiance of its citizens. These wily tyrants will find support for their position in arguments put forth by influential theorists to the effect that regimes with the rule of law, even if oppressive, should be obeyed since the alternative might be worse. Jeremy Waldron made such an argument: "a system that comes close to satisfying the ideal [of the rule of law] may make a reasonable claim on our support if there is a real danger that disobedience and protest against its (admitted) injustices and imperfections may precipitate a collapse into a type of regime that has no respect for legality whatsoever."[26] Thus may an odious regime use the rule of law to legitimate its tyranny by pointing out – ominously – that there are even more tyrannical possibilities. To see formal legality as moral in itself can have hazardous consequences for a populace. "Repressive law is perhaps less terrible than lawless repression, but it can be terrible all the same."[27]

A sensible resolution accepts the insights of both sides. Formal legality enhances the dignity of citizens by allowing them to predict and plan, no doubt a moral positive.[28] Just as importantly, however, any moral evaluation of the law, any determination of whether it generates a moral obligation of compliance on the part of citizens, must also consider the moral implications of the content of the rules and their effects.

The emptiness of formal legality, to make a broader point, runs contrary to the long tradition of the rule of law, the historical inspiration of which has been the restraint of tyranny by the sovereign. Such restraint went beyond the idea that the government must enact and abide by laws that take on the proper form of rules, to include the understanding that there were certain things the government or sovereign could not do. The limits imposed by law were substantive, based upon natural law, shared customs, Christian morality, or the good of community. Formal legality discards this orientation. Consistent with formal legality, the government can do as it wishes, so long as it is able to pursue those desires in terms consistent with (general, clear, certain, and public) legal rules declared in advance. If the government is moved to do something not legally permitted, it must simply change the law first, making sure to meet the requirements of the legal form.

With this in mind, it is correct to conclude that formal legality has more in common with the idea of rule *by* law than with the historical rule of law tradition.

Formal legality is a matter of rules

It is of paramount significance to recognize that the rule of law understood in terms of formal legality boils down to the nature of rules. A reconstruction of the implicit chain of reasoning involved is as follows.

"Law" in essence is comprised of rules (rules are the distinctive form that law takes). The function (and definition) of rules is to serve as general guides of behavior. The qualities of generality, certainty, clarity, and prospectivity are all connected to the nature of rules. Generality is an aspect of what it means to be a "rule," in contrast to a particular "order."[29] That is the essential difference between following a rule or taking an ad hoc action, or making a context-specific decision. Uncertain or unclear rules have limited efficacy in guiding behavior. A retroactive rule is an oxymoron, for it cannot be followed. Rules can consist of any kind of content. The rule of law is open to any kind of content. Rules are formal by nature; so law is formal by nature; so the rule of law is formal by nature.

Hence the qualities of formal legality are the same characteristics that all rules possess. Philosophical and sociological analyses of rules and rule-following highlight the same considerations and elements as the formal version of the rule of law.[30] In the end there is nothing distinctive about the formal rule of law as a separate ideal. It is about (legal) rules.[31]

Keeping in mind this last point will help more carefully to evaluate claims theorists have made about the formal rule of law. Max Weber argued that capitalism requires a formal rule-oriented legal system in order to provide the security and predictability necessary for market transactions. Hayek's formal approach to the rule of law ties into the same set of arguments about the predictability of rule-following as the key to individual liberty.[32] Capitalism, liberalism, and the rule of law are thus tightly wrapped together, licensing Hayek's assertion that the rule of law cannot operate in the context of a socialist economic system or the social welfare state.

Social welfare systems, however, as well as socialist ones, also rely upon rules to function. When rules exist and are honored by the legal system formal legality operates.[33] The essential question is: in what areas, or with respect to what activities, should legal rules govern? Formal legality has nothing to say about this question.[34] It offers no dictates about the proportion or types of government activities that ought to be rule bound. These are matters of social choice. Decisions must be made about when predictability and individual autonomy are highly valued, about the costs and benefits of applying legal rules to a given arena of social intercourse, about whether rules fit, are efficient, are effective, are socially beneficial, in what proportion and to what extent. Rules can be applied in all situations in which it is deemed socially beneficial, regardless of the nature of the surrounding economic or political system. The historical rule of law tradition, with its emphasis on restraining state tyranny, would indicate that formal legality should apply at least in those areas subject to severe government coercion, that is, at a minimum in the context of criminal punishment.

Contrary to what Hayek and Unger suggested, the social welfare state did not necessarily threaten the rule of law. It created areas of government action not cabined by detailed legal restrictions. Many of these involved newly established initiatives relating to government-sponsored programs. Previously law-governed matters, especially those relating to the application of criminal laws, mostly offenses to public order or to the persons and property of others, were not touched by the growth of the administrative bureaucracy. If anything, there has been an increase in the scope and application of criminal laws since Hayek wrote, which spells an expansion of the reach of formal legality, not a reduction, an expansion which might actually have reduced liberty of action rather than enhanced it. To be sure, many administrative initiatives contain punitive aspects analogous to criminal sanctions, like fines, but these often come within a rule-governed framework.

Owing to the overall expansion of government activities, much of it policy oriented requiring that discretionary judgments be made, there may have been a reduction in the total proportion of government actions bound by legal rules. However, Hayek cannot resort to formal legality to complain about this development, as formal legality only addresses the form that law should take, not the proportion or circumstances of its application. Outside the administrative context, in areas of private law there has been an increase in the use of open-ended standards, like fairness and reasonableness, and an increased orientation of judges to achieving justice in individual cases. Yet these changes have not altered the overall rule-bound character of the legal system; nor have they led to any significant reduction in the degree of predictability, nor have they had any evident adverse consequence on commercial transactions. If anything, modern complaints are about too much law – the vast bulk of which satisfies formal legality – not too little.

Western societies have confirmed for more than a century now that the social welfare state can indeed be combined with formal legality. Administrative discretion can be contained within restraints imposed by legislative mandates and procedural requirements. Asking judges to apply broad standards like fairness or reasonableness, or to make policy decisions or engage in interest balancing, does not inevitably destroy the legal character of an otherwise predominantly rule-based legal system. Predictability can still come about if there are shared background understandings or customs – either within society or within the legal culture – that inform the application of the broad standards. As long as the orientation of government officials remains rule-bound when governing rules exist, discretion allowed to government officials to further policy goals is not necessarily a start down a headlong slide to lawless oppression. Legal theorist Martin Krygier, familiar with formerly Communist Eastern Europe, observed that "there is a world of difference between, on the one hand, the unconstrained political voluntarism and instrumental use of law found in despotisms, and on the other, welfare states that mix bureaucratic interventions with political democracy and strong and long legal traditions."[35]

Democracy and formal legality

The third and last formal version of the rule of law adds democracy to formal legality. Like formal legality, democracy is substantively empty in that it says nothing about what the content of law must be. It is a decision procedure that specifies how to determine the content of law.

A common refrain in Western political thought, initiated by the Athenian democrats and repeated by Rousseau and Kant, among many others, is that freedom is to live under laws of one's own making. This is the notion of political liberty. According to philosopher Jurgen Habermas, who has provided the most sophisticated account of the link between formal legality and democracy, "the modern legal order can draw its legitimacy only from the idea of self-determination: citizens should always be able to understand themselves also as authors of the law to which they are subject as addressees."[36] Law obtains its authority from the consent of the governed. Judges, government officials, and citizens, must follow and apply the law as enacted by the people (through their representatives). Under this reasoning, formal legality, especially its requirements of certainty and equality of application, takes its authority from and serves democracy. Without formal legality democracy can be circumvented (because government officials can undercut the law); without democracy formal legality loses its legitimacy (because the content of the law has not been determined by legitimate means).

Habermas characterized this combination within Western liberal democracies as the only legitimate arrangement given contemporary beliefs and conditions.[37] The loss of faith in natural law and the fact of moral pluralism leave us no alternative. "Democratic genesis, not a priori principles to which the content of norms would have to correspond, provides the statute with its justice: 'The justice of a law is guaranteed by the particular procedure by which it comes about.'"[38] Under this arrangement, he asserted, the "legitimacy of positive law is conceived as procedural rationality,"[39] meaning that, in the absence of higher standards against which to judge the moral rightness of the law, the law is good if it is made pursuant to good procedures. Rational democratic mechanisms must accord everyone affected by the law an equal opportunity to participate, and must secure everyone's consent.

Persistent issues arise regarding what kind of consent is required. These issues would not arise in a direct democracy that requires unanimous agreement, but law-making in any large group cannot be run that way. Kant argued that the consent of *all* citizens (restrictively defined) does not mean what they would agree to if actually consulted, but instead what they would agree to if they acted consistent with reason.[40] Habermas explicitly called for unanimity: "the legitimacy of law ultimately depends on a communicative arrangement: as participants in rational discourses, consociates under law must be able to examine whether a contested norm meets with, or could meet with, the agreement of all those possibly affected."[41] In the final analysis, however, Habermas did not really mean actual unanimous consent, which is impracticable if not impossible. Nor is it evident that the unanimity requirement – which vindicates individual political freedom above all else – is wise, for it enables one person to hold the rest hostage, blocking initiatives that might benefit the collective or extracting disproportionate rewards as the price of securing the holdout's assent. These theorists were presenting a regulative ideal, setting up as a goal that legal systems should strive toward enacting laws all persons affected would agree to, without actually expecting that this would be achieved in practice.

Locke assumed a pragmatic stance on these issues: requiring direct participation and unanimity are recipes for paralysis, so representative democracy and majority rule will have to do. What is required of each citizen is individual consent to be governed according to democratic mechanisms – agreement about the procedure utilized to make decisions about the content of laws, not consent as to the content of each law produced. So long as a person or group on the losing side of one issue has a fair chance of prevailing on another issue, the system will be free.

In closing, it should be noted that resort to democracy as a procedural mode of legitimation for law carries a limitation identical to that of formal legality. Just as formal legality can effectuate evil laws, systems that use democratic procedures to determine the content of the law can produce evil laws. When democratic mechanisms are implemented in a society without a democratic tradition or without efforts to build one, or when antagonistic subcultures or communities coexist, democracy may serve as the means by which an organized cabal or subgroup in society seizes the reigns of government power, then utilizes the law to advance its particular agenda, while claiming the legitimacy conferred by democracy. Formal legality cannot prevent this from occurring. It should also be recognized that the rule of law is not the sole determinant of the degree of pre-dictability in a given system. Democratic systems can register dramatic swings in public mood and attitude. A democratic system with the rule of law therefore can be less certain and predictable and more tyrannical than a stable authoritarian regime without the rule of law;[42] this is not a reason to recommend the latter, but to be cognizant that all aspects of the surrounding social-political-economic-legal-cultural complex matter. Since a democratic legislature has the power to effectuate change in law whenever it desires, it poses a standing threat to the certainty of the law in a way that was not the case in classical and medieval understandings, in which the rule of law (natural, customary) consisted of an enduring body of rules.[43]

Democracy is a blunt and unwieldy mechanism that offers no assur-ances of producing morally good laws. Aside from vindicating the political liberty of individual citizens (at least in theory), perhaps its strongest jus-tification, not an inconsiderable one, is that it is less fraught with risk than any other system that can be presently imagined. Certainly it is the best way yet devised to change political leaders, but that is an entirely separate issue from how best to make law. This is hardly a reassuring endorsement. When democracy is cited as grounds for the legitimacy of law, and the values of formal legality are offered as additional reasons for legitimacy, the moral claim of law to obedience might seem weighty. It should not be forgotten, however, that neither of these formal mechanisms ensure that the laws enacted and carried out will be moral in content or effect.

8   Substantive theories

Individual rights

All substantive versions of the rule of law incorporate the elements of the formal rule of law, then go further, adding on various content specifications. The most common substantive version includes individual rights within the rule of law. Ronald Dworkin made a sophisticated case for this:

> I shall call the second conception of the rule of law the "rights" conception. It is in several ways more ambitious than the rule book conception. It assumes that citizens have moral rights and duties with respect to one another, and political rights against the state as a whole. It insists that these moral and political rights be recognized in positive law, so that they may be enforced *upon the demand of individual citizens* through courts or other judicial institutions of the familiar type, so far as this is practicable. The rule of law on this conception is the ideal of rule by an accurate public conception of individual rights. It does not distinguish, as the rule book conception does, between the rule of law and substantive justice; on the contrary it requires, as a part of the ideal of law, that the rules in the rule book capture and enforce moral rights.[1]

Dworkin insisted that these rights are not granted by the positive law, but instead form a background for and integral aspect of positive law.

He avoided resort to metaphysics by identifying the source of those rights in the community. The rule book "represents the community's effort to capture moral rights."[2] But the rule book is not the exclusive source of these rights, and the rule book can be silent or can produce conflicting interpretations. In such instances it is the responsibility of the judge to make the decision which "best fits the background moral rights of the parties" by framing and applying an overarching political principle that is consistent with the body of existing rules and principles.[3] These principles can go beyond the rules, and they can resolve apparent conflicts between the rules. When engaging in this task judges ask what legislators *should* have done had they been acting consistent with the political principles underlying the system and infusing the community.

Dworkin acknowledged the obvious objection to his rights conception: it is "often the case" that "it is controversial within the community what moral rights they have."[4] If that is so, how is the judge to formulate the prevailing political principles? Dworkin rested upon the faith that the application of a controlling principle will usually be evident.

To suggest that society's views on these subjects cohere at the highest level of political and moral principle, such that a correct legal answer can be found if only the judge studies the issue with sufficient acuity and dedication, denies the ultimately contestable nature of the disputes. As moral philosopher Alastair MacIntyre recently observed, "no fact seems to be plainer in the modern world than the extent and depth of moral disagreement, often enough disagreement on basic issues."[5] Contemporary US society, for example, is deeply divided over abortion, affirmative action in employment and education, rights of homosexuals, the death penalty, hate speech, access to pornography, public funding for religious schools, and more, all being played out in the legal arena in terms of rights. Furthermore, controversy goes beyond the content of rights to disagreements about appropriate remedies. For example, while a majority of citizens may have supported the Supreme Court's *Brown* decision invalidating legally enforced segregation – although a sizable group disagreed, especially in the southern USA – a clear majority of white citizens were vehemently opposed to busing children out of district as a remedy for segregated schools.[6] Resistance to abortion has gone as far as bombing clinics and the murdering of doctors. The battle over affirmative action and the treatment of homosexuals is taking place at every level in political and legal arenas.

These are not peripheral issues but disputes that cut to the core of the political principles and morals circulating in the USA and in other liberal societies. When a community is divided in its moral sense there is little reason for confidence that the collection of legal rules, political principles, or the community morality will be coherent or internally consistent. Perhaps no single or majority community moral view exists; different moral views might win out in contests over the law at different times or in different subjects. It should not, furthermore, be assumed that those empowered to make the law are always or primarily motivated to create law that faithfully mirrors the community morality. The influence of special interests in securing favorable legislation is notorious.

These objections strike not only at Dworkin but at all substantive versions of the rule of law that incorporate individual rights. There is no uncontroversial way to determine what these rights entail. All general ideals – like equality, liberty, privacy, the right to property, the freedom of contract, freedom from cruel punishment – are contestable in meaning and reach. In particular contexts of application conflicts between rights can arise. And no right is absolute, so consideration of social interests must always be involved, which cannot be answered through consultation of the right alone.

The most troublesome implication of Dworkin's approach is that it promises to remove disputed issues from the political arena and gives them over to judges.

Anti-democratic implications of rights

Individual rights inevitably have anti-democratic implications. Every Western liberal democracy struggles to find a balance. This struggle has been shaped by battles over the rule of law. There are two interrelated but distinguishable facets to this: the limits imposed on democracy, and the power accorded to judges.

As indicated, early liberals had an ambivalent attitude toward democracy. Liberty understood in terms of self-rule – political liberty – insists that citizens are entitled to govern themselves. But liberty understood as the right to property and the right of minorities (a label initially appended to religious groups and the wealthy, not to racial or ethnic groups) to be free from majority oppression – personal liberty – fears popular democracy. In the heyday of early liberalism it was widely assumed that, given the chance, "[t]he poor majority would of course pass laws taking from the rich minority their wealth until wealth was equally distributed."[7] For liberalism, and for the rule of law in its service, fear of mass democracy has predominated. Consequently, the "Rule of Law is more concerned with and committed to individual liberty than democratic governance."[8] Individual rights trump democracy when they come into conflict.

Democracy still rules, it might be said, when individual rights are explicitly contained within popularly enacted constitutions or bills of rights, because such clauses are themselves the products of democratic forces. Limits of this sort are self-imposed by the demos on the demos, and can be removed by the demos (by constitutional amendment) if it so desires, so striking legislation to vindicate rights is not anti-democratic. This answer does not work, however, for the many rights theorists, from Locke to Dworkin, who insist that individuals possess these rights – as a grant from God, or attached to our status as human beings, or as members of a moral community – independent of any explicit recognition in constitutional provisions or statutes.

Another sophisticated response to the anti-democratic objection is that individual rights are required to preserve the integrity of democracy; that is, only free people can exercise the self-determination of democracy.

Freedom is foremost self-determination (democracy), but to be genuinely self-determining one must first be free (individual rights). The rights of property, of free association, and free speech, in this view, are all necessary prerequisites for the realization of the self-determining person that democracy presupposes.[9] Democracy is therefore restrained by individual rights for the greater good of democracy. This account, however, reverses the liberal tradition, which historically situated democracy secondary to individual rights: "The existence and extent of democratic governance is only justified insofar as it better serves the enhanced liberty of individuals; it is a recent recruit on the proclaimed march to the truly liberal state."[10] The weaknesses of this reconciliation of rights and democracy are that the full list and scope of individual rights cannot be justified in terms of functional benefits to democracy, and it fails to do justice to the independent value attached in liberal societies to such rights.

A separate set of concerns about individual rights, the second facet of anti-democratic implications, relates to the power accorded to judges. Rights are not self-applying. *Someone* must say what individual rights mean in particular contexts of application. Someone must identify the limits they impose on the law-making power. In most Western liberal democracies final say over the content of rights is accorded to judges, typically sitting either as ordinary courts, constitutional courts, or human rights courts, engaging in what is known as judicial review of legislation. When judges are not elected, this confers on a group of individuals not accountable to democracy the power to veto democratic legislation.

Nothing mandates that the last word on the interpretation of rights be reposited in the judiciary. It could be given to a democratic body instead, like the parliament, or to a review council created for this purpose. However, it has become increasingly common to allocate this power to courts. The interpretation of law and legal rights is thought to be the special preserve of the judiciary. Furthermore, being anti-majoritarian by design, it appears logically required that rights not be entrusted to a democratically accountable body, for that would defeat their purpose.

No concern would arise from this allocation of authority if the content and implications of rights were readily apparent, but as already indicated that is often not the case. Here the indeterminacy problem discussed in Chapter Six is most acute. If judges consult their own subjective views to fill in the content of the rights, the system would no longer be the rule of law, but the rule of the men or women who happen to be the judges. Substitute one judge for another with different views, or get a different mix of judges, and the result might be different. It amounts to a clutch of Platonic Guardians presiding over the common people and their representatives.

Defenders pursue one of three main avenues to preserve the integrity of law from these charges of anti-democracy and subjectivity. Some legal theorists insist, consistent with the democratic consent argument, that judges interpret rights according to their plain meaning, in fidelity to the intentions of the delegates and voters who drafted and ratified them. The judge's task is not to answer subjective questions about values, but factual questions: What do the words mean? And in support of that inquiry, what did those who enacted the right intend? By virtue of this interpretive orientation, the subjectivity of the judge is obviated; the legal right rules, not the individual judge, and the political liberty of citizens who enacted the right, is vindicated. Unfortunately, the plain meaning of a right in a given context of application is often far from evident. Sometimes plain meaning and original intent point in different directions. Three further problems with this approach stand out: evidence of intention (especially for rights enacted a century or two ago) often is spotty or non-existent; there may well have been no intention at all (the problem at hand was not contemplated at the moment of enactment); or there may have been a variety of intentions among those who voted. Instead of dealing directly with the issues at hand, judges grapple with historical questions and speculate about states of mind, for which they are ill-qualified.

Another strategy tracks the position staked out by Dworkin.[11] He denied that judges consult their *own* subjective views of the governing principles but instead should seek to find the community's latent or emergent principles immanent within the complex of legal rules. Since the source of these principles is the community, this task is construed by Dworkin as democratic in nature.[12] The court, like the legislature, is a political institution participating in and reflecting the political process.[13] Judges should step in to enforce rights especially under circumstances where democracy is failing accurately to represent the principles underlying the polity, or to achieve justice. Judges, according to this argument, even as they invalidate democratic legislation on the ground that it oversteps individual rights, actually support democracy. Skeptics of this argument point out – in addition to the aforementioned arguments that conflicting or competing principles might circulate within a pluralistic community – that it is still the judge's view of the community's principles, which is difficult to keep separate from the judge's own principles. The suspicion that the personal views of the judges have a determinative role in shaping the content of the rights is difficult to repress considering that judges often disagree among themselves on what appears to be ideological grounds. Studies of the US Supreme Court have demonstrated a measurable correlation between the personal views of judges and their decisions in certain categories of cases.[14] Furthermore, it is odd to characterize judges as democratic actors when the thrust of the institutional design supporting the rule of law – especially an independent judiciary – is to insulate judges from political forces in order that they may render decisions based exclusively upon the law. Indeed, judges are universally condemned if seen to be acting politically. Dworkin's response is that this condemnation is merited only when judges base decisions on political "policy" as opposed to political "principle," and the latter is what he advocates as consistent with democracy. It is an exceedingly elusive line to locate and consistently maintain.

The third avenue is to assert that when the implications of rights are not evident, the judge must in good faith render what he or she believes to be the correct decision, supporting the decision with reasoned justifications which demonstrate that it is the most defensible interpretation (all things considered) of the rights at issue. A regrettable deviation from democratic authority it might be, but one that is inevitable regardless what system is devised. Presumably judges' views will be shaped by the surrounding society and the legal culture, so the decision will not be out of place. The virtue of this response is candor, and it may be the most pragmatic solution, given indeterminacy. However, it concedes that these kinds of decisions are not distinctively legal, renewing questions about the appropriateness of allocating them to judges.

None of the three foregoing avenues attempts the most ambitious response to the charge of subjectivity: that the rights are objective, either as a matter of natural law or correct moral philosophy (metaphysical or naturalistic), and the task of the judge is to work out this objective meaning. Two or more centuries ago this view was common. The American Declaration of Independence confidently asserted: "We hold these truths to be self-evident, that all men are created equal, that they are endowed by the Creator with certain unalienable Rights, that among these are Life, Liberty and the pursuit of Happiness." Contemporary skepticism – encapsulated in Bentham's pithy remark that natural rights are "nonsense on stilts"[15] – renders this path largely unavailable. A few theorists continue to propound versions of it,[16] so far none successfully garnering much assent. Again, the dilemma we find ourselves in has come about because central elements of the rule of law ideal were initially constructed upon faiths that no longer hold.

Revealingly, the actual practice of rights analysis in the USA and elsewhere is a mixture of all four of the above possibilities. Even the final one, which might not always be frankly acknowledged owing to the difficulty of defending it, still exerts a residual hold on the beliefs of many. Each has something to recommend it. None is immune to a skeptical retort. That is the modern condition.

Finally, defenders aver that questions about the interpretation of rights and judicial invalidation of democratic legislation do not occur so often that this is tantamount to rule by Platonic Guardians. By comparison to the multitude of cases judged, its frequency is indeed miniscule. Even so, it is disproportionately consequential when it occurs on issues that society holds dear and over which it is most divided. Self-rule is defeated if the most heart-felt decisions are made by someone else.

Perhaps the greater danger is to the judiciary itself. Believing politics to be an inevitable aspect of rights interpretation, and seeing the inordinate power judges have to issue ramifying social decisions, political forces might systematically apply ideological litmus tests to screen candidates in the appointments process in an attempt to stock the judiciary with loyalists to their view. Signs of this are presently occurring with respect to the US federal judiciary. If continued over the long run, this promises thoroughly to politicize the judiciary, ruining its credibility as a distinctively legal organ. A member of the US Supreme Court observed, when expressing dismay over the Court's apparently political decision seating George W. Bush as President, that the clear loser in the election was "the Nation's confidence in the judge as an impartial guardian of the rule of law."[17]

The judicialization of politics

The contemporary German version of the rule of law, the *Rechtsstaat*, manifests dramatically the tensions between democracy and individual rights. The notion of the *Rechtsstaat* has gone through several phases.[18] Early on it was influenced by Kant's liberalism, with an emphasis on formal rights that insured equal liberty for all. From the mid-nineteenth century, up through the mid-twentieth century, it came to be understood more in terms of rule *by* law. The atrocities committed through law by the Nazi regime, and the failure of law to serve as a barrier against Nazi terror, however, led to marked changes in the understanding of the *Rechtsstaat* following the World War II. In the post-War period of German self-recrimination, the prevailing legal positivist understanding of law was blamed as the primary culprit in the participation of judges and the legal profession in state tyranny. If law and rights are whatever the state says they are, as legal positivism holds, there appears to be no way to set legal limits on state action.

The Basic Law, Germany's post-War constitution, altered this by re-injecting substantive content into the rule of law with a vengeance. Rainer Grote summarized the changes:

The concern with the substantive elements of the rule of law is one of the most important features of the Basic Law. While including some of its widely recognized formal and procedural aspects, like the principle of legality . . . , the right to a fair hearing before the courts . . . , and the prohibition of retro-active criminal laws . . . , it goes at the same time beyond a merely formal understanding of the rule of law by establishing the *respect for and the protection of the dignity of man as the guiding principle of all state action* . . . The protection of individual dignity is recognized as the supreme value of the constitutional order created by the Basic Law . . . Art. 1, para. 2 acknowledges inviolable and inalienable human rights as the basis of every community, of peace and justice in the world, thereby recognizing the *universal and extralegal character of these rights which exist prior to and irrespective of their official recognition by the state* . . . Finally, it tries to make sure that the core guarantees which shape the liberal character of the state and its federal structure cannot be abolished by way of future constitutional amendments. Among other things, art. 79 declares amendments to the Basic Law which affect the basic principles laid down in articles 1 and 20, including the inviolability of human dignity as the central element of each of the more specific fundamental rights guarantees, inadmissible in any circumstances (save the adoption of a completely new constitution).[19]

A special Constitutional Court was created to enforce these individual rights. "In sum, the rule of law appears under the Basic Law as shorthand for the concept of fundamental rights, which is complemented by the fragmentation of political power within the framework of a parliamentary democracy and a strong role for the judiciary."[20]

These features situate the preservation of individual rights solidly within the notion of the rule of law, beyond the reach of the legislature, and even, with respect to the right of dignity, beyond the reach of constitutional amendment. The declaration that rights are independent of constitutional recognition is a rebuke of legal positivism that raises rights above law-makers and the demos. No longer is there doubt over whether limits exist on the power to legislate and on government action more generally; the only questions are about the content and application of those limits. In effect, this construction revived a form of natural law limits *sans* its religious underpinnings. It resurrected the Medieval understanding of the rule of law, and handed over enforcement to a judicial body.

Only two consequences resulting from this approach will be related. The first is that the right to dignity has proven especially susceptible to a broad reading by the judges on the Constitutional Court, covering all sorts of subjects, imposing negative as well as positive duties on the government.[21] Once again, the problem of indeterminacy raises disquieting questions about how judges specify the content and implications of such rights in situations of application.[22] The second is that many political disputes have been transformed into constitutional questions, such that there has been "a marked judicialization of politics in Germany."[23] The effect of this expansion of rights has been "a reduction in the legislative discretion"[24] of the Parliament. Through this understanding of the rule of law, the realm of politics, the reach of democracy, is being circumscribed by and in favor of judicial power.

This phenomenon is by no means limited to Germany. "Throughout Europe both national and supranational courts have begun to play a much more active and important role in deciding important and controversial social questions, questions traditionally decided by governments."[25] In several post-communist Eastern European countries judges have aggressively invalidated legislation in the name of a substantive understanding of a rule of law.[26] Increasingly assertive courts making decisions with political ramifications have begun to appear in Latin America as well.[27] Around the world today, riding on the wave of the spreading adoption of judicial review of legislation by constitutional courts, there is a marked trend toward the "global expansion of judicial power."[28]

When it occurs at the expense of abusive authoritarian institutions this phenomenon might be less alarming. But when it occurs at the expense of democratic institutions, or when the judiciary is disproportionately staffed by members from the socio-economic elite or some other unrepresentative subgroup, it may pose a serious threat to the self-rule of political liberty. More to the point, according such power to the judiciary may be detrimental to the rule of law itself, when the judiciary is highly politicized, intimidated by external pressure, singularly motivated by personal or group agendas, corrupt, or lacking in expertise or experience.[29]

Formal legality, democracy, and individual rights

Notwithstanding the aforementioned tensions amongst them, when the phrase the rule of law is uttered it is typically understood to include democracy and individual rights along with formal legality.[30] This triumvirate need not be conceptually necessitated under this view – they cluster together in liberal democracies as a unified complementary package. English legal theorist T. R. S. Allan made an argument like this on behalf of his thick substantive conception of the rule of law:

> [T]he term "rule of law" seems to mean primarily a corpus of basic principles and values, which together lend some stability and coherence to the legal order . . . The rule of law is an amalgam of standards, expectations, and aspirations: it encompasses traditional ideas about individual liberty and natural justice, and, more generally, ideas about the requirements of justice and fairness in the relations between government and governed. Nor can substantive and procedural fairness

be easily distinguished: each is premised on respect for the dignity of the individual person . . .

The idea of the rule of law is also inextricably linked with certain basic institutional arrangements. The fundamental notion of equality, which lies close to the heart of our convictions about justice and fairness, demands an equal voice for all adult citizens in the legislative process: universal suffrage may today be taken to be a central strand of the rule of law.[31]

Allan limited his conception to the British understanding of the rule of law, but it is representative of broader views. Confirmation of this came in the Declaration of the 1990 Conference on Security and Cooperation in Europe, with representatives from almost three dozen European countries, along with the USA and Canada: "the rule of law does not mean merely a formal legality which assumes regularity and consistency in the achievement and enforcement of democratic order, but justice based upon the recognition and full acceptance of the supreme value of the human personality and guaranteed by institutions providing a framework for its fullest expression;" and "democracy is an inherent element of the rule of law."[32]

While formal legality is the dominant understanding of the rule of law among legal theorists, this thick substantive rule of law, which includes formal legality, individual rights, and democracy, likely approximates the common sense of the rule of law within Western societies (assuming a common understanding exists). Widespread opinion is a weighty factor in the contest over what an ideal represents, regardless of whether theorists assert, as they are wont to do, that the popular understanding is confused.

A lesson can be taken from the regular instantiation of formal legality, individual rights, and democracy as a package. The anti-democratic implications of individual rights, in both of its facets, while formidable, can be balanced successfully in the flux of social and political forces. That it can work cannot be doubted in the face of so many current examples, each different in its own way. When courts, in the name of protecting individual rights, squelch democratic law-making too much, their conduct can result in a backlash that prompts the judiciary to restrain its conduct. A notorious example of this was the 1930s US Supreme Court, which invalidated social welfare legislation until President Roosevelt proposed to enlarge the Court as a means to appoint more compliant Justices; this "court packing plan" failed to obtain Congressional support, but the Court took notice and halted its obstructionist practice.[33] Although subsequent events have colored this affair favorably, as a triumph of democratic will and practicality over ideological judicial intransigence, it points out the attendant risks. Under different circumstances pressure can be brought to bear on courts with anti-democratic consequences. And each time such pressure is exerted successfully it threatens, or encourages further threats to, the integrity of the legal process.

There is no single formula for the achievement of a workable balance. At a minimum there must be a potentially active public exercising a degree of vigilance over government officials, prepared to rise up in protection of individual rights *and* democracy, and of the idea that everyone, including the government, is bound by the law. There must also be a well-established legal tradition dedicated to preserving the integrity of law, accepting that the interpretation, utilization, and application of legal rules is their particular mission, while committed to the proposition that the making of legal rules in a democratic society is properly allocated to the political arena. Above all else, it is essential that the government officials share in these ideals. They must become taken for granted.

The strongest objection to understanding the rule of law this way – as conjoining formal legality, democracy, and individual rights – is that those who preach it often forget its basis. It cannot be justified as the necessary or inherent meaning of the rule of law; rather it is as a common understanding of the phrase that developed only because those three elements came to work together in Western liberal democracies. This understanding of the rule of law does not necessarily travel. Societies that lack elements of this package cannot be instructed that to live up to the rule of law they must implement the full package of formal legality, democracy, and individual rights. To present just two contemporary examples: China can implement formal legality without democracy,[34] and Iran without human rights,[35] if that is what is desired, with no risk of incoherence.

Thickest substantive versions

The thickest substantive versions of the rule of law incorporate formal legality, individual rights, and democracy, but add a further qualitative dimension that might be roughly categorized under the label "social welfare rights." The outstanding example of this remains the findings of the International Commission of Jurists on the meaning of the rule of law following a 1959 Conference on the subject:

The "dynamic concept" which the Rule of Law became in the formulation of the Declaration of Delhi does indeed safeguard and advance the civil and political rights of the individual in a free society; but it is also concerned with the establishment by the state of social, economic, educational and cultural conditions under which man's legitimate aspirations and dignity may be realized. Freedom of expression is meaningless to an illiterate; the right to vote may be perverted into an instrument of tyranny exercised by demagogues over an unenlightened electorate;

freedom from government interference must not spell freedom to starve for the poor and destitute.[36]

The classical liberal view, with its obsession on preventing government tyranny, had a negative thrust geared to setting limits on the government, freeing individuals to do as they please. In the social welfare conception, the rule of law imposes on the government an affirmative duty to help make life better for people, to enhance their existence, including effectuating a measure of distributive justice. A version of this was mentioned in Chapter Six when it was suggested that self-determination of the right to liberty could be read to impose an obligation on the government to help individuals develop the capacity to be self-determining. The German *Rechtsstaat* took a partial step in this direction with its recognition of the right of dignity.

Wonderful as these aspirations are, incorporating them into the notion of the rule throws up severe difficulties. There are already potential conflicts among individual rights and between rights and democracy; adding social welfare rights to the mix multiplies the potential clashes, particularly in setting up a confrontation between personal liberty and substantive equality. Raz opposed this substantively rich conception of the rule of law for the reason that "to explain its nature is to propound a complete social philosophy."[37] Debates over social values are thereby reformulated into fights over the meaning of the rule of law. The rule of law then serves as a proxy battleground for a dispute about broader social issues, detracting from a fuller consideration of those issues on their own terms, and in the process emptying the rule of law of any distinctive meaning.

The rule of law cannot be about everything good that people desire from government. The persistent temptation to read it this way is a testament to the symbolic power of the rule of law, but it should not be indulged.

9   Three themes

This exploration of the history, politics, and theories surrounding the notion of the rule of law has presented a tale of continuity and change, shared understandings and sharp disputes. Moreover, each theory of the rule of law examined, whether formal or substantive, raises serious objections or concerns. This is to be expected of any ideal that has survived over two millennia, playing a pivotal role in so many contexts, from Medieval struggles between kings and popes to the global contest between socialism and liberalism. It would be facile to suggest that there is an overarching coherence to the subject. Disagreement exists about what the rule of law means among casual users of the phrase, among government officials, and among theorists. The danger of this rampant uncertainty is that the rule of law might devolve to an empty phrase, so lacking in meaning that it can be proclaimed with impunity by malevolent governments.

A surfeit of definitions of the rule of law has been presented in this work. Adding another in the hope that it would win the day would be redundant and naive. Instead this chapter will isolate and address three familiar themes that run through the rule of law tradition, drawing out the lessons to be taken from the foregoing exploration. They are characterized here as themes or clusters of meaning because, while interrelated, indeed almost inseparable, they revolve around distinct ideas, each with its own specific tilt. Focusing on these themes will lead to a number of informative conclusions, especially along the liberal/non-liberal divide. The next Chapter, an overview of the rule of law on the international level, will further demonstrate the usefulness of these three themes as an analytical framework.

Government limited by law

The broadest understanding of the rule of law, a thread that has run for over 2,000 years, often frayed thin, but never completely severed, is that the sovereign, and the state and its officials, are limited by the law.

The immediate inspiration underlying this idea was not the preservation of individual liberty, but restraint of government tyranny. Restraining the tyranny of the sovereign has been a perennial struggle, one which long pre-existed the emergence of the idea of individual liberty. This understanding of the rule of law dominated until the triumph of liberalism, when the emphasis shifted to formal legality.

There are two distinct senses of the notion that government officials must operate within a limiting framework of the law. The first sense is that officials must abide by the currently valid positive law. The law may be changed by properly authorized officials, but until it is changed it must be complied with. The second sense is that even when government officials wish to change the law, they are not entirely free to change it in any way they desire. There are restraints on their law-making power. There are certain things they cannot do with or in the name of law. These restraints have been understood in terms of the dictates of natural or divine law, or a timeless customary law, which were the dominant views in the Middle Ages, or in terms of human or civil rights, which is the common phraseology today. The fundamental import of this second sense is that the sovereign's power over the positive law is itself restricted in legal terms.

The puzzle presented by the idea that the sovereign is limited by the law is this: how can the very power that creates and enforces the law be limited by the law? Theorists as diverse as Aquinas and Hobbes thought that the rule of law in this sense was impossible, at least conceptually. If the law is declared by the sovereign, the sovereign cannot be limited by law, for that would mean the sovereign limits itself: "He that is bound to himself only, is not bound."[1] The problem of how to limit the law arises with respect to any person or body accorded the power to make or enforce law, whether the "sovereign" is the king or a parliament. In pre-modern times this puzzle applied only to the first sense of government limited by law, precisely because the state was not the source of the legal restraints – primarily natural law and customary law – that restricted its law-making ability, and enforcement was not by the state itself but left to God or to popular revolt (the right of resistance). In the modern period, when the restraint comes in the form of enacted rights, this puzzle exists in both senses of limits.

In the pre-modern period, subjecting monarchs and government officials to restraints imposed by law came about in three basic ways. The first way was that the monarch explicitly *accepted* or *affirmed* that the law was binding, though not always voluntarily. A prime example was the oath-taking of monarchs upon ascending to office. The typical oath bound monarchs to abide by divine, positive, and customary law. Another version of an accepted legal limitation was the Magna Carta, in which King John agreed to be bound, albeit under duress, and many future English monarchs reaffirmed their commitment to the document.

The second way was that it was widely *understood* or *assumed* that the monarch, and government officials, operated within a framework of laws that applied to everyone. The supreme example of this was Germanic customary law. Kings were thought by all to live within the strictures of this law. During the Christian dominance of the Medieval period everyone, king included, also understood and assumed that ("Divine") kings operated within divine and natural law restraints. Claims about and arguments over the propriety of official conduct were regularly articulated, by all groups within society, in terms of legality and illegality (according to divine, customary or positive law).

The third way was, as a matter of *routine conduct*, when engaging in ordinary activities, monarchs and government officials operated within legal restraints like everyone else (though often on more favorable terms). This third way complements and overlaps with the preceding two, but bears separate mention to emphasize the weight of mundane regularized conformity. A king or nobleman who had rights to fees or services from feudal holdings, also had duties and obligations that had to be satisfied. Kings or government officials who wanted to borrow money would have to live up to the agreement if they hoped to obtain future loans. Nobles, if not monarchs, could be held to answer in court proceedings for a breach of obligations. The public-private distinction was not sharply drawn during earlier periods, so the implicit message was that the kings and government officials operated on a daily basis within a legal framework, regardless of their status.

These three ways provided a powerful combination of ideals and practice. In the first way sovereigns and government officials held themselves out as law bound. Even if initially this claim was made opportunistically, after centuries of repetition it had real import. They felt law bound, so they were law bound. In the second way everyone in society shared in the belief that officials were bound by the law, which insured that this attitude remained constant through changes in regimes and officials. The third way provided daily reinforcement and confirmation that the sovereign, nobles, and government officials were law bound. Owing to these sources, operating within legal restraints became a measure of legitimacy for the conduct of these officials. Opposition to existing regimes, whether by popes, rivals seeking to supplant the sovereign, recalcitrant aristocrats resisting scutage, merchants striving to protect their activities from interference or ad hoc financial exactions, or the masses engaged in a popular revolt, would cite breaches of law (natural, divine, customary, or positive) to justify their resistance. The American Declaration of Independence, to cite a historic example, reads like a legal indictment against the King of England.

A skeptic will assert, correctly, that often monarchs and government officials did not in fact abide by the law, regardless of oaths, affirmations, and common understandings. When an objective was important enough to a sovereign, a law standing in the way was little more than an inconvenience to be circumvented. More often than not, the law was a weapon in their hands wielded to achieve their objectives, facilitated by judges beholden to or intimidated by them. This is all true. Nonetheless, the sovereign and government officials regularly did operate within the law. When they disregarded the law, it at least gave them pause, and they made strenuous efforts to construe their actions as law conforming. That rulers submitted to the restraints of the law largely for self-interested reasons does not detract from the reality that legal restrictions mattered.[2]

Although the sovereign and its officials regularly operated within the law, it must be underscored that in many instances there were no effective *legal* remedies for violation. When the law was repudiated or violated by the sovereign or government officials, there were *political* consequences to be paid. The threat of excommunication (which had political implications) was the means by which popes enforced divine law against kings; the threat of revolt was the mode of enforcement for Germanic customary law; against some monarchs it was the looming threat of being deposed or beheaded. Allegations about violations of the law were a rhetorical resource that helped rally support for those who opposed regal actions. In such cases, then, the sanction that served to enforce the law against the sovereign – the source of the law – was not a legal sanction, but a political one.

The two different senses of legal limitations on government officials, identified at the outset of this section, play out differently. Despite arguments that it is logically or conceptually impossible, there is no impediment in practice to imposing legal sanctions on the sovereign and government officials for violations of positive law (the first sense). Dicey identified as a mainstay of the rule of law in England that government officials could be brought before ordinary common law courts by private citizens to answer for violations of the law.[3] For this kind of restraint, the essential prerequisite is that the judiciary must possess a degree of independence from the rest of the governmental apparatus. This solution to the puzzle involves dividing up and partitioning the state apparatus, giving one part, the judiciary, the capacity to hold the other parts answerable on legal grounds. The autonomy and findings of the judiciary must be respected if this is to work. Notwithstanding skepticism about the prospects of this being successful, it can indeed function effectively, as is proven daily in many societies around the world.

Placing legal limitations on the law-making power of the sovereign – the second sense – is another matter altogether. The second sense of limits is far more ambitious than the first. Government officials can circumvent the first sense of legal limitation by simply amending the law not to stand in the way of desired objectives. The second sense restricts the law-maker's ability to mould the positive law to its will. There are certain things the sovereign cannot do, no matter what. In the Middle Ages, all of these sources of law – natural, divine, and customary – existed apart from and beyond the reach of the law-maker.

In contemporary non-liberal societies, at least those that continue to hold pervasively shared views of divine, natural, or customary law, limitations of this kind on state law can still be viable. In certain Muslim societies,[4] for example: "Government may not cross the boundaries firmly established by the Islamic Shari'a; rulers are held accountable to God's law."[5] The new constitution of Afghanistan creates a democratic Islamic Republic that assures equal rights for men and women, and disallows the enactment of any law contrary to Islam. Specific institutional arrangements vary, with final interpretive authority sometimes accorded to secular judges and sometimes to clerical judges or councils, or to a supreme religious leader. Perplexing problems are generated when modern circumstances are not addressed by traditional legal principles and rules and when these societies are internally pluralistic (with a sizeable group of citizens influenced by modern liberal views, or with distinct cultural or religious sub-communities coexisting), or when the law combines elements of modern and traditional, as every such system must. Workable arrangements are achievable, but the challenges are immense and cannot be met without a prevailing desire on all sides to make it work for the entire society.

In contemporary liberal societies, by contrast, the notion that there are legal limits on the government's law-making power (second sense), if it is to operate at all, must operate differently for the plain reason that natural law, divine law, and customary law no longer have the standing they once did. The modern equivalents of legal limits on law-makers in liberal societies are bills of rights or human rights declarations. Bills of rights come in two conceptually distinct versions. Those that are seen to exist independent of enactment – bills of rights that are understood to recognize but not give rise to said rights – are indistinguishable from natural law in setting limits on law-makers, with the notable exception that in the modern version courts have been accorded the power to interpret and apply them.

Bills of rights can, in the alternative, be understood as a form of positive law, whereby constitutional enactment is what gives rise to the right. The limits they set on law-makers can be altered. Thus they are conceptually akin to the first version of legal limits. When higher procedural barriers must be hurdled to amend bills of rights (like a super-majority vote), set so high that amendments become rare, bills of rights can operate *de facto* like the second version, with one further caveat. Medieval limits on legislation were considered absolute, whereas bills of rights are sometimes understood in procedural terms, allowing rights to be overcome if strict necessity or weighty justification is demonstrated.

The key to the successful implementation of the rule of law understood as setting limitations on government – is simply a pervasive belief, on the part of the populace and officials, that this is so. This point is perhaps as obvious as it is difficult to achieve.

Formal legality

The second cluster of meaning revolves around the construal of the rule of law as formal legality. The rule of law in this sense entails public, prospective laws, with the qualities of generality, equality of application, and certainty. As indicated earlier, these formal qualities are characteristic of rules as such. Formal legality emphasizes a rule-bound order established and maintained by government. The fullest procedural sense of formal legality also includes the availability of a fair hearing within the judicial process.

Most favored by legal theorists, this is the dominant understanding of the rule of law for liberalism and capitalism. Above all else it is about predictability. As Hayek put it, the rule of law makes "it possible to foresee with fair certainty how the authority will use its coercive powers in given circumstances and to plan one's individual affairs on the basis of this knowledge."[6] This means people know in advance which actions will expose them to the risk of sanction by the governmental apparatus. One is thereby apprised of the range of free action. There can be no criminal punishment without a preexisting law that specified the action as prohibited.

With respect to capitalism, public, prospective laws, with the qualities of generality, equality of application, and certainty, are well suited to facilitating market transactions because predictability and certainty allows merchants to calculate the likely costs and benefits of anticipated transactions. A growing body of evidence indicates a positive correlation between economic development and formal legality that is attributable to these characteristics.[7]

One limitation of the rule of law understood in these terms is that it is compatible with a regime of laws with inequitable or evil content. It is consistent with slavery, legalized segregation, and apartheid, as confirmed by the historical examples of the USA and South Africa. It is also consistent with authoritarian or non-democratic regimes, as illustrated by the respective examples of Singapore and China.[8] An effective system of the rule of law in this sense may actually strengthen the grip of an authoritarian regime by enhancing its efficiency and by according it a patina of legitimacy. This is not to deny that formal legality places crucial restraints on such regimes, but to emphasize that these restraints are nevertheless compatible with iniquity, because they are devoid of substantive content. An unjust set of laws is not made just by adherence to formal requirements.

There is another limitation to this version of the rule of law. Formal legality, according to its supporters and critics, requires that one forego the objectives of distributive equality (a more equal distribution of social goods) and doing justice in the individual case. These objectives require that case-by-case, context-sensitive determinations be made, which threatens generality, formal equality, certainty, and predictability.

While it is correct that formal legality exists in tension with these other social values and objectives, it is an erroneous overstatement to set them apart as mutually exclusive. Greater distributive equality could be advanced (albeit not perfectly achieved) through general rules applied equally to all, for example, by setting a limit on the amount of assets that can be passed to legatees upon death; and government resources can be allocated in a way that helps achieve greater equality by creating an excellent public education system, which would ameliorate the single most important disadvantage suffered by the poor. Rule of law systems can also accommodate doing justice in an individual case, so long as the rules of law are departed from to achieve justice infrequently, under compelling circumstances. Owing to the potential for tyranny by government, in the context of criminal punishment this departure can only occur in favor of defendants; rule-mandated injustices in defendants' favor – as when the guilty go free – must be accepted. The US legal system (and perhaps others, including the UK),[9] as suggested by Nonet and Selznick, would appear to have already made this adjustment without losing its overall rule-bound character. And the social welfare systems of the West, which have matured in the sixty years since Hayek first wrote, have shown that administrative discretion can be contained within legal restraints, and that formal legality may coexist with a substantial presence of discretionary, policy-oriented actions by government officials. The key guarantor of legal liberty is to maintain the restrictions of formal legality most rigidly as against the government whenever government coercion against person or property is threatened.

A final limitation is that there are many circumstances in which formal legality is not appropriate or socially beneficial. Many areas of government policy, especially where uncertainties or a great deal of variation prevails, will be defeated or severely undermined by attempts at restriction in advance by legal rules. Furthermore, in small-scale communities with a strong communitarian orientation, to offer another important context, adherence to formal legality, to rule by rules, might be harmful. Or in situations that threaten an eruption of uncontrollable violence, peace might better be achieved through political efforts, not resort to rules. When responding to such disputes, the primary concern often is to come to a solution that everyone can live with; long-term relationships and shared histories matter more than what the rules might dictate. Coming to a compromise may better achieve this goal than strict rule application (which is not to deny that rules will have an important role even under these circumstances). Contemporary Asian and African societies, in particular, notwithstanding penetration by Western ideas and practices, continue to have significant communitarian cultural strains which may in various ways and in various contexts clash with aspects of formal legality.

These observations also have application with regard to commercial transactions, with which formal legality has been closely associated. Locally as well as internationally, business partners have regularly demonstrated a desire to resort to arbitration, mediation, or other forms of resolution over court proceedings.[10] This in part owing to the expense, delay, and sometimes to the unreliability of local, national, and international courts, but it is also owing to the fact that business partners desire to continue profitable relationships and to maintain good reputations in the business community by demonstrating a willingness to come to a mutually acceptable resolution. Rules frequently have an-all-or-nothing consequence, resulting in winners and losers, but communities, whether social, political, or commercial, are often better served by both sides going away from a dispute satisfied.

This recitation of the disadvantages of formal legality should not be interpreted to denigrate its value. The observation that merchants can under certain circumstances function without resorting to legality, does not suggest that legality is irrelevant to commercial enterprise and markets. To the contrary, the establishment of a background framework of reliable legality is an important ingredient to capitalism as currently constituted.[11] Having this background to fall back upon in case of failure helps merchants work toward achieving an acceptable compromise.

The close connection between formal legality and capitalism contains an important lesson that ought to be made explicit, one well understood by classical liberals. While all members of society enjoy some benefit from formal legality, it is property owners who stand to benefit the most: their property is protected and they are most likely to enter into contracts. They can hire lawyers to vindicate their rights. A society in which property ownership is universal is one in which all enjoy the fullest benefits offered by formal legality.

Formal legality is perhaps best appreciated by comparison with when it is lacking. In the absence of some other source of predictability (like widely shared morals or customs), not to know how government officials will react to one's conduct, commercial or otherwise, is to be perpetually insecure. Societies that implement formal legality should be lauded for reducing this unpleasant state of uncertainty.

Before governments claiming to live up to formal legality become too self-congratulatory, however, they should be put to a reality test rarely entertained by Western theorists, one that takes cognizance of the complexity of modern legal regimes and their overflowing profusion of rules. Beyond general awareness that it is impermissible physically to harm others or their property, and that contracts create obligations, to what extent do citizens really have foreknowledge of the legal implications of their actions? A (nervous) retort might be: "that's what lawyers are for." This leads to additional unsettling questions about the cost and availability of legal counsel. If formal legality is truly about predictability for citizens, then attention must also be directed at discerning whether such predictability is actually conferred by the legal system.

Rule of law, not man

The third cluster of meaning sets out the rule of law by way of contrast to the rule of man. This oft-repeated contrast is presented as an antithesis: "the rule of law, not man;" "a government of laws, not men;" law is reason, man is passion; law is non-discretionary, man is arbitrary will; law is objective, man is subjective. The inspiration underlying this idea is that to live under the rule of law is not to be subject to the unpredictable vagaries of other individuals – whether monarchs, judges, government officials, or fellow citizens. It is to be shielded from the familiar human weaknesses of bias, passion, prejudice, error, ignorance, cupidity, or whim. This sense of the rule of law is grounded upon fear and distrust of others. It reflects a choice, which extends as far back as Aristotle, to prefer rule by law to unrestrained rule by another, even by a wise person, out of concern for the potential abuse that inheres in the power to rule.

The idea of "the rule of law, not man," powerful as it is, has been forever dogged by the fact that laws are not self-interpreting or applying. The operation of law cannot be sequestered from human participation. Hobbes considered it a delusive ideal for this reason. The inevitability of such participation provides the opportunity for the reintroduction of the very weaknesses sought to be avoided by resorting to law in the first place. The indeterminacy of law and language suggest that this opening can never be shut completely.

The standard twofold construction is, first, to identify the judiciary (comprised of legal experts) as the special guardians of the law, and, second, to deny the presence of the individual who is the judge. These two are connected: as the judge becomes indoctrinated in the ways of the law and the judicial role, the judge *becomes* the law personified. In the ideal, the judge is to be unbiased, free of passion, prejudice, and arbitrariness, loyal to the law alone. Whence come the reassuring declarations that the judge is the mouthpiece of the law, or the judge speaks the law, or the judge has no will. This image licenses the formalist assertion that judges engage in mechanistic rule application when rendering decisions. Final say in the interpretation and application of the law properly rests with the judiciary, in this view, because no other government official undergoes this necessary transformation in which the subjective individual is replaced with the objective judge. Although the rule of law in this third sense applies to all government officials operating in relation to legally governed activities, in the final analysis, owing to this reasoning, it is the special preserve of judges. In the last resort, they are the ones who insure that other government officials are held to the law.

This chain of reasoning supported, and was supported by, two additional social developments. First, a major role was played by the extraordinary growth of the legal tradition and its extensive social penetration. This included the establishment of the academic study of law, the increased complexity of law as a specialized body of knowledge with its own language and concepts accessible only to initiates, the consolidation of the legal profession as a self-regulating guild with a monopoly over legal services, the insinuation of lawyers as indispensable participants in the criminal law system, in establishing property ownership, and in facilitating commercial transactions, and the central role that persons trained in law came to play as advisors to kings and popes, and as advisors to, as well as becoming, government officials and legislators, among other positions of public and private authority. This expansion in social presence and power made lawyers, as a group, a formidable social force. It also bolstered the prestige held by judges, for judges stood at the pinnacle of the legal profession as the model and highest achievement toward which one might aspire. The claim made by those in this profession, its ideology as well as core self-identity, is that law is objective, apart, special, possessing its own integrity, insulated from the messiness of politics, the preserver of social order and facilitator of social intercourse.

The second contribution came from the spread of the notion of the separation of powers, which established the independence of judges. To be effective this required institutional arrangements that protected the judiciary from interference by others. The common formula for achieving this involved the selection of judges based upon legal qualifications (legal training and experience), long-term appointments for judges, procedural and substantive protections against the removal of judges, reasonable compensation for judges, and sufficient resources to maintain a functioning court system (support staff, books, courtrooms, etc.). The aforementioned professionalization of law made possible this separation, but this separation also represented the profession's highest achievement, amounting to institutional recognition and preservation of its specialness. These institutional factors were not alone enough, however, to assure the autonomy of judges. They were complemented by attitudes external to the judiciary, among government officials and the public at large, that it is improper to meddle with the judiciary as it fulfills its role interpreting and applying the law, matched by reciprocal attitudes among judges that it is improper to allow themselves to be influenced by considerations or pressure external to the law. The separation of powers did more than protect the judiciary; it simultaneously lessened the potential for abuse that might come from judges' having too much power. Judges depended upon cooperation from other branches of the government, and upon the voluntary compliance of citizens, for the enforcement of their decisions.

The ultimate risk of this theme of the rule of law, and the social, political, and ideological developments that accompanied it, is that the *rule of law* might become *rule by judges*. Whenever rules of law have authority, and judges have the final say over the interpretation and application of the law, judges will determine the implications of those rules of law. Recall that the theoretical debate over legal indeterminacy expired with a consensus that a degree of indeterminacy coexists with a substantial amount of predictability, at least in the US legal system. Once any degree of indeterminacy is recognized, it follows that the claim that judges merely speak the law is implausible. When, in addition, ignorance, weakness, subconscious bias, corruption, and the desire for power are admitted as natural human traits, the possibility that rule by law may become rule by judges is no longer a benign possibility but a matter of real concern.

This is a warning that judges must be selected with the utmost care, not just focusing on their legal knowledge and acumen, but with at least as much attention to their commitment to fidelity to the law (not inclined to manipulate the law's latent indeterminacy), to their willingness to defer to the proper authority for the making of law (accepting legislative decisions even when the judge disagrees), to their social background (to insure that judges are not unrepresentative of the community), to their qualities of honesty and integrity (to remain unbiased and not succumb to corruption), to their good temper and reasonable demeanor (to insure civility), and to their demonstrated capacity for wisdom. Law cannot but speak through people. Judges must be individuals who possess judgment, wisdom, and character, or the law will be dull-minded, vicious, and oblivious to its consequences. It was Aristotle who first insisted that the character and orientation of the judge is the essential component of the rule of law.

Whether the prospect of being ruled by judges elicits a positive or negative reaction depends upon the historical and contemporary circumstances of a given society, as well as upon one's politics. In France, where the pre-revolutionary practices of judges' buying the judicial office and using it for rent seeking has left a deep scar in the collective memory (though it may be fading), the idea that the rule of law might become the rule of judges would be anathema. In Indonesia, where the courts are renowned for corruption, this notion would be abhorrent.[12] In Iran, where the judiciary, whose membership is dominated by religious hardliners, has conducted closed trials of political dissidents, shut news publications, and jailed members of opposition parties, all in the name of consistency with the Constitution, this notion would be generate dismay.[13] In certain Latin American countries where the judiciary is seen as sympathetic to the propertied elite, this prospect would be considered reactionary.[14] There are many more examples around the world today where the prospect of rule by judges would be greeted with trepidation. Also in the USA, where the current Rehnquist Supreme Court is presently engaged in an aggressive reinterpretation of the respective powers of the state and federal governments, invalidating a number of congressional enactments, and more recently invalidated state legislation relating to treatment of homosexuals and application of the death penalty, there are great concerns about rule by judges. Rule by judges poses the specter of the usurpation of power by an unaccountable elite, treating political issues as if they were matters of law, hiding political decisions under the guise of purely legal interpretations.

This cautionary skepticism about the contrast between rule by law and rule by man is not a rejection of the difference it captures, only of the sharply drawn contrast between the two. At the moment of application, rules cannot do without the injection of human reason, insight and judgment, and can never be insulated completely from abuse at the hands of bad-faith individuals. But there is a vast difference between instructing persons (whether government officials or judges) to follow or apply a relevant body of rules to a situation, versus instructing them to do as they please or to do what they consider right without regard to rules. This large difference is appropriately captured by the contrast between rule of law and rule of man and must not be forgotten by critics who puncture it with such ease because it claims too much. There are innumerable examples every day around the world of government officials and judges faithfully complying with their duty to apply the law.

10 International level

Historian Paul Johnson opined that the great undertaking of the last millennium was the establishment of the rule of law within nation states, and that the project for this new millennium is to build the rule of law on the international or global level.[1] The first project remains a work in progress; the second has only just begun. Rather than hazard to prognosticate – on such time scales anything is possible, more than once – this chapter will offer an overview of the current state of the rule of law on the international level, organized in terms of the three themes set out in the preceding chapter. These offerings are tentative and brief, reflecting what is an uncertain and early state of affairs; for nigh every positive sign there is a concomitant reason for doubt.

Let us begin generally with the reasons for optimism. International lawyers (jurists, scholars, practitioners) are fond of reiterating that: "around the world today the vast majority of governments abide by the dictates of international law an overwhelming majority of the time."[2] Furthermore, an already impressive and ever-expanding range of subject matters are governed by international law, especially when increasingly common regional arrangements – like the European Union and the North American Free Trade Agreement (NAFTA) – are included in the estimation. International regulation of the commercial realm is particularly active, with global or transnational regional regimes covering all aspects of trade, intellectual property, commercial transactions, banking, foreign investment, telecommunications, securities, and more; global or regional rules, regulations, or principles also address the sea, space, pollution, the ozone, aviation, labor, territorial disputes, cross-border travel, treatment of migrant or displaced people, political refugees, diplomats, weapons of mass destruction, conduct of war, and more; civil, political, and human rights are explicitly set forth in multiple international and regional declarations. To apply and enforce these legal regimes, various international and regional tribunals have been created, many in the last few decades, including the International Court of Justice (the World Court), the International Tribunal for the Law of the Sea, the World Trade Organization's

(WTO) Dispute Settlement Body and Appellate Body, the International Centre for Settlement of Investment Disputes (ICSID), the International Court of Arbitration of the International Chamber of Commerce (ICC Court), the European Court of Justice, the Central American Court of Justice, the European Court of Human Rights, the Inter-American Court of Human Rights, the War Crimes Tribunals for Former Yugoslavia and Rwanda, the International Criminal Court, and more.[3]

Thus is an infrastructure of global law being laid. A growing multitude of subjects is being addressed by international or regional regulation. Most states comply with most of the regulations most of the time. And an array of courts and tribunals is being established to provide fora for these legal regimes. This steady foundation-laying is occurring both in what is called public international law (law involving relations among states, and human rights) and private international law (law involving relations among private parties from different nations, mostly commercial).[4] The primary sources and forms of law-making are multilateral and bilateral agreements (treaties), international customs, shared general principles, rules and regulations issued by international bodies (agencies or tribunals), decisions by international tribunals, model codes and contracts, widely utilized standard terms in private agreements, and coordinated law-making at the national level, which includes planned convergence or harmonization among national and transnational legal orders.[5]

Prudence counsels caution, however, when according significance to the above-cited factors. While it might be correct that most laws are followed most of the time, the most powerful states, and less powerful states when it matters most to them, nonetheless disregard international law by their leave when they consider it necessary for perceived national interest or to preserve the regime in power. *Realpolitik* remains a predictable mainstay of international law. Moreover, while certain subjects, especially commercially related ones, have indeed undergone remarkable growth in effective transnational legalization, other subjects, like human rights, have a largely paper or symbolic presence, at least in those states that reject them or respect them least. Although the list of tribunals is lengthy, the raw number of cases being handled is still relatively slight (but growing rapidly in recent years, especially in human rights and commercial contexts); the World Court, for example, operates on an annual budget of $11 million and has issued a little over a hundred decisions in its entire existence. Furthermore, the proliferation of international and regional tribunals – constituted to handle discrete subject matters, with no official mechanisms for coordination – may portend a coming non-systematic mish-mash of legal regimes operating in competition or overlap, with potentially contradictory or conflicting bodies of law and results.[6]

These concerns do not dent the confidence of international lawyers, who are cognizant of the hurdles to be overcome. Steadfastly projecting the inevitability of a positive outcome (at least in the long run) is implicitly understood by this group to be a necessary promotional step in its realization. The single strongest ground to believe that their optimism will be vindicated is the seemingly irresistible contemporary phenomenon of globalization of the economy. Advancements in technology, communication, media, transportation of goods and people, financial instruments and markets, have connected the world in ways never before seen and now hard to imagine without.[7] Huge transnational corporations, just one of the many manifestations of this globalization, now manufacture, assemble, distribute, market, locate offices, and sell around the globe, with no true or single national home or loyalty. A transnational legal infrastructure is developing apace with this economic globalization.

Sovereign limited by law

Law at the global level possesses unique characteristics that disrupt easy analogy to the rule of law in the context of nation states. The public international law system is conceptually constructed in terms of relations among sovereign states. There is no real legislature or executive. With limited exceptions (universal principles, and customary international law to which a state has not objected), the legal regimes that apply to a given sovereign state are only those that the state chooses to accept as applicable. Most international tribunals operate on a consent basis, such that they have jurisdiction to hear a case only if the states involved in a dispute agree to allow them to hear the case (although certain treaty regimes include compulsory jurisdiction). There is no effective standing institutionalized apparatus to enforce sanctions, so compliance with adverse decisions is often left to the good faith or self-interest of the losing party. Specific sanctions may be sought and imposed for instances of non-compliance, but the losing party may incur these consequences without conforming. Regional arrangements like the European Union are intermediate forms, with some characteristics akin to those above and in other respects more like ordinary nation states.

If public international law were envisioned in terms of a community of individuals – all monarchs in their own right – it would be one in which given sets of laws apply only to individuals who agree to be bound; there would be different sets of laws, various of which apply to some individuals and not to others (except for a short list of universal principles that apply to all). Any particular individual can refuse to be called before a court, and can later disregard a court determination even when the court does exercise jurisdiction. Described in this way it sounds odd, to say the least. In such a community, setting aside the possibility of a pervasive ethic that law should be respected owing to its status as law, individuals will agree to be bound by and will abide by law only if and when it is in their interest to do so. It is also evident that the most powerful individuals, those who have no fear of or need for others, would have the greatest capacity and incentive to act without regard to legal restraints.

Public international law in practice resembles what this scenario would predict. International legal limitations on sovereigns operate most effectively in the commercial realm precisely because the global economy has an impact on the economic health of virtually every state. States voluntarily encumber themselves with these legal restrictions, however reluctantly, for otherwise they would not be allowed to participate fully. Economic sanctions imposed by other states can inflict pain when coordinated, and therefore help motivate compliance with adverse decisions. Not coincidentally, the WTO Dispute Settlement Body exercises compulsory jurisdiction that is not contingent upon the consent of the parties.

The prime exemplar cited by international lawyers for the willingness of powerful states to disregard the rule of law is the USA (also generally credited as a key contributor to building the international rule of law), [8] the world's sole current superpower. A regularly cited instance involved the complaint lodged by Nicaragua before the World Court in the mid-1980s challenging the legality of US military actions. The USA filed notice with the Court that it was withdrawing its consent to jurisdiction. In response, the Court held that the withdrawal was untimely, jurisdiction was proper, and proceeded to hear the case; whereupon the USA belligerently refused to appear.[9] In a more recent example, a determination by the World Court to stay the execution of a foreign national pending compliance with international laws requiring consular notification was not honored by the US Supreme Court; the US Administration took the position that the World Court's provisional order was not binding; the executions went ahead, provoking recriminations from international lawyers and commentators around the world.[10] The highly contestable legality of the recent USA-led invasion of Iraq, and President Bush's doctrine of preemptive self-defense, cemented the image abroad of the USA as a nation that flouts international law whenever it so desires.

The USA is far from the only exhibitor of such conduct. Doubts about the realization of the rule of law in terms of legal limits on sovereigns on the global level are therefore understandable. In particular, many international lawyers hold that the "fundamental limitation of the rule of law in international adjudication is its voluntary nature."[11] States cannot be effectively bound by international laws if they must consent prior to being hauled before a court to answer for purportedly illegal conduct. It is not entirely persuasive to counter that most states comply most of the time, for that highlights that the rule of law applies mainly with respect to the weak or well-behaved, when the thrust of this theme of the rule of law is to constrain the mighty and rapacious. Put in terms of Locke's analysis, the nations that override or refuse to accept international law whenever they deem it necessary exist in a state of nature vis-a-vis the other countries, judging their own cases in ways inherently biased towards their own interests.

The conclusion that this is far from the rule of law appears almost obligatory, but it would be too shallow. Here is why: that most states (including powerful and rogue ones) do comply most of the time with international law, except when it really matters to them, even in the absence of the threat of effective institutional sanctions (facing mostly political or economic consequences), was roughly the scenario with respect to sovereigns in the Medieval period when the rule of law tradition took hold. Similar to monarchs under those circumstances, when sovereign states today violate international law, they nonetheless make every effort to construe their action as if consistent with the law, an effort which confirms that the law matters even as it is being circumvented.

The above discussion relates to legal restrictions on states, as sovereign entities. A qualitatively different kind of legal limitation on sovereigns on the international level holds government leaders personally accountable for especially egregious conduct. This is a relatively new development, the precedent for which was established by the Nuremberg trials that followed World War II. To punish and serve as a deterrent, the War Crimes Tribunals of Former Yugoslavia and Rwanda, and the International Criminal Court, have been set up to conduct criminal prosecutions of government officials who perpetuate gross atrocities, primarily genocide and crimes against humanity. Presently the list of leaders who have escaped responsibility for terrible crimes against their people far exceeds the handful who have been called to answer, but the International Criminal Court has only just been created (with the USA vehemently refusing to sign).

Formal legality

In relation to the second cluster of meaning surrounding the rule of law – requiring public, prospective rules with the qualities of generality, equality of application, and certainty – several issues particular to international legal regulation will be summarily identified. This and the following cluster of the rule of law apply to both public and private international law contexts. First, the circumstances mentioned in the preceding section, and more generally the role that power and politics have in influencing international law, have adverse implications for the equality of application and certainty of the law.

Second, the proliferation of uncoordinated tribunals and the disaggregation of international law along subject-specific lines – the result of the law being created piecemeal through treaties with a particular focus, and of the fact that transnational commercial law is substantially created by private contracting parties – generates problems with consistency and coherence, which have already arisen,[12] detracting from equality of application and certainty. "It is not possible to keep up with all the new treaties, decisions of international organizations, and cases of international courts and tribunals."[13] Particular complications for consistency are presented in overlapping areas between separate treaty regimes, as when environmental issues have implications for trade. International law will not facilitate predictability if a given context is potentially governed by conflicting bodies of legal rules and subject to incompatible policies.

Third, the process of international law application is not always transparent. WTO dispute settlement decisions, for example, are made in closed secret hearings;[14] arbitration decisions by the ICC Court are generally not published, and those by ICSID are published only upon agreement of the parties. Non-transparency arguably runs afoul of the publicity aspect of formal legality, renders it impossible to monitor equality of application, and inhibits the development of certainty based upon consistent interpretation.

Fourth, problems for clarity, coherence, and consistency of application are created by the fact that national legal regimes and their domestic courts interact in a multitude of planned and unplanned ways with public and private international law: national courts interpret international or transnational laws and decisions by courts and arbitrators, and vice versa; national legal regimes incorporate, refer to, rely upon, coordinate with, ignore, contradict, and sometimes override, international or transnational laws, and vice versa.

A final point relevant to formal legality is that the primary orientation of international law – by design – has been to keep peace between sovereign nations, a goal which often is advanced more by compromise than by strict rule-orientation. Under GATT, predecessor to the WTO, conflicts were resolved in a conciliatory manner involving negotiation of the parties. Some of this orientation was carried over to the new arrangement, with the WTO tribunal named the "Dispute Settlement Body," although in practice decisions have become more formally legal. It has been argued, furthermore, that disputes before the World Court "are frequently dangerous enough that it is understandable that the Court gives a higher priority to settling them than to issuing sweeping legal pronouncements."[15] In the European Union, a concerted effort is made to find an acceptable solution when dealing with complaints about human rights violations by member states. In a variety of international legal contexts a premium is placed upon resolving disputes in a manner satisfactory to all parties. These are context-specific arrangements not always susceptible to general rule application. Considering what is at stake, considering the political nature of the disputes that arise, considering that so much depends upon voluntary compliance, it makes sense that fidelity to rules should not always be the primary value. This orientation detracts from the achievement of formal legality, to be sure, but for prudent reasons.

Rule of law, not man

Major rule of law concerns emerge in the international legal arena with respect to the third cluster of meaning, the notion that judges – and legal officials more generally – must interpret and apply the law in an unbiased fashion. A threshold difficulty is that international lawyers do not share a professional tradition and culture to the same depth and degree that permeates most national legal systems.[16] It could not be expected otherwise given that participants in international law have been educated in different legal traditions – civil law, common law, socialist, Islamic, and various other types and combinations.[17] To identify just one contrast, the more active inquisitorial judging model of civil law systems is markedly different from the neutral-umpire judging style of common law adversarial systems.[18] Most international lawyers specialize in international law during their education and later in practice, which has its own shared body of knowledge; still, palpable differences in approach and attitude feed into how international law is understood and constituted.

As indicated in earlier chapters, a shared legal culture reduces indeterminacy in the context of application, enhancing predictability and certainty, making it possible to hold judges more accountable for their decisions. A thick and pervasively shared legal culture thus helps insure that the outcome of a case does not turn on which person happens to be the judge. Judging from the explosive growth of international and transnational legal institutions and practices in recent decades, the emergence of global law firms, the increasing practice of obtaining advanced legal training abroad,[19] and the solidification and enhanced prestige of international law (especially private) as an academic specialty, a mature international legal culture promises eventually to develop, solving this problem. However, the international legal profession is currently dominated by Western-trained lawyers; it is important, for reasons stated in the concluding section of this chapter, that it draws participants from around the world to render it broadly influenced and representative.

A more troublesome threat to this aspect of the rule of law is posed by a characteristic peculiar to international law tribunals. In a number of these tribunals – including the World Court, the International Law of the Sea Tribunal, and the European Court of Human Rights – parties have a right to have a judge from their own country sit on the judicial panel that decides the case; if no judge from that nation is available, the party may appoint an ad hoc judge to sit for that case only. Providing for national representation on judicial panels has historical roots: early on parties acceded to arbitration to resolve international disputes, with this provision included to assure them that their national interests would be taken seriously. This arrangement became common for international tribunals (although the WTO is a notable exception that prohibits citizens from the nation of a party in dispute from hearing the case, unless all parties agree otherwise). Not surprisingly, the process of appointing judges to these international courts has become "highly politicized."[20]

Obvious questions arise about the impartiality of "national" judges on panels. Indeed it appears that an implicit component of the judges' role, while they are told to decide the case according to law, is to act as guardian of the parties that appointed them. There is a tension between these two roles; more so, it is contrary to the fundamental ideal underlying the rule of law that judges not be biased toward or against a party in a case. Ad hoc judges are especially suspect, as they are not ordinary members of the bench and thus are perhaps less inured to the neutral stance demanded by the judicial role. "There tends to be an assumption that judges chosen by parties are not truly independent of them and will naturally receive indications or instructions."[21] Empirical studies of World Court decisions have shown a pattern in which judges tend to decide disproportionately in favor of their own country (though not exceedingly so), a pattern which is more pronounced for ad hoc judges.[22] These judges are placed in an untenable position. Even judges who pride themselves on possessing the capacity for rendering objective judgments may be tempted super-critically to scrutinize their own nation's position, to appear scrupulous in meeting their duty of neutrality. Whatever the case, an extraneous, non-legal consideration is weighing in the decision of these judges. Achievement of the rule of law in the third sense is rendered more tenuous by this concession to politics in the design of international judicial tribunals.

A final concern has to do with the impact of personal interests of judges and arbitrators on decisions. This problem is most acute in international arbitration between private parties. Arbitrators tend to come from, and return to, the same circles of transnational commerce as the parties, or their counsel, in the cases they decide. "This may give rise to suspicions that an arbitrator may favor a party (or counsel) who has provided frequent employment in the past and may do so again in the future."[23] Compounding this concern, for some forms of arbitration (most prominently ICSID) each party picks one arbitrator (and agree upon a third), which raises anew all the concerns in the preceding paragraph, now from the standpoint of personal interest rather than national bias. International judges are commonly appointed to serve relatively short terms, or act as part-time judges, which again means that they preside over parties or counsel with whom they may have interacted in the past or may do so in the near future.[24] None of this suggests that arbitrators and judges in these situations are necessarily corrupt (some domestic judges and arbitrators operate in similar conditions), only that undue temptations are at play that might compromise the neutrality of the person presiding, again, at the expense of the rule of law.

Hesitations about the capacity of international judges to act in an unbiased fashion are magnified on the international level when it is recognized that the process of judicialization of domestic politics remarked upon in Chapter Eight has also been observed on the international arena. "[T]he international decisions are themselves removed from the political control of states and put into the hands of what is, in effect, a new international player: the international judiciary."[25] The danger of a distant unaccountable elite rendering decisions that affect international and national political interests is manifest.

An international law for all

Perhaps the greatest barrier to the development of a truly international rule of law lies not in any of the specific problems identified above, all of which can be resolved or massaged. A consistent girding underlying the historical development of the rule of law for nation states have been supportive beliefs that the law was just, made by the people, and/or for the good of the entire community. These characteristics are what make law deserving of respect. The problem is that the world today manifests a chasm of gargantuan proportions. Notwithstanding the much-ballyhooed "Asian miracle," which suffered a severe setback in the late 1990s, in the world today the rich countries are getting richer and the poor ones are becoming poorer. Three billion people live on less than $2 a day, with

1.2 billion of them surviving on half that amount; 2 billion people lack electric power, and 1.5 billion lack safe water.[26] By comparison, the conditions in the West are luxurious to an extreme.

There is a material danger that the international legal regime will be perceived by the rest of the world as a Western invention and tool that primarily serves to perpetuate the advantages held by the West. Blatantly self-interested, hypocritical, or power-based actions in the international arena by the West encourage this suspicion. Examples are plentiful. Western countries insist upon the virtues of free trade, but award massive subsidies to support their own farmers, who then over-produce goods that are dumped below cost on the international market, wiping out already impoverished farmers from developing countries, harvesting a backlash of resentment.[27] Western countries refuse to include such subsidies within the ambit of the WTO. The World Bank and International Monetary Fund have forced a straightjacket of painful and politically destabilizing economic constraints on countries seeking grants or loans, constraints that Western countries do not themselves observe,[28] and would reject as an infringement upon their sovereignty. International efforts to implement various restrictions to reduce pollution and slow the destruction of rain forests are viewed as attempts to hobble countries that are finally getting started in the process of industrialization, trying to impose restrictions that the West did not honor on its own path to development. International labor regulations are seen as measures designed to protect Western laborers from competition from cheaper laborers in non-Western countries by increasing production costs. The mostly Western permanent members of the UN Security Council possess veto power over decisions of the international community. Even human rights are suspect: "there are a number of countries that regard human rights and human rights instruments as forms of cultural imperialism of the West."[29]

If there is to be an enduring international rule of law, it must be seen to reflect the interests of the entire international community. Otherwise there is little prospect of pervasively entrenching the requisite belief that international law is worthy to rule.

11   A universal human good?

At the outset of this book it was observed that politicians, government officials, political and legal theorists, business leaders, development experts,
the World Bank and IMF, and many others around the globe, from liberal and non-liberal societies, from developed countries and developing countries, promote the rule of law as offering worldwide benefit. A
quarter century ago noted Marxist historian E. P. Thompson incited a
stormy academic debate among the far left when he declared, following a detailed historical study of liberalism in England, that the rule
of law was an unqualified, universal good.[1] Coming from one of their
heroes, fellow Marxists considered this conclusion almost traitorous.
Thompson confirmed that law served the interests of the ruling class,
and that judges were drawn from the ruling class and showered it with
favoritism. English liberal law, in the guise of neutrality, concealed and
reinforced many iniquities. But that was not the whole story. He also
discovered that the ideology of being bound by the law had a restraining effect on those with power, whether the monarchy or the wealthy.
They claimed to be bound by the law, and the effect of this claim –
because they and others around them came to believe and act upon this
claim – was to place them within legal restraints. Rhetoric became reality.
With this in mind, Thompson concluded that the rule of law was "a cultural achievement of universal significance."[2] As complicit as law often
was in perpetuating domination and inequality, Thompson nonetheless
found that "the rule of law itself, the imposing of effective inhibitions upon
power and the defence of the citizen from power's all-intrusive claims,
seems to me to be an unqualified human good."[3]

When the rule of law is understood to mean that the government is
limited by the law, the first cluster of meaning, Thompson is correct that
it is a universal human good. The heritage of this idea, which first became
firmly established in the Middle Ages, preexists liberalism; it is not inherently tied to liberal societies, or to liberal forms of government. Everyone
is better off, no matter where they live and who they are, if government
officials operate within a legal framework in both senses described, in the

sense of abiding by the law as written, and in the sense that there are limits on law-making power.

Opponents of this assertion have argued that the government is an extension of the community, so protection against it is not just unnecessary but will inhibit the benevolent exercise of government power.[4] This argument is dangerously naïve. Nowhere today can it be asserted plausibly that the government is just the community personified. The state system, and governments in their modern form, are of relatively recent invention, no more than several centuries old, a development initially of the West, which then spread by colonization or imitation.[5] As such, the government has never been an extension of the community, at least not outside the imaginings of political theorists, but rather has everywhere been an institutionalized apparatus of concentrated power that constitutes the active operating mechanism of the state. In situations of social, cultural, ethnic, moral, or religious pluralism, a condition which is common around the world today in liberal and non-liberal societies, the government cannot be an extension of the community because no single community exists. Moreover, in pluralistic situations characterized by competition among discrete groups, there is a heightened risk that the governmental apparatus will be seized by one of the sub-communities in society and applied to oppress others. The reality, demonstrated many times over, is that people in society have at least as much reason to fear the power wielded by government officials as they do to look forward to its fruits.

There is nothing inherently individualist about this understanding of the rule of law. It will protect the integrity of the community from government oppression, if a communitarian orientation prevails, just as it will protect the individual, if an individualist orientation prevails, and it may even protect both in situations of pluralism. The legal limits on the government are the limits that society and its political institutions generate. A religion-steeped society, as existed in the Medieval period and exists today in many Islamic societies, or a society in which custom is still a dominant social force, would produce legal limits on government officials – in both senses, as positive law, and as limits on law-making power – that respect and support these social-cultural views.

Daunting complications arise when substantial parts of the positive law, or limits on the law (like bills of rights), are transplanted from a Western society onto a non-Western culture in a manner that conflicts with prevailing views. In situations like this, Western theories (like Dworkin's) that assume a match between background morality and law are plainly inapt. The law will not match the morality of society and there will be no overarching coherence. There is no standard formula for dealing with a situation like this other than to tread with care.

Leaders of some Asian societies have raised objections to Western-derived bills of rights or human rights declarations as individualist in orientation, contrary to their communitarian cultures. Many Muslim leaders reject Western liberal societies as "materialist, corrupt, decadent, and immoral."[6] Personal liberty does not have the same salience in these cultures, it is said, so these rights should not impose limits on non-Western governments. These views cannot be dismissed outright.[7] Cultures are indeed different and personal liberty, as much as the West takes it for granted, cannot be justified in universalist terms.

Although the conversation often ends with a standoff, there is another way to approach these issues. Do not start with a zone of protected individual autonomy to identify the limitations on government, as is done with individual rights in liberalism. Instead begin with the idea of preventing government tyranny, and decide what limits on this modern behemoth are desirable and match prevailing social-cultural views and arrangements. This is consistent with how legal limits on the state developed – though not intentionally – in the pre-liberal Medieval period. It is likely that important components of Western bills of rights – like the prohibition against torture or the summary imposition of criminal penalties – those that protect against the most grievous forms of government oppression, would be carried over with this alternative orientation.

Preventing government tyranny was a concern in ancient Athens, a concern throughout the Medieval period, and continues to be a concern everywhere today. The nature of the limitations will vary with the society, culture, political and economic arrangements, but the need for limitations on the government will never be obsolete. The great contribution to human existence of the rule of law in this sense is that it provides one answer to this need.

When the rule of law is understood as formal legality, the second cluster of meaning, it is a supremely valuable good, but it is not necessarily a universal human good. In no society is it thought that rules, the essence of formal legality, should dominate in all circumstances. Formal legality follows whenever legal limits on government, just mentioned, exist. Formal legality is essential whenever government coercion against person or property is threatened, especially in the imposition of criminal sanctions. Formal legality is also valuable in providing security and predictability of transactions, commercial and otherwise, among strangers or among members of different communities, though it is possible that formal legality need not be applied even in market contexts if other functionally equivalent social mechanisms are efficacious, as when relationships and prevailing cultural understandings generate security and predictability.[8] In all instances where social ties and shared understandings are thin, leading to less security and predictability, as is the case in urban areas around the world, formal legality will offer important advantages.

Outside of these situations, especially in non-liberal societies and cultures, the question of the applicability of formal legality must be examined closely. Formal legality – rule by rules – is counter-productive in situations that require discretion, judgment, compromise or context-specific adjustments. It may have limited application to the family realm and little if any to the sphere of community activities. Often orientations other than formal legality will be less disruptive of existing relationships and social bonds. Strict adherence to the dictates of formal legality can be alienating and destructive when it clashes with surrounding social understandings, particularly when there are strongly shared communitarian values and when everyone expects justice to be done. An emphasis on formal legality potentially creates particular difficulties in situations where a substantial bulk of the law and legal institutions is transplanted from elsewhere, as is common in post-colonial societies, for the reason that the legal norms and institutions may clash with local norms and institutions.[9] Especially complex problems will arise in hybrid situations, where both liberal and non-liberal orientations circulate. Here the mix must be determined following negotiation among the interests involved. Blanket "all or nothing" strategies should be avoided. The proper application of formal legality can be determined only in the context at hand, by the people involved. Otherwise it will fail, or inflict harm.

The third cluster of meaning – the rule of law, not man – follows whenever the first or second is adopted. A society that adopts the view that the government is limited by law and that the law should satisfy the qualities of formal legality, is also necessarily, in those contexts in which the law applies, embracing the rule of law, not persons. Whether this can successfully be accomplished without descending to rule by judges depends upon whether that particular society is able to maintain the necessary balance, a crucial element of which is self-restraint on all sides.

It should be recognized that all three takes on the rule of law, discussed in abstract terms, are open with respect to content. Saying that there are legal limitations on the government does not say what those limits are; the requirements of formal legality specify the form but not content of the laws; the "rule of law, not man" says that government officials must sublimate their views to the applicable laws but does not specify what those laws should be. Neither democracy, nor individual rights, nor justice is necessarily implicated in any of these themes. This reminder is important because often the rule of law is discussed in a manner that claims its own legitimacy without respect to whether the law is just or conforms to the interests of the community. In the classical period and the

Medieval period the supremacy accorded to the rule of law was directly linked to the belief that the content of the law was morally right and was oriented to the good of the community. During these pre-modern periods people thought law to be infused with moral content. The idea that the rule of law is a moral good without respect to this underpinning would have seemed bizarre to them, and should be rejected by us. Whenever implemented, the rule of law (understood in terms of all three aspects) should always be subject to evaluation from the standpoint of justice and the good of the community.

All of the requirements, and the strengths and limitations, of each of these meanings of the rule of law were stated earlier and will not be repeated here. This exploration will end by proposing what is *the* essential ingredient to establishing the rule of law, however it is understood. Pervasive societal attitudes about fidelity to the rule of law – in each of the three meanings – is the mysterious quality that makes the rule of law work. Grounds for optimism in this respect can be found in an observation I made at the outset of the book, that no government in the world today openly rejects the rule of law, while many government leaders pay public homage to it. Even when this is more rhetoric than reality, it is of fundamental significance, for the reasons articulated by Thompson. Those in power repeatedly espoused the virtue of being bound by the law; in the course of time this rhetoric became a prime cultural value, a view of government and law shared by most everyone. Precisely the same process courses through the development of the rule of law in the Medieval period. Recent disappointment over the apparent lack of progress following the past several of decades of efforts to build the rule of law is therefore premature. The rule of law tradition has been centuries in the making. Throughout history an indispensable element of it was that government officials and the general populace accepted, and came to take for granted, the value and propriety of the rule of law. Around the world today there are signs of this beginning to happen in many societies that heretofore have lacked the rule of law tradition. Therein lies the hope.

Notes

INTRODUCTION

1. Fancis Fukuyama, *The End of History and the Last Man* (New York: Avon Books 1992).
2. "Declaration of Democratic Values," reprinted in *Washington Post*, 9 June 1984, A14.
3. State of Union Address, quoted in Steve H. Hanke, "Point of View: Legalized Theft," *Forbes*, 4 March 2002, vol. 169, issue 5.
4. Judith N. Shklar, *Legalism* (Cambridge, Mass.: Harvard Univ. Press 1964) p. 22.
5. "World Bank Sees Rule of Law Vital," *United Press International*, 9 July 2001 (statements of World Bank President James Wolfensohn); Lawrence Tshuma, "The Political Economy of the World Bank's Legal Framework for Economic Development," 8 *Social & Legal Studies* 75 (1999).
6. "A World Free of Poverty," by Jim Boyd, *Star Tribune*, 25 June 2000, A27.
7. "Gulags Give Way to the Rule of Law," by Robert Cordy, *Boston Herald*, 18 November 2002, A25.
8. "China Sign UN Pact on Rights and Rule of Law," by Eric Eckholm, *New York Times*, 21 November 2000, A4.
9. "Chinese Movement Seeks Rule of Law to Keep Government in Check," by Steven Mufson, *Washington Post*, 5 March 1995, A25.
10. "Keeping Economic Drive on Track will Require Huge Effort, Warns Hu," by Wang Xiangwei and Gary Cheung, *South China Morning Post*, 8 March 2003.
11. "Mugabe Told He has Lost Moral Right to Govern," by Marie Woolf, *Independent*, 1 August 2002, A8.
12. "We Are Beginning the Rule of Law," *Business Week*, 29 May 2000, p. 70.
13. "Hiding Behind the Rule of Law," by Azar Nafisi, *New York Times*, 19 December 1997, A39.
14. "A Farmer Learns About Mexico's Lack of the Rule of Law," by Tim Weiner, *New York Times*, 27 October 2000, A3.
15. "Makeover for a Warlord," by Anthony Davis, *Time*, 3 June 2002.
16. International Commission of Jurists, *The Rule of Law in a Free Society* (Geneva 1959) p. VII.
17. "Chinese Movement Seeks Rule of Law to Keep Government in Check," by Steven Mufson, *Washington Post*, 5 March 1995, A25.

18. Olufemi Taiwo, "The Rule of Law: The New Leviathan?," 12 *Canadian Journal of Law & Jurisprudence* 151, 152 (1999).
19. Jeremy Waldron, "Is the Rule of Law an Essentially Contested Concept (in Florida)?," 21 *Law & Philosophy* 137 (2002).
20. Judith N. Shklar, "Political Theory and the Rule of Law," in Allan C. Hutcheson and Patrick Monahan, eds., *The Rule of Law: Ideal or Ideology* (Toronto: Carswell 1987) p. 1.
21. Thomas Carothers, "The Rule of Law Revival," 77 *Foreign Affairs* 95 (1998).

1   CLASSICAL ORIGINS

1. See Richard E. Rubenstein, *Aristotle's Children: How Christians, Muslims, and Jews Rediscovered Ancient Wisdom and Illuminated the Dark Ages* (New York: Harcourt 2003).
2. Martin Ostwald, *From Popular Sovereignty to Sovereignty of Law: Law, Society and Politics in Fifth-century Athens* (Berkeley: Univ. of California Press 1987) p. 5–15.
3. J. W. Jones, *The Law and Legal Theory of the Greeks* (Oxford: Clarendon Press 1956) p. 90.
4. See J. M. Kelly, *A Short History of Western Legal Theory* (Oxford: Oxford Univ. Press 1992) p. 29–30.
5. Aristotle, *Politics*, edited by Stephen Everson (Cambridge: Cambridge Univ. Press 1988) 1292a, p. 89.
6. Jones, *The Law and Legal Theory of the Greeks*, p. 69–70.
7. Philip Brook Manville, *The Origins of Citizenship in Ancient Athens* (Princeton: Princeton Univ. Press 1997) p. 107.
8. Ostwald, *From Popular Sovereignty*, p. 509–24; Jones, *Law and Legal Theory of the Greeks*, p. 102–15.
9. Bruno Leoni, *Freedom and the Law* (Indianapolis: Liberty Fund 1991) p. 79.
10. Otswald, *From Popular Sovereignty*, p. 497.
11. Plato, *The Laws*, translated by Trevor Saunders (London: Penguin 1970) 715, p 174.
12. Aristotle, *Politics*, Book III, 1286, p. 78.
13. See Ernest J. Weinreb, "The Intelligibility of the Rule of Law," in *The Rule of Law: Ideal or Ideology*, p. 60.
14. Judith N. Shklar, "Political Theory and the Rule of Law," in *The Rule of Law: Ideal or Ideology*, p. 3.
15. Plato, *The Laws*, 715, at 713.
16. Aristotle, *Nichomachean Ethics*, edited by Terence Irwin (Indianapolis: Hackett 1985) 5.13, p. 117.
17. Aristotle, *Politics*, 1282b, p. 68.
18. Ibid.
19. Ibid., 1307b, p. 124.
20. See David Cohen, *Law, Violence and Community in Classical Athens* (Cambridge: Cambridge Univ. Press 1995) p. 34–57.
21. See Ostwald, *From Popular Sovereignty*, p. 83.
22. Aristotle, *Politics*, 1286a., p. 75–76.

23. Jones, *The Law and Legal Theory of the Greeks*, p. 7 (quoting Plato).
24. Asitotle, *Politics*, 1286b, p. 76.
25. See Cohen, *Law, Violence and Community*, p. 4–57.
26. Werner Jaeger, *Paideia: The Ideals of Greek Culture*, vol. III, translated by G. Highet (Oxford: Oxford Univ. Press 1944) p. 137, 222.
27. Cohen, *Law, Violence and Community*, p. 56–57.
28. See Blandine Kriegel, *The State and the Rule of Law* (Princeton: Princeton Univ. Press 1995) p. 93 ("It is a singular error . . . to believe that in the ancient cities men enjoyed liberty. They had not even the idea of it.").
29. Cicero, *The Republic and The Laws*, translated by Niall Rudd (Oxford: Oxford Univ. Press 1998), *The Republic*, Book Two, 48, p. 50.
30. Ibid.
31. Janet Coleman, *A History of Political Thought: From Ancient Greece to Early Christianity* (Oxford: Blackwell 2000) p. 274.
32. Cicero, *The Laws*, Book Three, 2–3, p. 151.
33. Ibid., Book Three, 4, p. 151.
34. Ibid., Book Two, 13, p. 126.
35. Ibid., Book Two, 11, p. 125.
36. Coleman, *A History of Political Thought*, p. 284–87.
37. John Julius Norwich, *A Short History of Byzantium*, p. 17.
38. Peter Stein, *Roman Law in European History* (Cambridge: Cambridge Univ. Press 1999) p. 59.
39. See Brian Tierney, "'The Prince is Not Bound by the Laws.' Accursius and the Origins of the Modern State," 5 *Comparative Studies in Society and History* 378, 392 (1963).
40. Stein, *Roman Law in European History*, p. 32–37; Norwich, *A Short History of Byzantium*, p. 63.
41. Digest 1.4.1 and Digest 1.3.1, cited in Stein, *Roman Law in European History*, p. 59; Tierney, "Origins of the Modern State."
42. Jill Harris, *Law and Empire in Late Antiquity* (Cambridge: Cambridge Univ. Press 1999) p. 14–19.
43. Ibid., p. 21.
44. Digest 1.3.31 and Code 1.14.4, reprinted in Tierney, "Origins of the Modern State," p. 386.
45. See Leoni, *Freedom and Law*, p. 83–85.

2   MEDIEVAL ROOTS

1. In addition to the specific sources hereafter cited, the following general description was substantially informed by Henri Pirenne, *Mohammed and Charlemagne* (Mineola, NY: Dover Pub. 2001); Henri Pirenne, *Economic and Social History of Medieval Europe* (New York: Harcourt 1937); R. W. Southern, *The Making of the Middle Ages* (London: Hutchinson Ltd 1968). Among medievalists there is a continuing controversy over Pirenne's thesis that the Moslem invasions caused the Medieval period. Although I rely heavily on his account of medieval conditions, especially the situation of the towns and the nature of commerce, which are highly regarded, I taken no position on the specific point of dispute.

2. See Henri Pirenne, *Medieval Cities* (Garden City, NY: Doubleday 1925).

3. Pirenne, *Medieval Cities*, p. 28–29.

4. Marc Bloch, *Fedual Society: Social Classes and Political Organization*, vol. 2 (Chicago: Univ. of Chicago Press 1961).

5. Pirenne, *Medieval Cities*, p. 46–47.

6. See Joseph R. Strayer, *On the Medieval Origins of the State* (Princeton, NJ: Princeton Univ. Press 1970).

7. See Norwich, *A Short History of Byzantium*.

8. See Rubenstein, *Aristotle's Children*, Chaps. 4 and 5.

9. Thomas Aquinas, *Treatise on Law*, 95. Art. 1 (Wash., DC: Regnery Gateway 1987) p. 76.

10. Ibid., 95. Art. 4, p 97.

11. Ibid., 96. Art. 5, p. 100–01.

12. Ibid., p. 100.

13. Ibid.

14. Stein, *Roman Law in European History*, p. 30.

15. Ibid., p. 42.

16. Walter Ullmann, *A History of Political Thought: The Middle Ages* (Middlesex: Penguin 1965) p. 33.

17. Ibid., p. 35.

18. Quoted in Pirenne, *Mohammed and Charlemagne*, p. 230.

19. Richard Tarnas, *The Passion of the Western Mind* (New York: Ballantine Books 1991) p. 158.

20. Norman F. Cantor, *The Civilization of the Middle Ages* (New York: Harper Perennial 1994) p. 258.

21. Ibid., p 177.

22. Johan Huizinga, The Waning of the Middle Ages (Mineola, NY: Dover Pub. 1999) p. 57.

23. For discussions of the relationship between popes and kings, see Joseph Canning, *A History of Medieval Political Thought 300–1450* (London: Routledge 1996); Ullmann, *A History of Political Thought*.

24. Huizinga, Waning of the Middle Ages, p. 140.

25. Cantor, *Civilization of the Middle Ages*, p. 176.

26. Ibid., p. 181.

27. Ibid.

28. Ibid., p. 265–76.

29. Canning, *A History of Medieval Political Thought*, p. 58.

30. John B. Morrall, *Political Thought in Medieval Times* (Toronto: Univ. Toronto Press 1980) p. 24.

31. Andre Tunc, "The Royal Will and the Rule of Law," in *Government Under Law*, p. 404.

32. Ibid., p. 408.

33. Ullmann, *A History of Political Thought*, p. 103.

34. Ibid., p.183.

35. Frits Kern, *Kingship and Law in the Middle Ages* (New York: Harper Torchbooks 1956) p. 70–71.

36. Morrall, *Political Thought in Medieval Times*, p. 16.

37. Kern, *Kingship and Law in the Middle Ages*, p. 182.

38. John N. Figgis, *Studies of Political Thought: From Gerson to Grotius, 1414–1625* (Bristol: Thommes Press 1998 [1916]) p. 153.
39. Morrall, *Political Thought in Medieval Times*, p. 16; Kern, *Kingship and Law in the Middle Ages*, p. 85–97.
40. Kern, *Kingship and Law in the Middle Ages*, p. 87–88.
41. Kenneth Pennington, *The Prince and the Law, 1200–1600* (Berkeley: Univ. of California Press 1993) p. 119–64.
42. Bloch, *Feudal Society*, p. 451.
43. Pennington, *The Prince and the Law*, p. 117.
44. See generally J. C. Holt, *Magna Carta*, 2nd edition (Cambridge: Cambridge Univ. Press 1992) p. 1–22.
45. Max Radin, "The Myth of Magna Carta," 60 *Harvard Law Review* 1060, 1062 (1947).
46. Holt, *Magna Carta*, p. 461. Two versions of the Magna Carta were issued, the first in 1215 with King John, which he repudiated a month later, with the support of Pope Innocent III, on the grounds that it was invalid because entered into under duress. The second version was issued in 1225, confirmed by King Henry III. Clause 39 in the original became clause 29 in the second version.
47. William H. Dunham, "Magna Carta and British Constitutionalism," in *The Great Charter*, Introduction by Erwin N. Griswold (New York: Pantheon 1965) p. 26.
48. See Norman F. Cantor, *Imagining the Law: Common Law and the Foundations of the American Legal System* (New York: Harper Perennial 1997) p. 120–63.
49. Historians now dispute whether Bracton actually wrote these words, which are, however, contained in his book. See John Morrow, *History of Political Thought* (New York: NYU Press: 1998) p. 279. They have been attributed to him for centuries, and questions about authorship in no way lessen their influence.
50. Henry Bracton, *On the Laws and Customs of England*, vol. III (Cambridge, Mass.: Harvard Univ. Press 1968) p. 305–06.
51. See Philip B. Kurland, "Magna Carta and Constitutionalism in the United States: 'the Noble Lie,'" in *The Great Charter*.
52. See Holt, *Magna Carta*, p. 10, 18.
53. See Dunham, "Magna Carta and British Constitutionalism," and Kurland, "Magna Carta and Constitutionalism in the United States."
54. Arthur R. Hogue, *Origins of the Common Law* (Indianapolis: Liberty Fund 1986) p. 57.
55. R. W. Carlyle, *Medieval Political Theory in the West* (1928), p. 457, quoted in Joseph M. Snee, "Leviathan at the Bar of Justice," in *Government Under Law*, edited by Arthur E. Sutherland (Cambridge, Mass.: Harvard Univ. Press 1956) p. 118.
56. Figgis, *Studies of Political Thought: From Gerson to Grotius, 1414–1625*, p. 75.
57. Cantor, *Imagining the Law*, p. 145.
58. See E. N. Williams, *The Ancient Regime in Europe* (Middlesex: Penguin 1972).
59. Figgis, *Studies of Political Thought: From Gerson to Grotius, 1414–1625*, p. 63.
60. Richard Pipes, *Property and Freedom* (New York: Vintage 2000) p. 136.

61. See Kriegel, *State and the Rule of Law*, p. 64–90.
62. See Hogue, *Origins of the Common Law*.
63. 12 Coke's Reports 63 [1607], quoted in John Ferejohn and Pasquale Pasquino, "Rule of Democracy and Rule of Law," in Jose Maria Maravall and Adam Przeworski, eds. *Democracy and the Rule of Law* (Cambridge: Cambridge Univ. Press 2003) p. 244.
64. An abbreviated sociological account of this shift can be found in Gianfranco Poggi, *The Development of the Modern State* (Stanford: Stanford Univ. Press 1978).
65. Poggi, *The Development of the Modern State*, p. 79–85.
66. See Carl Stephenson, *Medieval Feudalism* (Cornell: Cornell Univ. Press 1965) p. 97–107; Pirenne, *Economic and Social History of Medieval Europe*. For a description of the economic activities of the towns in a later period, and its social implications, see John Hale, *The Civilization of Europe in the Renaissance* (New York: Touchstone 1993) p. 372–92
67. For an account of the financial and power conflicts between nobles and monarchs in England, see Pipes, *Property and Freedom*, Chap. 3.
68. Pirenne, *Medieval Cities*, Chaps. 6, 7, 8.
69. Ibid., p. 141.
70. Max Weber, *On Law in Economy and Society*, edited by Max Rheinstein (New York: Simon and Schuster 1967) p. 353.
71. Pirenne, *Economic and Social History of Medieval Europe*, p. 25.
72. Roberto M. Unger offers an account of the various historical pathways for the emergence of liberalism in Roberto M. Unger, *Law in Modern Society* (New York: Free Press 1976).

3   LIBERALISM

1. For accounts of liberalism which include many of these various aspects, see Harry K. Girvetz, *The Evolution of Liberalism* (New York: Collier Books 1963); Roberto M. Unger, *Knowledge and Politics* (New York: Free Press 1976).
2. See Jeremy Waldron, "Theoretical Foundations of Liberalism" 37 (No. 147) *Philosophical Quarterly* 127 (1987).
3. John Stuart Mill, *On Liberty and Other Writings* (Cambridge: Cambridge Univ. Press 1989) p. 16.
4. Ronald Dworkin, *A Matter of Principle* (Harvard: Harvard Univ. Press 1985) p. 191.
5. Isaiah Berlin, *Four Essays on Liberty* (Oxford: Oxford Univ. Press 1969) p. 129.
6. Jean-Jacques Rousseau, *The Social Contract* (Middlesex: Penguin 1968) p. 65.
7. Ibid., p. 83.
8. Baron de Montesquieu, *Spirit of Laws*, edited by J. V. Pritchard, vol. 1 (London: Bell and Sons 1914) p. 161 (Book XI, s. 3).
9. *Lawrence v. Texas*, 123 S Ct 2472, 2475 (2003) (holding that homosexuals have a right to engage in private consensual sexual conduct free from government interference).

10. Ian Shapiro, *The Evolution of Rights in Liberal Theory* (Cambridge: Cambridge Univ. Press 1985) p. 271.

11. Unger, *Law In Modern Society*, p. 191.

12. Joseph Raz, "The Rule of Law and Its Virtue," in Robert L. Cunningham, ed., *Liberty and the Rule of Law* (College Station: Texas A&M Univ. Press 1979) p. 4.

13. Hutchinson and Monahan, "Democracy and the Rule of Law," p. 100.

14. Quoted in Leoni, *Freedom and the Law*, p. 152.

15. Berlin, *Four Essays on Liberty*, p. 130. Berlin made a famous distinction between "negative liberty" and "positive liberty" that is different from but converges at certain points with my contrast between, respectively, private liberty and political liberty. To avoid a confusion of terminology, I have not referred to his distinction, informative as it is.

16. Ibid., p. 118–72.

17. Ibid., p. 166.

18. Immanuel Kant, *Metaphysical Elements of Justice*, 2nd edition, translated by John Ladd (Indianapolis: Hackett Publishing 1999) p. 120–21.

19. See Leoni, *Freedom and Law*.

20. Pipes, *Property and Freedom*, p. 231.

21. See Immanuel Kant, *Political Writings* (Cambridge: Cambridge Univ. Press 1991) p. 79.

22. John Gray, *Liberalism*, 2nd edition (Minneapolis: Univ. of Minneapolis Press 1995) p. 17–25.

23. This account of the Enlightenment and its implications is informed by a number of texts, predominantly Ernst Cassirer, *The Philosophy of the Enlightenment* (Princeton: Princeton Univ. Press 1951); Carl Becker, *The Heavenly City of Eighteen Century Philosophers* (New Haven: Yale Univ. Press 1932); Peter Gay, *The Enlightenment: The Science of Freedom* (New York: Norton & Co. 1996); Norman Hampson, *The Enlightenment* (London: Penguin 1990); Isaiah Berlin, *The Roots of Romanticism* (Princeton: Princeton Univ. Press 1999).

24. See Thomas Munch, *The Enlightenment: A Comparative Social History* (London: Arnold 2000) p. 132–42.

25. Isaiah Berlin, *The Crooked Timber of Humanity* (Pinceton: Princeton Univ. Press 1990) p. 40.

26. See Hampson, *The Enlightenment*, p. 73–127.

27. See John Gray, *The Two Faces of Liberalism* (Cambridge: Polity Press 2000).

28. See Shapiro, *The Evolution of Rights in Liberal Theory*, p. 282–84.

29. See Stephen Mulhall and Adam Swift, *Liberals and Communitarians* (Oxford: Blackwell 1992) p. 9–33; Ronald Dworkin, "Liberalism," in *A Matter of Principle* (Cambridge, Mass. Harvard Univ. Press 1985).

30. See Mulhall and Swift, *Liberals and Communitarians*.

31. In legal theory this view of law was known as historical jurisprudence, most prominently expressed in F. von Savigny, *Of the Vocation of Our Age for Legislation and Jurisprudence* (New York: Arno 1983).

32. The two most elaborate accounts of this connection are Harold J. Lasky, *The Rise of European Liberalism* (New Brunswick: Transaction 1997) and C. B.

Macpherson, *The Political Theory of Possessive Individualism* (Oxford: Oxford Univ. Press 1962).

33. Lasky, *The Rise of European Liberalism*, p. 161–96.
34. See Poggi, *The Development of the Modern State*, p. 119.
35. See Weber, *On Law in Economy and Society*, p. 39–40; David Trubek, "Max Weber on Law and the Rise of Capitalism," [1972] *Wisconsin Law Review* 720.
36. See Lasky, *The Rise of European Liberalism*, p. 175–91; Robert L. Heilbroner, *The Worldly Philosophers* (New York: Touchstone 1981) p. 42–74.
37. Lasky, *The Rise of European Liberalism*, p. 181.
38. Shapiro, *The Evolution of Rights in Liberal Theory*, p. 303.
39. See Macpherson, *The Political Theory of Possessive Individualism*, p. 57–59.
40. F. A. Hayek, *The Road to Serfdom* (Chicago: Univ. of Chicago Press 1944) p. 21.
41. Ibid., p. 44.
42. Ibid., p. 133.
43. Ibid., p. 134.
44. Jeremy Bentham, "Bentham Manuscripts, LXIX", 44, quoted in A. J. Ayer and Jane O'Grady, eds., *A Dictionary of Philosophical Quotations* (Oxford: Blackwell 1992) p. 48.
45. Hobbes made this point. See Shapiro, *The Evolution of Rights in Liberal Theory*, p. 39.
46. See Brian Z. Tamanaha, *Realistic Socio-Legal Theory: Pragmatism and a Social Theory of Law* (Oxford: Clarendon Press 1997) p. 123–27

4   LOCKE, MONTESQUIEU, THE FEDERALIST PAPERS

1. Thomas Hobbes, *Leviathan*, edited by J. C. A. Gaskin (Oxford: Oxford Univ. Press 1996) p. 176, 215.
2. Ibid., p. 179, 175.
3. Ibid., p. 176–77.
4. Ibid., p. 215.
5. Jean Hampton, "Democracy and the Rule of Law," in Ian Shapiro, ed., *The Rule of Law* (New York: NYU Press 1994) p. 16 (emphasis in original); see also Michael P. Zuckert, "Hobbes, Locke, and the Problem of the Rule of Law," in Ibid., p. 63–79.
6. Waldron, "Is the Rule of Law and Essentially Constested Concept (In Florida)?," p. 143 (articulating Hobbes' position).
7. See Hampton, "Democracy and the Rule of Law," p. 18.
8. John Locke, *Second Treatise of Government* (Indianapolis: Hackett 1980) Chap. 2, p. 8–14.
9. Leo Strauss, *Natural Right and History* (Chicago: Univ. of Chicago Press 1965) p. 248–51.
10. Locke, *Second Treatise of Government*, Ibid., p. 47 (ss. 88–89); p. 65–66 (ss. 123–24).
11. Ibid., p. 46–47 (s. 87).
12. Ibid., p. 48–51 (ss. 90–94).

13. Ibid., p. 52 (ss. 95–96).
14. Ibid., p. 103 (s. 202).
15. Ibid., p. 17 (s. 23).
16. Ibid., p. 72–73 (s. 137).
17. Zuckert, "Hobbes, Locke, and the Problem of the Rule of Law," p. 74.
18. Locke, *Second Treatise of Government*, p. 66 (s. 124).
19. Laski, *The Rise of European Liberalism*, p. 156.
20. Macpherson, *The Political Theory of Possessive Individualism*, p. 194–262.
21. Strauss, *Natural Right and History*, p. 234.
22. Robert A. Heineman, *Authority and the Liberal Tradition* (Durham, NC: Carolina Academic Press 1984) p. 29.
23. Macpherson, *The Political Theory of Possessive Individualism*, p. 252.
24. Strauss, *Natural Right and History*, p. 257.
25. Ibid., p. 246.
26. Adam Smith, *Lectures on Jurisprudence*, edited by R. L. Meek, D. D. Raphael, and P. G. Stein (Oxford: Clarendon Press 1978) p. 208.
27. Karl Marx and Friedrich Engels, *The Communist Manifesto* (Oxford: Oxford Univ. Press 1998) p. 21.
28. Friedrich Engels, *The Origins of the Family, Private Property and the State* (New York: International Publishers 1942) p. 156–57.
29. Baron de Montesquieu, *Spirit of Laws*, edited by J. V. Pritchard, vol. 1 (London: Bell and Sons 1914) p. 161 (Book XI, s. 2).
30. Ibid., p. 161 (Book XI, s. 3).
31. Thomas L. Pangle, *Montesquieu's Philosophy of Liberalism: A Commentary on the Spirit of the Laws* (Chicago: Chicago Univ. Press 1989) p. 109.
32. Montesquieu, *Spirit of Laws*, p. 161 (Book XI, s. 4).
33. Ibid.,
34. Ibid., p. 162 (Book XI, s. 6).
35. Judith N. Shklar, "Political Theory and the Rule of Law," in *The Rule of Law: Ideal or Ideology*, p. 5.
36. Pangle, *Montesquieu's Philosophy of Liberalism*, p. 132.
37. Montesquieu, *Spirit of Laws*, p. 103 (Book XI, s. 6).
38. Pangle, *Montesquieu's Philosophy of Liberalism*, p. 198.
39. Montesquieu, *Spirit of Laws*, p. 331 (Boox XIX, s. 27).
40. Pangle, *Montesquieu's Philosophy of Liberalism*, p. 147.
41. Ibid., p. 148.
42. Montesquieu, *Spirit of Laws*, p. 50 (Book V, s. 6).
43. Ibid., Books XIX and XX; Pangle, *Montesquieu's Philosophy of Liberalism*, p. 198–99.
44. Gottfried Dietze, *The Federalist: A Classic on Federalism and Free Government* (Baltimore: John Hopkins Univ. Press 1965) p. 255–56.
45. James Madison, Alexander Hamilton, and John Jay, *The Federalist Papers* (New York: Arlington House 1966) No. 10, p. 82.
46. Dietze, *The Federalist*, p. 41–102.
47. Madison, Hamilton, and Jay, *Federalist Papers*, No. 10, p. 81.
48. Berlin, *Four Essays on Liberty*, p. 163. In this passage Berlin presents Mills' criticism of the idea of self-rule.

49. Madison, Hamilton, and Jay, *Federalist Papers*, No. 51, p. 320–25.

50. Ibid., No. 51, p. 324.

51. Ibid., No. 78, p. 466.

52. Ibid., No. 78, p. 467.

53. Ibid., No. 78, p. 467.

54. Ibid., No. 84, p. 512–15.

55. To counter this possibility, the Ninth Amendment was included in the Bill of Rights, which says: "The enumeration in the Constitution, of certain rights, shall not be construed to deny or disparage others retained by the people." The problem, however, is discerning precisely what are these retained rights entail.

56. See Leonard W. Levy, *Origins of the Bill of Rights* (New Haven: Yale Nota Bene 2001) Chap. 1.

57. *Marbury v. Madison*, 1 Cranch 137,177 (1803).

58. For background on this incorporation and its implications, see Eugene Cotran, "The Incorporation of the European Convention on Human Rights into the Law of the United Kingdom," in Eugene Cotran and Adel Omar Sherif, eds., *Democracy, the Rule of Law, and Islam* (The Hague: Kluwer 1999) p. 135–60.

59. See C. H. McIlwain, "The English Common Law, Barrier Against Absolutism," XLIX *American Historical Review* 23 (1934).

60. See J. G. A. Pocock, *The Ancient Constitution and the Feudal Law* (Cambridge: Cambridge Univ. Press 1957).

61. Howard Nenner, *By Color of Law: Legal Culture and Constitutional Politics in England, 1660–1689* (Chicago: Univ. Chicago Press 1977).

62. See A. V. Dicey, *Introduction to the Law of the Constitution* (Indianapolis: Liberty Fund 1982 [1908]).

63. See James R. Stoner, *Common Law and Liberal Theory: Coke, Hobbes, and the Origins of American Constitutionalism* (Lawrence: University Press of Kansas 1992); Friedrich Hayek, *Law, Legislation and Liberty: Rules and Order*, vol. 1 (Chicago: Chicago Univ. Press 1973) p. 84–85.

64. Cited in Stoner, *Common Law and Liberal Theory*, p. 52.

65. See Brian Z. Tamanaha, *A General Jurisprudence of Law and Society* (Oxford: Oxford University Press 2001) p. 44–50.

66. Dicey, *Introduction to the Law of the Constitution*, p. 24.

67. English participation in the European Union, and its recent incorporation of the European Convention on Human Rights, has altered this arrangement in complicated ways that are not yet clear, at least to this author.

68. Hayek, *The Constitution of Liberty*, p. 206.

69. Dicey, *Introduction to the Law of the Constitution*, p. 26–35.

70. Berlin, *Four Essays on Liberty*, p. 166 n. 2.

71. Alex de Tocqueville, *Democracy in America* (NY: Mentor Books 1900) p. 122.

72. Shklar, *Legalism*, p. 8–9.

73. Jeremy Bentham, *A Fragment on Government* (Cambridge: Cambridge Univ. Press 1988) p. 117.

74. Weber, *On Law in Economy and Society*, p. 203.

5   CONSERVATIVES WARN

1. See Eric Hobsbawm, *The Age of Capital: 1848–1875* (New York: Vintage 1996). The entire nineteenth century is covered by Hobsbawm with two additional volumes: Eric Hobsbawm, *The Age of Revolution: 1789–1848* (New York: Vintage 1996), and *The Age of Empire: 1875–1914* (New York: Vintage 1989).

2. Hobsbawm, *The Age of Capital*, p. 245.

3. See John Stuart Mill, "Chapters on Socialism," in Stefan Collins, ed., *On Liberty and Other Writings* (Cambridge: Cambridge Univ. Press 1989).

4. Ibid., p. 224–48.

5. Ibid., p. 233.

6. Hobsbawm, *The Age of Capital*, p. 108–15; Hobsbawm, *The Age of Empire*, p. 112–41.

7. Hobsbawm, *The Age of Capital*, p. 99; Hobsbawm, *The Age of Empire*, p. 84–111.

8. Mill, "Chapters on Socialism," p. 223–24.

9. Hobsbawm, *The Age of Capital*, p. 305; see also Hobsbawm, *The Age of Empire*, p. 84–141.

10. An informative account of the origin of the phrase and influences on Dicey's formulation is contained in H. W. Arndt, "The Origins of Dicey's Concept of the 'Rule of Law,'" 31 *Australian Law Journal* 117 (1957).

11. Dicey, *Introduction to the Study of the Law of the Constitution*, p. 110.

12. E. Barker, "The 'Rule of Law,'" [1914] *Political Quarterly* 116, 118.

13. *Osborn v. Bank of United States*, 22 US (9 Wheaton) 736,866 (1824).

14. Dicey, *Introduction to the Study of the Law of the Constitution*, p. 115.

15. Ibid., p. 146–68.

16. Ibid., p. lv.

17. Barker, "The 'Rule of Law,'" p. 116.

18. Ibid., p. 124.

19. See Ivor Jennings, *The Law and the Constitution*, 5th edition (London: Univ. of London Press 1959); Paul Craig, *Public Law and Democracy in the United Kingdom and the United States of America* (Oxford: Oxford Univ. Press 1990).

20. An informative historical argument regarding the shared underpinnings of far left and far right political positions is provided in Stephen J. Tonsor, "The Conservative Origins of Collectivism," in, Robert L. Cunningham, ed., *Liberty and the Rule of Law* (College Station: Texas A&M Univ. Press 1979).

21. F. A. Hayek, "Preface 1956," in *The Road to Serfdom* (Chicago: Univ. of Chicago Press 1994) p. xliii.

22. Ibid., p. 80.

23. F. A. Hayek, *The Political Idea of the Rule of Law* (Cairo: National Bank of Egypt 1955) p. 34.

24. Rousseau, *The Social Contract*, p. 82.

25. Hayek, *The Constitution of Liberty*, p. 210–12.

26. Ibid., p. 207–08.

27. Ibid., p. 153.

28. Frederic William Maitland, *A Historical Sketch of Liberty and Equality* (Indianapolis: Liberty Fund 2000 [1875]) p. 110.

29. Hayek, *The Constitution of Liberty*, p. 212–17.

30. Ibid., p. 214–15.
31. Hayek, *Law, Legislation and Liberty*, vol. 1, p. 142.
32. Hayek, *The Political Ideal of the Rule of Law*, p. 56.
33. Ibid., p. 46–59.
34. Hayek, *The Road to Serfdom*, p. 80–111. Although he presses this argument elsewhere, its most concise articulation is still in this initial text. See also Hayek, *Law, Legislation and Liberty: The Mirage of Social Justice*, vol. 2 (Chicago: Univ. of Chicago Press 1976) p. 62–100.
35. See John Gray, *Hayek on Liberty* (New York: Routledge 1998) p. 72–75.
36. Hayek, *The Road to Serfdom*, p. 87–88.
37. Hayek, *Law, Legislation and Liberty*, vol. 3 (Chicago: Univ. of Chicago Press 1979) p. 41–64.
38. Hayek, *The Political Ideal of the Rule of Law*, p. 19.
39. See Hayek, *Law, Legislation and Liberty*, vol. 1, especially Chaps. 4 and 5. An excellent study of Hayek's concept of the market and the law is Gray, *Hayek on Liberty*.
40. Hayek, *Law, Legislation and Liberty*, vol. 1, p. 80
41. Ibid., p. 86.
42. Ibid., p. 119.
43. Ibid., p. 117–18.
44. Bruno Leoni made the related argument that the common law is superior to legislation in that case-by-case development generates more certainty that legislative initiatives, which can be altered wholesale at will. Leoni, *Freedom and Law*.
45. Hayek, *Law, Legislation and Liberty*, vol. 1, p. 89.
46. Ibid., p. 31–44.
47. Ibid., p. 38.
48. Hayek, *Law, Legislation and Liberty: The Political Order of a Free Society*, vol. 3, p. 1–19.
49. His model constitution proposed a special body to fulfill this role, Ibid., p. 109–24.
50. Hayek, *The Constitution of Liberty*, p. 216–18.
51. Ibid., p. 210.
52. Hayek, *Law, Legislation and Liberty*, vol. 3, p. 110.
53. Ibid., p. 150.
54. See Theodore J. Lowi, "The Welfare State, The New Regulation, and The Rule of Law," in *The Rule of Law: Ideal or Ideology*.
55. See Jeffrey Jowell, "The Rule of Law Today," in Jeffrey Jowell and Dawn Oliver, eds. *The Changing Constitution*, 3rd edition (Oxford: Oxford Univ. Press 1994).
56. Bill Scheuerman, "The Rule of Law and the Welfare State: Toward a New Synthesis," 22 *Politics & Society* 195 (1994).

6   RADICAL LEFT ENCOURAGES DECLINE

1. See Alexander M. Bickel, *The Least Dangerous Branch* (New York: Bobbs-Merrill 1962); Philip B. Kurland, "Egalitarianism and the Warren Court," 68 *Michigan Law Review* 629 (1970).

2. Lester Mazor, "The Crisis of Legal Liberalism," 81 *Yale Law Journal* 1032 (1972).
3. Ibid., p. 1049.
4. See Robert Unger, *Knowledge and Politics* (New York: Free Press 1976) p. 145–190.
5. Mill, *On Liberty and Other Writings*, p. 227.
6. Hayek was especially alarmed about the damage inflicted upon the rule of law ideal by Legal Realists in the name of social justice. See Hayek, *The Political Ideal of the Rule of Law*, p. 46–59.
7. See William M. Wiecek, *The Lost World of Classical Legal Thought* (Oxford: Oxford Univ. Press 1998) Chap. Two.
8. See Felix Cohen, "Transcendental Nonsense and the Functional Approach," 35 *Columbia Law Review* 809 (1935).
9. 198 US 45 (1904).
10. David Dudley Field, *Magnitude and Importance of Legal Science* (1859), reprinted in George Christie and Patrick Martin, *Jurisprudence*, 2nd edition (St. Paul, Minn.: West Pub. 1995) p. 713.
11. See Robert Summers, *Instrumentalism and American Legal Theory* (Ithaca, NY: Cornell Univ. Press 1982).
12. See Tamanaha, *A General Jurisprudence of Law and Society*, p. 44–50.
13. See Morton Horwitz, *The Transformation of American Law: 1870–1960* (New York: Oxford Univ. Press 1992).
14. 347 US 483 (1954).
15. Alexander M. Bickel, "The Original Understanding and the Segregation Decision," 69 *Harvard Law Review* 1 (1955).
16. 163 US 537 (1896).
17. See Herbert Wechsler, "Toward Neutral Principles of Constitutional Law," 73 *Harvard Law Review* 1 (1959).
18. Ronald Dworkin, *Taking Rights Seriously* (London: Duckworth 1977); *A Matter of Principle* (Cambridge, Mass.: Harvard Univ. Press 1985); *Law's Empire* (Cambridge, Mass.: Harvard Univ. Press 1986).
19. Dworkin, *Taking Rights Seriously*, p. 269.
20. See Tamanaha, *A General Jurisprudence of Law and Society*, Chap. 2.
21. Philippe Nonet and Philip Selznick, *Law and Society in Transition: Toward Responsive Law* (New York: Octagon Books 1978) p. 79.
22. See Tamanaha, *Realistic Socio-Legal Theory*, Chap. 8.
23. Unger, *Law in Modern Society*, p. 273 n. 11.
24. Ibid., p. 192.
25. Ibid., p. 291 n. 40.
26. Ibid., p. 200.
27. Ibid., p. 197.
28. Ibid., p. 198.
29. Ibid., p. 199.
30. Unger, *Knowledge and Politics*, p. 99.
31. Ibid.,
32. See Michael J. Sandel, *Liberalism and the Limits of Justice* (Cambridge: Cambridge Univ. Press 1982); Alastair MacIntyre, *After Virtue* (Notre Dame: Univ. of Notre Dame Press 1984).

33. Duncan Kennedy, "Form and Substance in Private Law Adjudication," 89 *Harvard Law Review* 1685, 1685 (1976).

34. Unger, *Knowledge and Politics*, p. 220.

35. Ibid., Chap. 6.

36. See Leslie Bender, "A Lawyer's Primer on Feminist Theory and Tort," 38 *Journal of Legal Education* 3 (1988).

37. Martha Minow and Elizabeth Spelman, "In Context," 63 *Southern Calif. Law Review* 1597 (1990); Catherine Wells, "Situated Decisionmaking," 63 *Southern Calif. Law Review* 1727 (1990).

38. See Paul D. Carrington, "Of Law and the River," 34 *Journal of Legal Education* 222 (1984).

39. See Richard Delgado, "The Ethereal Scholar: Does Critical Legal Studies Have What Minorities Want?," 22 *Harvard Civil Rights-Civil Liberties Law Review* 301 (1987).

40. An informative discussion of these kinds of indeterminacy is in Christian Zapp and Eben Moglen, "Linguistic Indeterminacy and the Rule of Law: On the Perils of Misunderstanding Wittgenstein," 84 *Georgetown Law Review* 485 (1996).

41. The critical literature on this subject is substantial, consisting of general arguments on indeterminacies and specific demonstrations of indeterminacies. Several of the most useful general articles that helped inform this account will be cited below; interested readers can find their way into the literature through these general accounts. See Joseph William Singer, "The Player and the Cards: Nihilism and Legal Theory," 94 *Yale Law Journal* 1 (1984); Allan C. Hutchinson and Patrick J. Monahan, "Politics and the Critical Legal Scholars: The Unfolding Drama of American Legal Thought," 36 *Stanford Law Review* 199 (1984); James Boyle, "The Politics of Reason: Critical Legal Theory and Local Social Thought," 133 *Univ. Pennsylvania Law Review* 685 (1985); Mark Tushnet, "Defending the Indeterminacy Thesis," 16 *Quinnipiac Law Review* 339 (1996); John Hasnas, "Back to the Future: From Critical Legal Studies Forward to Legal Realism, or How Not to Miss the Point of the Indeterminacy Argument," 45 *Duke Law Journal* 84 (1995); Duncan Kennedy, "Freedom and Constraint in Adjudication: A Critical Phenomenology," 36 *Journal of Legal Education* 518 (1986).

42. There is a sizable body of literature contesting the indeterminacy thesis. The following were the most helpful sources of the points made in the text. Lawrence B. Solum, "On the Indeterminacy Crisis: Critiquing Critical Dogma," 54 *Univ. Chicago Law Review* 462 (1987); Ken Kress, "Legal Indeterminacy," 77 *California Law Review* 283 (1989); Jules L. Coleman and Brian Leiter, "Determinacy, Objectivity, and Authority," 142 *Univ. Pennsylvania Law Review* 549 (1995); Steven J. Burton, "Reaffirming Legal Reasoning: The Challenge From the Left," 36 *Journal of Legal Education* 358 (1986); Christopher L. Kutz, "Just Disagreement: Indeterminacy and Rationality in the Rule of Law," 103 *Yale Law Journal* 997 (1994).

43. See H. L. A. Hart, *The Concept of Law* (Oxford: Oxford Univ. Press 1961) Chap. VII.

44. See Solum, "On the Indeterminacy Crisis."

45. Singer, "The Player and the Cards," p. 22.

46. See Owen Fiss, Objectivity and Interpretation," 34 *Stanford Law Review* 739 (1982); Owen Fiss, "Conventionalism," 58 *Southern Calif. Law Review* 177 (1985); St. Burton, "Reaffirming Legal Reasoning: The challenge from the Left," 36 *Journal of Legal Education* 358.
47. See Tamanaha, *Realistic Socio-Legal Theory*, Chaps. 7 and 8.

7   FORMAL THEORIES

1. Paul Craig, "Formal and Substantive Conceptions of the Rule of Law," *Public Law* 467, 467 (1997). See also Robert S. Summers, "A Formal Theory of the Rule of Law," 6 *Ratio Juris* 127, 135 (1993). Although the use of this distinction is standard, there is not complete agreement on what falls into which category. For reasons that will be explained in the text, I include democracy in the formal category, while Summers places it in the substantive category. Nothing of significance follows from this categorization, which is for clarification, so disagreement about placement should not raise concern.
2. Noel B. Reynolds, "Grounding the Rule of Law," 2 *Ratio Juris* 1, 3 (1989).
3. Franz L. Neumann, "The Change in the Function of Law in Modern Society," in William E. Scheuerman, ed., *The Rule of Law Under Siege* (Berkeley: Univ. of California Press 1996) p. 104.
4. Joseph Raz, "The Rule of Law and Its Virtue," in *The Authority of Law* (Oxford: Clarendon Press 1979) p. 212–13.
5. See Michel Rosenfeld, "The Rule of Law and the Legitimacy of Constitutional Democracy," 74 *Southern California Law Review* 1307, 1318–29 (2001).
6. "Chinese Movement Seeks Rule of Law to Keep Government in Check," by Steven Mufson, *Washington Post*, 5 March 1995, A25.
7. Carothers, "The Rule of Law Revival," p. 97.
8. Raz, "The Rule of Law and its Virtue," p. 211.
9. Ibid., p. 221.
10. Raz, "The Rule of Law and its Virtue," p. 214.
11. See also Summers, "A Formal Theory of the Rule of Law"; Robert S. Summers, "Propter Honoris Respectum: The Principles of the Rule of Law," 74 *Notre Dame Law Review* 1691 (1999).
12. Lon L. Fuller, *The Morality of Law*, 2nd revised edition (New Haven: Yale Univ. Press 1969) Chap. 2.
13. See Jeremy Waldron, "The Rule of Law in Contemporary Liberal Theory," 2 *Ratio Juris* 79, 84–85.
14. Raz, "The Rule of Law and its Virtue," p. 220–21.
15. Ibid., p. 214.
16. Fuller, *The Morality of Law*, p. 153.
17. Summers, "A Formal Theory of the Rule of Law," p. 136.
18. Lawrence Tshuma, "The Political Economy of the World Bank's Legal Framework for Economic Development," 8 *Social and Legal Studies* 75, 83 (1999); World Bank, *Governance and Development* (Wash. DC: World Bank 1992).

19. Fuller, *The Morality of Law*, p. 209–10.
20. Ibid., p. 157–59.
21. Waldron, "The Rule of Law in Contemporary Liberal Theory," p. 93–94.
22. John Finnis, *Natural Law and Natural Rights* (Oxford: Clarendon Press 1980) p. 274.
23. Ibid., p. 273 (emphasis in original).
24. Raz, "The Rule of Law and Its Virtue," p. 225–26.
25. See Robert Barro, 'Dictatorship and the Rule of Law: Rules and Military Power in Pinochet's Chile," in Jose Maria Maravall and Adam Przeworski, eds., *Democracy and the Rule of Law* (Cambridge: Cambridge Univ. Press 2003) p. 188–219. It should be added that this military dictatorship ultimately gave way to a democratic government, perhaps in part owing to the force of legal ideals it espoused.
26. Waldron, "The Rule of Law in Contemporary Liberal Theory," p. 94.
27. Martin Krygier, "Marxism and the Rule of Law: Reflections After the Collapse of Communism," 15 *Law and Social Inquiry* 633, 641 (1990).
28. See Robert P. George, "Reason, Freedom, and the Rule of Law," 15 *Regent Univ. Law Review* 187 (2002).
29. Frederick Schauer, *Playing By the Rules: A Philosophical Examination of Rule-Based Decision-Making in Law and Life* (Oxford: Clarendon Press 1991) Chap. 2 ("Rules as Generalizations").
30. See Schauer, *Playing by the Rules*; Frederick Schauer, "Formalism," 97 *Yale Law Journal* 509 (1988); Robert S. Summers, "The Formal Character of Law," 51 *Cambridge Law Journal* 242 (1992); Weber, *On Law in Economy and Society*.
31. See Shklar, *Legalism* ("legalism is the morality of rule following"), p. 87; Antonin Scalia, "The Rule of Law as a Law of Rules," 56 *Univ. Chicago Law Review* 1175 (1989).
32. See David Trubek, "Max Weber on Law and the Rise of Capitalism," [1972] *Wisconsin Law Review* 720.
33. See Summers, "A Formal Theory of the Rule of Law," p. 136–37. An affirmative argument that the rule of law is compatible with socialism can be found in Christine Sypnowich, "Utopia and the Rule of Law," in *Recrafting The Rule of Law*.
34. See Timothy A. O. Endicott, "The Impossibility of the Rule of Law," 19 *Oxford Journal of Legal Studies* 1, 12 (1999) ("There is not necessarily any clear answer, from the legal point of view, to the question, *what ought to be regulated?*").
35. Martin Krygier, "Marxism and the Rule of Law: Reflections After the Collapse of Communism," 642 (1990).
36. Jurgen Habermas, *Beyond Facts and Norms*, translated by William Rehg (Cambridge: MIT Press 1996) p. 449.
37. Ibid., Chaps. Three, Four, Five, and Six.
38. Ibid., p. 189.
39. Ibid., p. 453.
40. Kant, *Political Writings*, p. 78–80.
41. Habermas, *Beyond Facts and Norms*, p. 104.

42. Gerard Alexander, "Institutionalized Uncertainty, The Rule of Law, and the Sources of Democratic Stability," 35 *Comparative Political Studies* 1145 (2003).
43. See Leoni, *Freedom and Law*.

8   SUBSTANTIVE THEORIES

1. Ronald Dworkin, "Political Judges and the Rule of Law," 64 *Proceedings of the British Academy* 259, 262 (1978).
2. Ibid., p. 269.
3. Ibid., p. 268.
4. Ibid., p. 263–64.
5. Alastair MacIntyre, "Theories of Natural Law in the Culture of Advanced Modernity," in E. B. McLean, ed., *Common Truths: New Perspectives on Natural Law* (Wilmington, Del.: ISI Books 2000).
6. See D. Adamany and J. Grossman, "Support for the Supreme Court as a National Policymaker," 5 *Law and Policy Quarterly* 405 (1983).
7. Frederic William Maitland, *A Historical Sketch of Liberty and Equality*, p. 153.
8. Allan C. Hutchinson and Patrick Monahan, "Democracy and the Rule of Law," in *The Rule of Law: Ideal or Ideology*, p. 100.
9. See Robert A. Dahl, *On Democracy* (New Haven: Yale Univ. Press 1998).
10. Hutchinson and Monahan, "Democracy and the Rule of Law," p. 100.
11. An excellent overview of Dworkin's position can be found in Brian Bix, *Jurisprudence: Theory and Context*, 3rd Edition (Durham, NC: Carolina Academic Press 2004) Chap. 7.
12. See Dworkin, "Political Judges and the Rule of Law."
13. See Allan C. Hutchinson, "The Rule of Law Revisited: Democracy and Courts," in *Recrafting the Rule of Law*. This article, construing courts' actions as consistent with democracy, indicates a turnaround for Hutchinson, who in a previous article argued that the rule of law was a restraint on democracy.
14. See Tamanaha, *Realistic Socio-Legal Theory*, Chap. 8.
15. Jeremy Bentham, "Anarchial Fallacies," *Works II*, p. 501, quoted in Ayer and O'Grady, *A Dictionary of Philosophical Quotations*, p. 47.
16. See Finnis, *Natural Law and Natural Rights*.
17. *Bush* v. *Gore*, 531 US 98, 129 (2000)(Stevens J.).
18. See Rosenfeld, "The Rule of Law and the Legitimacy of Constitutional Democracy," p. 1318–29.
19. Ranier Grote, "Rule of Law, Rechtsstaat and Etat de droit," in Christian Starck, ed., *Constitutionalism, Universalism and Democracy – Comparative Analysis* (Baden-Baden: Nomos Verlagsgesellschaft 1999) p. 286 (emphasis added).
20. Ibid., p. 288. See also Ulrich Karpen, "Rule of Law," in Ulrich Karpen, ed., *The Constitution of the Federal Republic of Germany* (Baden-Baden: Nomos Verlagsgesellschaft 1988).
21. Grote, "Rule of Law, Rechtsstaat and Etat de droit," p. 289.

22. See Habermas, *Between Facts and Norms*, p. 240–53.
23. Grote, "Rule of Law, Rechtsstaat and Etat de droit," p. 288.
24. Ibid., p. 291.
25. John Ferejon and Pasquale Pasqino, "Rule of Democracy and the Rule of Law," in *Democracy and the Rule of Law*, p. 249.
26. See Kim Lane Scheppele, "When the Law Doesn't Count," 149 *Univ. Pennsylvania Law Review* 1361 (2001).
27. See Jose Maria Maravall, "The Rule of Law as a Political Weapon," in *Democracy and the Rule of Law*, p. 261–301.
28. See C. Neal Tate and Torbjorn Vallinder, *The Global Expansion of Judicial Power* (New York: NYU Press 1995).
29. See Leighton McDonald, "Positivism and the Formal Rule of Law: Questioning the Connection," 21 *Australian Journal of Legal Philosophy* 93, 105–06 (2001).
30. See Norman S. Marsh, "The Rule of Law as a Supra-National Concept," in A. G. Guest, ed., *Oxford Essays in Jurisprudence* (Oxford: Oxford Univ. Press 1961) p. 244.
31. T. R. S. Allan, *Law, Liberty, and Justice: The Legal Foundations of British Constitutionalism* (Oxford: Oxford Univ. Press 1993) p. 21–22.
32. Document of the Copenhagen Meeting of the Conference on the Human Dimension of the CSFE, June5–July 29, 1990, nors. 3 and 4. See also Ernest S. Easterly, "The Rule of Law and the New World Order," 22 *Southwestern Univ. Law Review* 161, 165–66 (1995); John Norton Moore, "The Rule of Law and Foreign Policy," [1993] *Harvard Journal of World Affairs* 92.
33. See William E. Leuchtenburg, *The Supreme Court Reborn* (Oxford: Oxford Univ. Press 1995) Chap. 5.
34. See Wei Pan, "Toward a Consultative Rule of Law Regime in China," 12 *Journal of Contemporary China* 3 (2003).
35. See Keyvan Tabari, "The Rule of Law and the Politics of Reform in Post-Revolutionary Iran," 18 *International Sociology* 96 (2003).
36. International Commission of Jurists, *The Rule of Law in A Free Society: A Report of the International Congress of Jurists* (Geneva 1959).
37. Raz, "The Rule of Law and its Virtue," p. 211.

9   THREE THEMES

1. Hobbes, *Leviathan*, p. 176–77.
2. See Stephen Holmes, "Lineages of the Rule of Law," in *Democracy and the Rule of Law*, p. 19–61.
3. Dicey, *Introduction to the Study of the Law of the Constitution*.
4. See Nathan J. Brown, "Shari'a and the State in the Modern Muslim Middle East," 29 *International Journal Middle Eastern Studies* 359 (1997).
5. Nathan J. Brown, "Islamic Constitutionalism in Theory and Practice," in *Democracy, the Rule of Law and Islam*, p. 491.
6. Hayek, *The Road to Serfdom*, p. 80.

7. See Robert J. Barro, *Determinants of Economic Growth: A Cross Country Empirical Study* (Cambridge, Mass.: MIT Press 1997).

8. See Kanishka Jayasuriya, "The Rule of Law and Governance in the East Asian State," 1 *Australian Journal of Asian Law* 107 (1999).

9. See Tamanaha, *Realistic Socio-Legal Theory*, p. 238–40.

10. See Yves Dezalay and Bryant Garth, *Dealing in Virtue: International Commercial Arbitration and the Construction of a Transnational Legal Order* (Chicago: Chicago Univ. Press 1996); Stuart Macaulay, "Non-Contractual Relations in Business: A Preliminary Study," 28 *American Sociological Review* 33 (1963).

11. See Ibrahim F. I. Shihata, *Complementary Reform: Essays on Legal, Judicial and Other Institutional Reforms Supported by the World Bank* (The Hague: Kluwer 1997).

12. For a recent expression of this, see Remarks of Mark Baird, "Indonesia's Corruption Assailed," in *New York Times*, 28 August 2002, World Business, section W.

13. See "Iran's President Trying to Limit Power of Clergy," by Nazila Fathi, *New York Times*, 29 August 2002, A 1, A 14; Tabari, "The Rule of Law and the Politics of Reform in Post-Revolutionary Iran."

14. See Jose Maria Maravall, "The Rule of Law as a Political Weapon," in *Democracy and the Rule of Law*.

10   INTERNATIONAL LEVEL

1. "Laying Down the Law," by Paul Johnson, *Wall Street Journal*, 10 March 1999, A22. The term "international law" traditionally understood means law between states, whereas "global law" includes all actors in the global arena. I use these terms interchangeably, as the meaning of international law is undergoing a transformation to the latter sense.

2. Louis Henkin, *How Nations Behave* (NY: Columbia Univ. Press 1979) p. 47.

3. For an excellent overview of these tribunals, see Philippe Sands, Ruth Mackenzie, and Yuval Shany, *Manual on International Courts and Tribunals* (London: Butterworths 1999).

4. "Private international law" is also used to mean "conflicts of laws," though I use it here in the broader sense described.

5. See Michael P. Malloy, "Bumper Cars: Themes of Convergence in International Regulation," 60 *Fordham Law Review* 1 (1992).

6. See generally Jonathan I. Charney, "Is International Law Threatened by Multiple International Tribunals?" 271 *Recueil Des Cours* 101 (1998). Charney concludes that there is substantial uniformity despite these problems, but not complete.

7. See generally Martin Albrow, *The Global Age: State and Society Beyond Modernity* (Stanford, Calif.: Stanford Univ. Press 1996); Tamanaha, *A General Jurisprudence of Law and Society*, p. 120–28.

8. See John Quigley, "The New World Order and the Rule of Law," 18 *Syracuse Journal of International and Comparative Law* 75 (1992).

9. *Nicaragua* v. *United States*, 1984 ICJ 22 (26 November).
10. See Bruno Simma, "International Adjudication and US Policy – Past, Present, and Future," in Norman Dorsen and Prosser Gifford, eds., *Democracy and the Rule of Law* (Wash., DC: CQ Press 2001) p. 554–55.
11. Jean Allain, *A Century of International Adjudication: The Rule of Law and its Limits* (The Hague: TCM Asser Press 2000) p. 7.
12. See Benedict Kingsbury, "Foreword: Is the Proliferation of International Courts and Tribunals a Systemic Problem?" 31 *New York University Journal of International Law and Politics* 679 (1999).
13. Philippe Sands, "Turtles and Torturers: The Transformation of International Law," 33 *New York University Journal of International Law and Politics* 527, 548 (2001).
14. See Michael J. Trebilcock, "Post-Seattle: A Qualified Defense of the WTO and an Unqualified Defense of the International Rule of Law," in *Democracy and the Rule of Law*, p. 326–27.
15. Kingsbury, "Foreword: is the Proliferation of International Courts and Tribunals a Systemic Problem?," p. 694.
16. See Detlev F. Vagts, "The International Legal Profession: A Need for More Governance?," 90 *American Journal of International Law* 250 (1996).
17. See Konrad Zweigert and Hein Kotz, *An Introduction to Comparative Law* (Oxford: Clarendon Press 1992).
18. Other differences in professional legal culture are discussed in David M. Trubek, Yves Dezalay, Ruth Buchanan, and John R. Davis, "Global Restructuring and the Law: Studies of the Internationalization of Legal Fields and the Creation of Transnational Arenas," 44 *Case Western Reserve Law Review* 407 (1994).
19. See Mary Daly, "Thinking Globally: Will National Borders Matter to Lawyers a Century From Now?," 1 *Journal Institute to Study Legal Ethics* 297 (1996).
20. Ruth Mackenzie and Philippe Sands, "International Courts and Tribunals and the Independence of the International Judge," 44 *Harvard International Law Journal* 271, 278 (2003).
21. Vagts, "The International Legal Profession: A Need for More Governance?," p. 258.
22. See Gilbert Guillaume, "Some Thoughts on the Independence of International Judges Vis-à-Vis States," 2 *Law and Practice of International Courts and Tribunals* 163 (2003).
23. Vagts, "The International Legal Profession: A Need for More Governance?," p. 258.
24. See Philippe Sands, "Introduction: Papers Presented at the Villa La Pietra Symposium on the Independence and Accountability of the International Judge," 2 *Law and Practice of International Courts and Tribunals* 3, 4 (2003). This symposium issue contains a number of papers considering issues about the independence of international judges.
25. Sands, "Turtles and Torturers," p. 555.
26. Ko-Yung Tung, "The World Bank's Role in a Global Economy," in *Democracy and the Rule of Law*, p. 330.

27. See Editorial, "The Unkept Promise," *New York Times*, 30 December 2003, A20.

28. See Joseph E. Stiglitz, *Globalization and its Discontents* (New York: W. W. Norton 2002).

29. Ratna Kapur, "Neutrality and Universality in Human Rights Law," in *Democracy and the Rule of Law*, p. 390.

11   A UNIVERSAL HUMAN GOOD?

1. E. P. Thompson, *Whigs and Hunters: The Origin of the Black Act* (New York: Pantheon Books 1975).

2. Ibid., p. 265.

3. Ibid., p. 266. For a critical response from the Left, see Morton Horwitz, "The Rule of Law: An Unqualified Human Good?," 86 *Yale Law Journal* 561 (1977).

4. See Morton Horwitz, "The Rule of Law: An Unqualified Human Good?."

5. See Finer, *The History of Government*, Chap. 7.

6. See Samuel P. Huntington, *The Clash of Civilizations: Remaking of World Order* (New York: Simon & Schuster 1996) p. 213.

7. Ibid., Chap. 9. Huntington draws the contrast between Western and non-Western societies in terms far too stark, as almost irreconcilable, but he is correct that the differences are real and not sufficiently appreciated by most Westerners.

8. See C. A. Jones, "Capitalism, Globalization and Rule of Law: An Alternative Trajectory of Legal Change in China," 3 *Social and Legal Studies* 195 (1994).

9. See Tamanaha, *A General Jurisprudence of Law and Society*, Chap. 4.

Bibliography

Adamany, D. and J. Grossman. (1983), "Support for the Supreme Court as a National Policymaker," 5 *Law and Policy Quarterly* 405.

Albrow, Martin. (1996), *The Global Age: State and Society Beyond Modernity* (Stanford, Calif.: Stanford Univ. Press).

Alexander, Gerard. (2003), "Institutionalized Uncertainty, The Rule of Law, and the Sources of Democratic Stability," 35 *Comparative Political Studies* 1145.

Allain, Jean. (2000), *A Century of International Adjudication: The Rule of Law and its Limits* (The Hague: T. C. M. Asser Press).

Allan, T. R. S. (1993), *Law, Liberty, and Justice: The Legal Foundations of British Constitutionalism* (Oxford: Oxford Univ. Press).

Aquinas, Thomas. (1987), *Treatise on Law* (Wash., DC: Regnery Gateway).

Aristotle. (1985), *Nichomachean Ethics*. Terence Irwin, ed. (Indianapolis: Hackett).

Aristotle. (1988), *Politics*. Stephen Everson, ed. (Cambridge, Mass.: Cambridge Univ. Press).

Arndt, H. W. (1957), "The Origins of Dicey's Concept of the 'Rule of Law,'" 31 *Australian Law Journal* 117.

Ayer, A. J. and Jane O'Grady, eds. (1992), *A Dictionary of Philosophical Quotations* (Oxford: Blackwell).

Baird, Mark. "Indonesia's Corruption Assailed," *New York Times*, 28 August 2002: World Business, Section W.

Barker, E. (1914), "The 'Rule of Law,'" *Political Quarterly* 116.

Barro, Robert. (1997), *Determinants of Economic Growth: A Cross Country Empirical Study* (Cambridge, Mass.: MIT Press).

Barro, Robert. (2003), "Dictatorship and the Rule of Law: Rules and Military Power in Pinochet's Chile," in Jose Maria Maravall and Adam Przeworski, eds., *Democracy and the Rule of Law* (Cambridge: Cambridge Univ. Press).

Becker, Carl. (1932), *The Heavenly City of Eighteenth Century Philosophers* (New Haven: Yale Univ. Press).

Bender, Leslie. (1988), "A Lawyer's Primer on Feminist Theory and Tort," 38 *Journal of Legal Education* 3.

Bentham, Jeremy. (1988), *A Fragment on Government* (Cambridge: Cambridge Univ. Press).

Berlin, Isaiah. (1969), *Four Essays on Liberty* (Oxford: Oxford Univ. Press).

Berlin, Isaiah. (1990), *The Crooked Timber of Humanity* (Princeton: Princeton Univ. Press).

Berlin, Isaiah. (1999), *The Roots of Romanticism* (Princeton: Princeton Univ. Press).

Bickel, Alexander M. (1955), "The Original Understanding and the Segregation Decision," 69 *Harvard Law Review* 1.

Bickel, Alexander M. (1962), *The Least Dangerous Branch* (New York: Bobbs-Merrill).

Bix, Brian. (2004), *Jurisprudence: Theory and Context* 3rd revised edition (Durham, NC: Carolina Academic Press).

Bloch, Marc. (1961), *Feudal Society: Social Classes and Political Organization*, vol. 2 (Chicago: Chicago Univ. Press).

Boyle, James. (1985), "The Politics of Reason: Critical Legal Theory and Local Social Thought," 133 *Univ. Pennsylvania Law Review* 685.

Bracton, Henry. (1968), *On the Laws and Customs of England* (Cambridge, Mass.: Harvard Univ. Press).

Brown, Nathan J. (1997), "Shari'a and the State in the Modern Muslim Middle East," 29 *International Journal Middle Eastern Studies* 359.

Brown, Nathan J. (1999), "Islamic Constitutionalism in Theory and Practice," in Eugene Cotran and Adel Omar Sherif, eds., *Democracy, The Rule of Law, and Islam* (The Hague: Kluwer).

Burton, Steven J. (1986), "Reaffirming Legal Reasoning: The Challenge From the Left," 36 *Journal of Legal Education* 358.

Bush v. Gore, 531 US 98 (2000).

Canning, Joseph. (1996), *A History of Medieval Political Thought 300–1450* (London: Routledge).

Cantor, Norman F. (1994), *The Civilization of the Middle Ages* (New York: Harper Perennial).

Cantor, Norman F. (1997), *Imagining the Law: Common Law and the Foundations of the American Legal System* (New York: Harper Perennial).

Carlyle, R. W. (1956), *A History of Medieval Political Theory in the West*, quoted in Joseph M. Snee, "Leviathan at the Bar of Justice," in Arthur E. Sutherland, ed., *Government Under Law* (Cambridge, Mass.: Harvard Univ. Press).

Carothers, Thomas. (1998), "The Rule of Law Revival," 77 *Foreign Affairs* 95.

Carrington, Paul D. (1984), "Of Law and the River," 34 *Journal of Legal Education* 222.

Cassirer, Ernst. (1951), *The Philosophy of the Enlightenment* (Princeton: Princeton Univ. Press).

Charney, Jonathan I. (1998), "Is International Law Threatened by Multiple International Tribunals?" 271 *Recueil Des Cours* 101.

Christie, George and Patrick Martin, eds., (1995), *Jurisprudence*, 2nd ed. (St. Paul, Minn.: West Pub.)

Cicero. (1998), *The Republic and The Laws*, trans. Niall Rudd (Oxford: Oxford Univ. Press).

Cohen, David. (1995), *Law, Violence and Community of Classical Athens* (Cambridge: Cambridge Univ. Press).

Cohen, Felix. (1935), "Transcendental Nonsense and the Functional Approach," 35 *Columbia Law Review* 809.

Coleman, Janet. (2000), *A History of Political Thought: From Ancient Greece to Early Christianity* (Oxford: Blackwell).

Coleman, Jules L. and Brian Leiter. (1995), "Determinacy, Objectivity, and Authority," 142 *Univ. Pennsylvania Law Review* 549.

Collins, Stefan, ed. (1989), *On Liberty and Other Writings* (Cambridge: Cambridge Univ. Press).

Cotran, Eugene. (1999), "The Incorporation of the European Convention on Human Rights into the Law of the United Kingdom," in *Democracy, The Rule of Law, and Islam* (The Hague: Kluwer).

Craig, Paul. (1990), *Public Law and Democracy in the United Kingdom and the United States of America* (Oxford: Oxford Univ. Press).

Craig, Paul. (1997), "Formal and Substantive Conceptions of the Rule of Law," *Public Law* 467.

Cunningham, Robert L., ed. (1979), *Liberty and the Rule of Law* (College Station: Texas A&M Univ. Press).

Dahl, Robert A. (1998), *On Democracy* (New Haven: Yale Univ. Press).

Daly, Mary. (1996), "Thinking Globally: Will National Borders Matter to Lawyers a Century From Now?" 1 *Journal Institute to Study Legal Ethics* 297.

Delgado, Richard. (1987), "The Ethereal Scholar: Does Critical Legal Studies Have What Minorities Want?" 22 *Harvard Civil Rights-Civil Liberties Law Review* 301.

Dezalay, Yves and Bryant Garth. (1996), *Dealing in Virtue: International Commercial Arbitration and the Construction of a Transnational Legal Order* (Chicago: Chicago Univ. Press).

Dicey, A. V. (1982 [1908]). *Introduction to the Law of the Constitution* (Indianapolis: Liberty Fund).

Dietze, Gottfried. (1965), *The Federalist: A Classic on Federalism and Free Government* (Baltimore: John Hopkins Univ. Press).

Document of the Copenhagen Meeting of the Conference on the Human Dimension of the CSFE, 5 June–29 July 1990, nos. 3 and 4.

Dunham, William H. (1965), "Magna Carta and British Constitutionalism," *The Great Charter*, Introduction by Erwin N. Griswold (New York: Pantheon).

Dworkin, Ronald. (1977), *Taking Rights Seriously* (London: Duckworth).

Dworkin, Ronald. (1978), "Political Judges and the Rule of Law," 64 *Proceedings of the British Academy* 259.

Dworkin, Ronald. (1985), *A Matter of Principle* (Cambridge, Mass.: Harvard Univ. Press).

Dworkin, Ronald. (1986), *Law's Empire* (Cambridge, Mass.: Harvard Univ. Press).

Dyzenhaus, David, ed. (1999), *Recrafting the Rule of Law* (Portland, OR: Hart Pub.).

Easterly, Ernest S. (1995), "The Rule of Law and the New World Order," 22 *Southwestern Univ. Law Review* 161.

Endicott, Timothy A. O. (1999), "The Impossibility of the Rule of Law," 19 *Oxford Journal of Legal Studies* 1.

Engels, Friedrich. (1942), *The Origins of the Family, Private Property and the State* (New York: International Publishers).

Ferejon, John and Pasquale Pasqino. (2003), "Rule of Democracy and the Rule of Law," in Jose Maria Maravall and Adam Przeworski eds., *Democracy and the Rule of Law* (Cambridge, Mass.: Cambridge Univ. Press).

Field, David Dudley. (1995 [1859]), "Magnitude and Importance of Legal Science," reprinted in George Christie and Patrick Martin, eds., *Jurisprudence*, 2nd ed. (St. Paul, Minn.: West Pub.).

Figgis, John N. (1998 [1916]), *Studies of Political Thought: From Gerson to Grotius, 1414–1625* (Bristol: Thommes Press).

Finer, Samuel E. (1999), *The History of Government* (Oxford: Oxford Univ. Press).

Finnis, John. (1980), *Natural Law and Natural Rights* (Oxford: Clarendon Press).

Fiss, Owen. (1982), "Objectivity and Interpretation," 34 *Stanford Law Review* 739.

Fiss, Owen. (1985), "Conventionalism," 58 *Southern Calif. Law Review* 177.

Fukuyama, Fancis. (1992), *The End of History and the Last Man* (New York: Avon Books).

Fuller, Lon L. (1969), *The Morality of Law*, 2nd revised ed. (New Haven: Yale Univ. Press).

Gay, Peter. (1996), *The Enlightenment: The Science of Freedom* (New York: Norton & Co.).

Girvetz, Harry K. (1963), *The Evolution of Liberalism* (New York: Collier Books).

George, Robert P. (2002), "Reason, Freedom, and the Rule of Law," 15 *Regent Univ. Law Review* 187.

Gray, John. (1995), *Liberalism*, 2nd ed. (Minneapolis: Minn. Univ. Press).

Gray, John. (2000), *The Two Faces of Liberalism* (Cambridge: Polity Press).

Grote, Ranier. (1999), "Rule of Law, Rechtsstaat and Etat de droit," in Christian Starck, ed., *Constitutionalism, Universalism and Democracy – A Comparative Analysis* (Baden-Baden: Nomos Verlagsgesellschaft).

Guest, A. G. (1961), *Oxford Essays in Jurisprudence* (Oxford: Oxford Univ. Press).

Guillaume, Gilbert. (2003), "Some Thoughts on the Independence of International Judges Vis-à-Vis States," 2 *Law and Practice of International Courts and Tribunals* 163.

Habermas, Jurgen. (1996), *Beyond Facts and Norms*, trans. William Rehg (Cambridge: MIT Press).

Hale, John. (1993), *The Civilization of Europe in the Renaissance* (New York: Touchstone).

Hampson, Norman. (1990), *The Enlightenment* (London: Penguin).

Hampton, Jean. (1994), "Democracy and the Rule of Law," in Ian Shapiro, *The Rule of Law* (New York: NYU Press).

Harris, Jill. (1999), *Law and Empire in Late Antiquity* (Cambridge: Cambridge Univ. Press).

Hart, H. L. A. (1961), *The Concept of Law* (Oxford: Oxford Univ. Press).

Hasnas, John. (1995), "Back to the Future: From Critical Legal Studies Forward to Legal Realism, or How Not to Miss the Point of the Indeterminacy Argument," 45 *Duke Law Journal* 84.

Hayek, F. A. (1955), *The Political Idea of the Rule of Law* (Cairo: National Bank of Egypt).

Hayek, F. A. (1973), *Law, Legislation and Liberty: Rules and Order*, vol. 1 (Chicago: Chicago Univ. Press).

Hayek, F. A. (1976), *Law, Legislation and Liberty: The Mirage of Social Justice*, vol. 2 (Chicago: Chicago Univ. Press).

Hayek, F. A. (1979), *Law, Legislation and Liberty: The Political Order of a Free Society*, vol. 3 (Chicago: Chicago Univ. Press).

Hayek, F. A. (1994 [1944]), *The Road to Serfdom* (Chicago: Chicago Univ. Press).

Heilbroner, Robert L. (1981), *The Worldly Philosophers* (New York: Touchstone).

Heineman, Robert A. (1984), *Authority and the Liberal Tradition* (Durham, NC: Carolina Academic Press).

Henkin, Louis. (1979), *How Nations Behave* (New York: Columbia Univ. Press).

Hobbes, Thomas. (1996), *Leviathan* (Oxford: Oxford Univ. Press).

Hobsbawm, Eric. (1989), *The Age of Empire: 1875–1914* (New York: Vintage).

Hobsbawm, Eric. (1996a), *The Age of Capital: 1848–1875* (New York: Vintage).

Hobsbawm, Eric. (1996b), *The Age of Revolution: 1789–1848* (New York: Vintage).

Hogue, Arthur R. (1986), *Origins of the Common Law* (Indianapolis: Liberty Fund).

Holmes, Stephen. (2003), "Lineages of the Rule of Law," in Jose Maria Maravall and Adam Przeworski, eds., *Democracy and the Rule of Law* (Cambridge: Cambridge Univ. Press).

Holt, J. C. (1992), *Magna Carta*, 2nd ed. (Cambridge: Cambridge Univ. Press).

Horwitz, Morton. (1977), "The Rule of Law: An Unqualified Human Good?" 86 *Yale Law Journal* 561.

Horwitz, Morton. (1992), *The Transformation of American Law: 1870–1960* (New York: Oxford Univ. Press).

Huizinga, Johan. (1999), *The Waning of the Middle Ages* (Mineola, New York: Dover Publishers).

Huntington, Samuel P. (1996), *The Clash of Civilizations: Remaking of World Order* (New York: Simon & Schuster).

Hutchinson, Allan C. and Patrick Monahan. (1984), "Politics and the Critical Legal Scholars: The Unfolding Drama of American Legal Thought," 36 *Stanford Law Review* 199.

Hutchinson, Allan C. and Patrick Monahan, eds. (1987), *The Rule of Law: Ideal or Ideology* (Toronto: Carswell).

Hutchinson, Allan C. and Patrick Monahan. (1999), "The Rule of Law Revisited: Democracy and Courts," in David Dyzenhaus, ed., *Recrafting the Rule of Law* (Oxford: Hart Pub.).

International Commission of Jurists. (1959), *The Rule of Law in A Free Society: A Report of the International Congress of Jurists* (Geneva).

Jaeger, Werner. (1944), *Paideia: The Ideals of Greek Culture*, vol. III, trans. G. Highet (Oxford: Oxford Univ. Press).

Jayasuriya, Kanishka. (1999), "The Rule of Law and Governance in the East Asian State," 1 *Australian Journal of Asian Law* 107.

Jennings, Ivor. (1959), *The Law and the Constitution*, 5th ed. (London: London Univ. Press).

Johnson, Paul. "Laying Down the Law," *Wall Street Journal*, 10 March 1999: A22.

Jones, C. A. (1994), "Capitalism, Globalization and Rule of Law: An Alternative Trajectory of Legal Change in China," 3 *Social and Legal Studies* 195.

Jones, J. Walter. (1956), *The Law and Legal Theory of the Greeks* (Oxford: Clarendon Press).

Jowell, Jeffrey. (1994), "The Rule of Law Today," in Jeffrey Jowell and Dawn Oliver, eds., *The Changing Constitution*, 3rd ed. (Oxford: Oxford Univ. Press).

Kant, Immanuel. (1991), *Political Writings* (Cambridge: Cambridge Univ. Press).

Kant, Immanuel. (1999), *Metaphysical Elements of Justice*, 2nd ed., trans. John Ladd (Indianapolis: Hackett Publishing).

Kapur, Ratna. (2003), "Neutrality and Universality in Human Rights Law," in Jose Maria Maravall and Adam Przeworski, eds., *Democracy and the Rule of Law* (Cambridge: Cambridge Univ. Press).

Karpen, Ulrich. (1988), "Rule of Law," in *The Constitution of the Federal Republic of Germany* (Baden-Baden: Nomos Verlagsgesellschaft).

Kelly, J. M. (1992), *A Short History of Western Legal Theory* (Oxford: Oxford Univ. Press).

Kennedy, Duncan. (1976), "Form and Substance in Private Law Adjudication," 89 *Harvard Law Review* 1685.

Kern, Fritz. (1956), *Kingship and Law in the Middle Ages* (New York: Harper Torchbooks).

Kingsbury, Benedict. (1999), "Foreword: Is the Proliferation of International Courts and Tribunals a Systemic Problem?," 31 *New York University Journal of International Law and Politics* 679.

Ko-Yung. (2003), "The World Bank's Role in a Global Economy," in Jose Maria Maravall and Adam Przeworski, eds., *Democracy and the Rule of Law* (Cambridge: Cambridge Univ. Press).

Kress, Ken. (1989), "Legal Indeterminacy," 77 *California Law Review* 283.

Kriegel, Blandine. (1995), *The State and the Rule of Law* (Princeton: Princeton Univ. Press).

Krygier, Martin. (1990), "Marxism and the Rule of Law: Reflections After the Collapse of Communism," 15 *Law and Social Inquiry* 633.

Kurland, Philip B. (1965), "Magna Carta and Constitutionalism in the United States: 'the Noble Lie,'" in William H. Dunham, ed., *The Great Charter* (New York: Pantheon).

Kurland, Philip B. (1970), "Egalitarianism and the Warren Court," 68 *Michigan Law Review* 629.

Kutz, Christopher L. (1994), "Just Disagreement: Indeterminacy and Rationality in the Rule of Law," 103 *Yale Law Journal* 997.

Lasky, Harold J. (1997), *The Rise of European Liberalism* (New Brunswick: Transaction).

Lawrence v. Texas, 539 US . . . (2003); 123 S Ct 2472 (2003).

Leoni, Bruno. (1991), *Freedom and the Law* (Indianapolis: Liberty Fund).

Leuchtenburg, William E. (1995), *The Supreme Court Reborn* (Oxford: Oxford Univ. Press).

Levy, Leonard W. (2001), *Origins of the Bill of Rights* (New Haven: Yale Nota Bene).

Lochner v. New York, 198 US 45 (1904).

Locke, John. (1980), *Second Treatise of Government* (Indianapolis: Hackett).

Lowi, Theodore J. (1987), "The Welfare State, The New Regulation, and The Rule of Law," in Allan Hutchinson and Patrick Monahan, eds., *The Rule of Law: Ideal or Ideology* (Toronto: Carswell).

Macauley, Stuart. (1963), "Non-Contractual Relations in Business: A Preliminary Study," 28 *American Sociological Review* 33.

MacIntyre, Alastair. (1984), *After Virtue* (Notre Dame: Notre Dame Univ. Press).

MacIntyre, Alastair. (2000), "Theories of Natural Law in the Culture of Advanced Modernity," in E. B. McLean, ed., *Common Truths: New Perspectives on Natural Law* (Wilmington, Del.: ISI Books).

Macpherson, C. B. (1962), *The Political Theory of Possessive Individualism* (Oxford: Oxford Univ. Press).

MacKenzie, Ruth and Philippe Sands. (2003), "International Courts and Tribunals and the Independence of the International Judge," 44 *Harvard International Law Journal* 271.

Madison, James, Alexander Hamilton, and John Jay. (1966), *The Federalist Papers* (New York: Arlington House).

Maitland, Frederic William. (2000 [1875]), *A Historical Sketch of Liberty and Equality* (Indianapolis: Liberty Fund).

Malloy, Michael P. (1992), "Bumper Cars: Themes of Convergence in International Regulation," 60 *Fordham Law Review* 1.

Manville, Philip Brook. (1997), *The Origins of Citizenship in Ancient Athens* (Princeton: Princeton Univ. Press).

Maravall, Jose Maria and Adam Przeworski, eds. (2003), *Democracy and the Rule of Law* (Cambridge: Cambridge Univ. Press).

Marbury v. Madison, 1 Cranch 137, 177 (1803).

Marsh, Norman S. (1961), "The Rule of Law as a Supra-National Concept," in A. G. Guest, ed., *Oxford Essays in Jurisprudence* (Oxford: Oxford Univ. Press).

Marx, Karl and Friedrich Engels. (1998), *The Communist Manifesto* (Oxford: Oxford Univ. Press).

Mazor, Lester. (1972), "The Crisis of Legal Liberalism," 81 *Yale Law Journal* 1032.

McDonald, Leighton. (2001), "Positivism and the Formal Rule of Law: Questioning the Connection," 21 *Australian Journal of Legal Philosophy* 93.

McIlwain, C. H. (1934), "The English Common Law, Barrier Against Absolutism," XLIX *American Historical Review* 23.

McLean, E. B., ed. (2000), *Common Truths: New Perspectives on Natural Law* (Wilmington, Del.: ISI Books).

Mill, John Stuart. (1989), *On Liberty and Other Writings* (Cambridge: Cambridge Univ. Press).

Minow, Martha and Elizabeth Spelman. (1999), "In Context," 63 *Southern California Law Review* 1597.

Montesquieu, Baron de. (1914), *Spirit of Laws*. J. V. Pritchard, ed. (London: Bell and Sons).

Moore, John Norton. (1993), "The Rule of Law and Foreign Policy," *Harvard Journal of World Affairs* 92.

Morrall, John B. (1980), *Political Thought in Medieval Times* (Toronto: Toronto Univ. Press).

Morrow, John. (1998), *History of Political Thought* (New York: NYU Press).

Mulhall, Stephen and Adam Swift. (1992), *Liberals and Communitarians* (Oxford: Blackwell).

Munch, Thomas. (2000), *The Enlightenment: A Comparative Social History* (London: Arnold).

Nafisi, Azar. "Hiding Behind the Rule of Law," *New York Times*, 19 December 1997: A39.

Nenner, Howard. (1977), *By Color of Law: Legal Culture and Constitutional Politics in England, 1660–1689* (Chicago: Chicago Univ. Press).

Neumann, Franz L. (1996), "The Change in the Function of Law in Modern Society," in William E. Scheuerman, ed., *The Rule of Law Under Siege* (Berkeley: Calif. Univ. Press).

Nicaragua v. United States, 1984 ICJ 22 (26 November).

Nonet, Philippe and Philip Selznick. (1996), *Law and Society in Transition: Toward Responsive Law* (New York: Octagon Books).

Norwich, John Julius. (1999), *A Short History of Byzantium* (New York: Vintage).

Osborn v. Bank of United States, 22 US (9 Wheaton) 736, 866 (1824).

Ostwald, Martin. (1986), *From Popular Sovereignty to the Sovereignty of Law: Law, Society and Politics in Fifth-Century Athens* (Berkeley, Calif.: Calif. Univ. Press).

Pan, Wei. (2003), "Toward a Consultative Rule of Law Regime in China," 12 *Journal of Contemporary China* 3.

Pangle, Thomas L. (1989), *Montesquieu's Philosophy of Liberalism: A Commentary on the Spirit of the Laws* (Chicago: Chicago Univ. Press).

Pennington, Kenneth. (1993), *The Prince and the Law, 1200–1600* (Berkeley, Calif.: Calif. Univ. Press).

Pipes, Richard. (2000), *Property and Freedom* (New York: Vintage).

Pirenne, Henri. (1925), *Medieval Cities* (Garden City, NY: Doubleday).

Pirenne, Henri. (1937), *Economic and Social History of Medieval Europe* (New York, Harcourt).

Pirenne, Henri. (2001), *Mohammad and Charlemagne* (Mineola, New York: Dover Publishers).

Plato. (1970), *The Laws*. Trans. Trevor Saunders (London: Penguin).

Plato. (1985), *The Republic*. Trans. Richard W. Sterling and William C. Scott (New York: Norton).

Plessy v. Ferguson, 347 US 483 (1954).

Pocock, J. G. A. (1957), *The Ancient Constitution and the Feudal Law* (Cambridge: Cambridge Univ. Press).

Poggi, Gianfranco. (1978), *The Development of the Modern State* (Stanford: Stanford Univ. Press).

Quigley, John. (1992), "The New World Order and the Rule of Law," 18 *Syracuse Journal of International and Comparative Law* 75.

Radin, Max. (1947), "The Myth of Magna Carta," 60 *Harvard Law Review* 1060.

Raz, Joseph. (1979), "The Rule of Law and Its Virtue," in *The Authority of Law* (Oxford: Clarendon Press).

Reynolds, Noel B. (1989), "Grounding the Rule of Law," 2 *Ratio Juris* 1.

Rosenfeld, Michel. (2001), "The Rule of Law and the Legitimacy of Constitutional Democracy," 74 *Southern Calif. Law Review* 1307.

Rousseau, Jean-Jacques. (1968), *The Social Contract* (Middlesex: Penguin).

Rubenstein, Richard E. (2003), *Aristotle's Children: How Christians, Muslims, and Jews Rediscovered Ancient Wisdom and Illuminated the Dark Ages* (New York: Harcourt).

Sandel, Michael J. (1982), *Liberalism and the Limits of Justice* (Cambridge: Cambridge Univ. Press).

Sands, Philippe. (2001), "Turtles and Torturers: The Transformation of International Law," 33 *New York University Journal of International Law & Politics* 527.

Sands, Philippe. (2003), "Introduction: Papers Presented at the Villa La Pietra Symposium on the Independence and Accountability of the International Judge," 2 *Law and Practice of International Courts and Tribunals* 3.

Sands, Philippe, Ruth Mackenzie, and Yuval Shany. (1999), *Manual on International Courts and Tribunals* (London: Butterworths).

Scalia, Antonin. (1989), "The Rule of Law as a Law of Rules," 56 *Univ. Chicago Law Review* 1175.

Schauer, Frederick. (1988), "Formalism," 97 *Yale Law Journal* 509.

Schauer, Frederick. (1991), *Playing By the Rules: A Philosophical Examination of Rule-Based Decision-Making in Law and Life* (Oxford: Clarendon Press).

Scheppele, Kim Lane. (2001), "When the Law Doesn't Count," 149 *Univ. Pennsylvania Law Review* 1361.

Scheuerman, William E. (1994), "The Rule of Law and the Welfare State: Toward a New Synthesis," 22 *Politics and Society* 195.

Scheuerman, William E., ed. (1996), *The Rule of Law Under Siege* (Berkeley, Calif.: Calif. Univ. Press).

Shapiro, Ian. (1985), *The Evolution of Rights in Liberal Theory* (Cambridge: Cambridge Univ. Press).

Shapiro, Ian, ed. (1994), *The Rule of Law* (New York: NYU Press).

Shihata, Ibrahim F. I. (1997), *Complementary Reform: Essays on Legal, Judicial and Other Institutional Reforms Supported by the World Bank* (The Hague: Kluwer).

Shklar, Judith N. (1964), *Legalism* (Cambridge, Mass.: Harvard Univ. Press).

Shklar, Judith N. (1987), "Political Theory and the Rule of Law," in Allan C. Hutcheson and Patrick Monahan, eds., *The Rule of Law: Ideal or Ideology* (Toronto: Carswell).

Simma, Bruno. (1984), "International Adjudication and U.S. Policy – Past, Present, and Future," in Norman Dorsen and Prosser Gifford, eds., *Democracy and the Rule of Law* (Wash., DC: CQ Press).

Singer, Joseph William. (1984), "The Player and the Cards: Nihilism and Legal Theory," 94 *Yale Law Journal* 1.

Smith, Adam. (1978), *Lectures on Jurisprudence*. R. L. Meek, D. D. Raphael, and P. G. Stein, eds. (Oxford: Clarendon Press).

Snee, Joseph M. (1956), "Leviathan at the Bar of Justice," in Arthur E. Sutherland, ed. *Government Under Law* (Cambridge, Mass.: Harvard Univ. Press).

Solum, Lawrence B. (1987), "On the Indeterminacy Crisis: Critiquing Critical
Dogma," 54 *Univ. Chicago Law Review* 462.

Southern, R. W. (1968), *The Making of the Middle Ages* (London: Hutchinson
Ltd.).

Starck, Christian, ed. (1999), *Constitutionalism, Universalism and Democracy –
A Comparative Analysis* (Baden-Baden: Nomos Verlagsgesellschaft).

Stein, Peter. (1999), *Roman Law in European History* (Cambridge: Cambridge
Univ. Press).

Stephenson, Carl. (1965), *Medieval Feudalism* (Cornell: Cornell Univ. Press).

Stiglitz, Joseph E. (2002), *Globalization and its Discontents* (New York: W. W.
Norton).

Stoner, James R. (1992), *Common Law and Liberal Theory: Coke, Hobbes, and the
Origins of American Constitutionalism* (Lawrence: Kansas Univ. Press).

Strauss, Leo. (1953), *Natural Right and History* (Chicago, IL: Chicago Univ.
Press).

Strayer, Joseph R. (1970), *On the Medieval Origins of the State* (Princeton, New
Jersey: Princeton University Press).

Summers, Robert S. (1982), *Instrumentalism and American Legal Theory* (Ithaca,
NY: Cornell Univ. Press).

Summers, Robert S. (1992), "The Formal Character of Law," 51 *Cambridge Law
Journal* 242.

Summers, Robert S. (1993), "A Formal Theory of the Rule of Law," 6 *Ratio
Juris* 127, 135.

Summers, Robert S. (1999), "Propter Honoris Respectum: The Principles of the
Rule of Law," 74 *Notre Dame Law Review* 1691.

Sutherland, Arthur, ed. (1956), *Government Under Law* (Cambridge, Mass.:
Harvard Univ. Press).

Sypnowich, Christine. (1999), Utopia and the Rule of Law," in David Dyzenhaus,
ed., *Recrafting the Rule of Law* (Oxford: Hart Pub.).

Tabari, Keyvan. (2003), "The Rule of Law and the Politics of Reform in Post-
Revolutionary Iran," 18 *International Sociology* 96.

Taiwo, Olufemi. (1999), "The Rule of Law: The New Leviathan?" 12 *Canadian
Journal of Law & Jurisprudence* 151.

Tamanaha, Brian Z. (1997), *Realistic Socio-Legal Theory: Pragmatism and a Social
Theory of Law* (Oxford: Clarendon Press).

Tamanaha, Brian Z. (2001), *A General Jurisprudence of Law and Society*, (Oxford:
Oxford Univ. Press).

Tarnas, Richard. (1991), *The Passion of the Western Mind* (New York: Ballantine
Books).

Tate, C. Neal and Torbjorn Vallinder. (1995), *The Global Expansion of Judicial
Power* (New York: NYU Press).

Thompson, E. P. (1975), *Whigs and Hunters: The Origin of the Black Act* (New
York: Pantheon Books).

Tierney, Brian. (1963), "'The Prince is Not Bound by the Laws.' Accursius and
the Origins of the Modern State," 5 *Comparative Studies in Society and History*
378, 392.

Tocqueville, Alex de. (1900), *Democracy in America*. Trans. Henry Reeve (New York: Mentor Books).

Tonsor, Stephen J. (1979), "The Conservative Origins of Collectivism," in Robert L. Cunningham, ed., *Liberty and the Rule of Law* (College Station: Texas A&M Univ. Press).

Trebilcock, J. (1972), "Post-Seattle: A Qualified Defense of the WTO and an Unqualified Defense of the International Rule of Law," in Jose Maria Maravall and Adam Przeworski, eds., *Democracy and the Rule of Law* (Cambridge: Cambridge Univ. Press).

Trubek, David M., Yves Dezalay, Ruth Buchanan, and John R. Davis. (1994), "Global Restructuring and the Law: Studies of the Internationalization of Legal Fields and the Creation of Transnational Arenas," 44 *Case Western Reserve Law Review* 407.

Tshuma, Lawrence. (1999), "The Political Economy of the World Bank's Legal Framework for Economic Development," 8 *Social and Legal Studies* 75. World Bank, Governance and Development (Wash., DC: World Bank 1992).

Tunc, Andre. (1956), "The Royal Will and the Rule of Law," in Arthur E. Sutherland, ed., *Government Under Law* (Cambridge, Mass.: Harvard Univ. Press).

Tushnet, Mark. (1996), "Defending the Indeterminacy Thesis," 16 *Quinnipiac Law Review* 339.

Ullmann, Walter. (1965), *A History of Political Thought: The Middle Ages* (Middlesex, NY: Penguin).

Ulrich, Karpen. (1988), "Rule of Law," *The Constitution of the Federal Republic of Germany* (Baden-Baden: Nomos Verlagsgesellschaft).

Unger, Roberto M. (1975), *Knowledge and Politics* (New York: Free Press).

Unger, Roberto M. (1976b), *Law in Modern Society* (New York: Free Press).

Vagts, Detlev F. (1996), "The International Legal Profession: A Need for More Governance?," 90 *American Journal of International Law* 250.

van de S. Centlivres, A. (1956), "The Constitution of the Union of South Africa and the Rule of Law," in Arthur Sutherland, ed., *Government Under Law* (Cambridge, Mass.: Harvard Univ. Press).

von Savigny, F. (1983), *Of the Vocation of Our Age for Legislation and Jurisprudence* (New York: Arno).

Waldron, Jeremy. (1987), "Theoretical Foundations of Liberalism" 37 (No. 147) *Philosophical Quarterly* 127.

Waldron, Jeremy. (1989), "The Rule of Law in Contemporary Liberal Theory," 2 *Ratio Juris* 79.

Waldron, Jeremy. (2002), "Is the Rule of Law an Essentially Contested Concept (in Florida)?" 21 *Law & Phil.* 137.

Weber, Max. (1967), *On Law in Economy and Society*. Max Rheinstein ed. (New York: Simon and Schuster).

Wechsler, Herbert. (1959), "Toward Neutral Principles of Constitutional Law," 73 *Harvard Law Review* 1.

Weinreb, Ernest J. (1987), "The Intelligibility of the Rule of Law," *The Rule of Law: Ideal or Ideology* (Toronto: Carswell).

Wells, Catherine. (1990), "Situated Decisionmaking," 63 *Southern California Law Review* 1727.

Wiecek, William M. (1998), *The Lost World of Classical Legal Thought* (Oxford: Oxford Univ. Press).

Williams, E. N. (1972), *The Ancient Regime in Europe* (Middlesex: Penguin).

Zapp, Christian and Eben Moglen. (1996), "Linguistic Indeterminacy and the Rule of Law: On the Perils of Misunderstanding Wittgenstein," 84 *Georgetown Law Review* 485.

Zuckert, Michael P. (1994), "Hobbes, Locke, and the Problem of the Rule of Law," in Ian Shapiro, ed., *The Rule of Law* (New York: NYU Press).

Zweigert, Konrad and Hein Kotz. (1992), *An Introduction to Comparative Law* (Oxford: Clarendon Press).

Index

abortion, 103
administrative actions, 64–65, 72, 98–99, 120
Afghanistan, 118
Alexander the Great, 8
Allan, T. R. S., 110–11
apartheid, 120
Aquinas, Thomas, 18–19, 25, 48, 115
arbitration, 121, 135
Aristotle, 7, 8–10, 12, 18–19, 87, 122, 125
Asian countries, 92–93, 135, 139
Augustus, 12
Austin, John, 57
authoritarian regimes, 85, 93, 95–96, 97, 115, 120, 139
autonomy of law, 83

Bentham, Jeremy, 45, 57, 59, 79, 107
Berlin, Isaiah, 32, 37, 58
bills of rights, 55, 71, 104, 118–19, 138–39
bishops, 21, 30
bourgeois, 28–31, 43–44, 51, 53, 61
Bracton, Henry of, 26
Burger Court, 74
Bush, George W, 1, 108, 130
Byzantium, 12, 17–18

Cambridge University, 18
capitalism
    19th century England, 60–62
    and formal legality, 119, 121–22
    and liberalism, 43–45, 73
    Radical Left, 73
    rules, 97
Central American Court of Justice, 128
certainty, legal certainty, 66, 83, 97, 119, 122
Charlemagne, 17, 20, 21
Charles the Bold, 22
Chicago, 2, 73
children, 7, 36
China, 2, 3, 92–93, 112, 120

Church, 19–23, 30, 39
Cicero, 11–12
civil disobedience, 74
civil liberties. *See* human rights
clarity of rules, 93, 97
clergy, Middle Ages, 17
Coke, Edward, 25, 29, 57
colonization, 138
colonized subjects, 36
commerce, 28–31, 43–44, 53, 119, 121, 130
common law, 27, 56, 57, 59, 64, 69–70
communism, 1
communitarianism, 42–43, 73, 84–86, 121
Conference on Security and Cooperation in Europe 1990, 111
conservatives. *See* Dicey; Hayek
Constant, Benjamin, 37
Constantine, Emperor, 12, 15, 19, 20–21
Constantinople, 12, 15, 18
constitutions, 36, 55, 56–57, 64, 104
contractual rights, 44, 103
Corpus Iuris Civilis, 12, 13–14, 18
criminal punishment, 98, 109, 120, 139
Critias, 10
Critical Legal Studies Movement, 74, 77
cruel punishment, 35
Crusaders, 18
customary law
    England, 26
    Germanic customary law, 23–25, 116, 117
    international law, 128, 129
    meaning, 23–24
    Middle Ages, 22, 115

Dark Ages, 15–17
death penalty, 103, 125
Declaration of Delhi, 112
democracy
    Cicero, 11
    early liberalism, 38